ANTHROPOLOGISTS IN THE PUBLIC SPHERE

ANTHROPOLOGISTS IN THE PUBLIC SPHERE

SPEAKING OUT ON WAR, PEACE, AND AMERICAN POWER

EDITED BY ROBERTO J. GONZÁLEZ

UNIVERSITY OF TEXAS PRESS
AUSTIN

Requests for permission to reproduce material from
this work should be sent to Permissions, University
of Texas Press, P.O. Box 7819, Austin, TX 78713-7819.

⊗ The paper used in this book meets the minimum
requirements of ANSI/NISO Z39.48-1992 (R1997)
(Permanence of Paper).

LIBRARY OF CONGRESS CATALOGING-IN-PUBLICATION DATA

Anthropologists in the public sphere : speaking out on
war, peace, and American power / edited by Roberto J.
González. — 1st ed.
    p.   cm.
Includes bibliographical references and index.
  ISBN 0-292-70235-3 (cl. : alk. paper) —
  ISBN 0-292-70169-1 (pbk. : alk. paper)
  1. Political anthropology. 2. War and society.
3. Peace. 4. Power (Social sciences) I. González,
Roberto J. (Roberto Jesús), date
GN492.A592 2004
306.2 — dc22

                       2003021093

FOR JORGE, ERNESTO, AND VERÓNICA

CONTENTS

ACKNOWLEDGMENTS

Research for this book was supported in part by a Junior Faculty Career Development Grant from San Jose State University. Roberto and Imelda González enthusiastically encouraged me to pursue the project in its earliest stages. C. Jay Ou and Kenji Tierney made suggestions that improved the manuscript. Theresa May of the University of Texas Press provided comments and directed the manuscript to two anonymous reviewers, who gave thorough and insightful suggestions. I also wish to thank colleagues from the San Jose State anthropology department for their support.

For the last ten years, Laura Nader and Gerald Berreman have been extraordinary mentors. By practicing and advocating a more relevant anthropology, they continue inspiring others to follow their example. I am especially grateful to Laura Nader for her generosity and encouragement.

ANTHROPOLOGISTS IN THE PUBLIC SPHERE

ANTHROPOLOGISTS IN
THE PUBLIC SPHERE
SPEAKING OUT ON
WAR, PEACE, AND
AMERICAN POWER

ROBERTO J.   *Every time intellectuals have the chance to*
GONZÁLEZ   *speak yet do not speak, they join the forces*
                that train men not to be able to think and
imagine and feel in morally and politically adequate ways. When
they do not demand that the secrecy that makes elite decisions
absolute and unchallengeable be removed, they too are part of
the passive conspiracy to kill off public scrutiny. When they do
not speak, when they do not demand, when they do not think
and feel and act as intellectuals . . . they contribute to the moral
paralysis, the intellectual rigidity, that now grip both leaders and
led around the world.
—C. WRIGHT MILLS, *THE CAUSES OF WORLD WAR III* (1958)

It is time to divert at least some of our research energies away
from the minutiae of diverse problems and to focus on their
broader context. What has been missing is perspective . . . *An-*
thropology appears to be a discipline that can show us how we
got where we are and suggest how we might get out.
—JOHN BODLEY, *ANTHROPOLOGY AND CONTEMPORARY HUMAN PROBLEMS*
(1985)

Anthropology for the General Public

This book is about anthropologists communicating what they know
about culture, society, history, and power with the general public. Their
statements are short, pointed, and passionate, based on experience and
immersion in the subject matter—not fly-by-night observations.

In the 1930s and 1940s, some American anthropologists were so
influential, and their work so well known, that they were literally

household names. In magazines and newspaper articles and in public debates, Franz Boas, Ruth Benedict, and Margaret Mead (all of Columbia University), as well as Ashley Montagu, regularly commented upon issues of national and international politics and culture using language that almost any literate person could understand.

It is not unusual for anthropologists in other countries to address broad audiences—for example, in Mexico, Rodolfo Stavenhagen, Margarita Nolasco, and Roger Bartra often contribute commentaries to daily newspapers such as *La Jornada* and *Reforma*. In France, Claude Lévi-Strauss and Pierre Bourdieu published frequently in *Le Monde* and other periodicals. Brazil, India, and other countries also have anthropologists who are national figures.

Today few anthropologists could be considered celebrities in the United States, but that does not mean that none speak to the public. The contemporary picture is more disperse, with hundreds of individuals reaching out to wider audiences—in local newspapers, on radio programs and television shows, at schools, museums, libraries, and bookstores, and with community organizations. As the discipline has expanded, it has become more diverse and eclectic. Not surprisingly, efforts at publicizing anthropological knowledge are more varied and decentralized.

There is a wide range of projects under way to disseminate anthropology within the United States. An anthropologist at Virginia Polytechnic, Samuel Cook, has spent years working with community groups in the Appalachian region to draw attention to the environmentally destructive practice of mountaintop removal by coal mining companies. Robert Borofsky of Hawaii Pacific University is revitalizing public anthropology by searching for new avenues to make anthropological knowledge accessible to nonspecialists. His projects include the compilation of concise summaries of articles published in the discipline's most widely circulated journals. Recently, anthropology graduate students at the University of California, Berkeley, edited an anthology, *September 11: Contexts and Consequences*, to help broaden public knowledge about the terrorist attacks on the World Trade Center and the Pentagon. Thousands of copies now circulate among those seeking a better understanding of fast-moving foreign policies. Eric Prokosch, whose anthropological analysis of antipersonnel weapons in *The Technology of Killing* (1995) provides critical information for researchers and the lay public, is perhaps best known for working with Amnesty International in campaigns to end torture and the death penalty. Still others, such as Jan English-Lueck from San Jose State University, are introducing anthropology to high school, junior high, and elementary school students, not only as a way of recruiting future generations of anthropologists, but also to train young minds to think comparatively and critically.

This collection of readings focuses on another group of anthropologists working to publicize their knowledge through the popular press. Specifically, they make use of mass media to diffuse information about U.S. foreign policy and its impact upon other societies. Most of the pieces included here have appeared in newspapers, magazines, or online journals, while a few others are from interviews on television or radio programs. These anthropologists are participant-observers and citizen-scholars whose work appeals directly to the American public.

Although all the contributors have been trained as anthropologists, not all are academics. Some are graduate students, while others are professors or professors emeriti. The collection also includes pieces by anthropologists working for nonprofit or nongovernmental organizations, popular magazines, radio stations, and activist groups. At first sight, it is striking that the majority of the articles have been written by anthropologists who are not based at the old prestige centers of the discipline—the academic departments of elite universities such as Columbia University. Yet an anthropology attuned to public audiences may well reemerge from the profession's peripheries, if greater tolerance for experimentation is permitted from off-center locations.

A common thread links the individual articles and interviews: they may be read as cultural critiques of American Empire. The emergence and extension of this empire and the corporatization of government are among the most important historical facts of our time and have inspired recent studies by social scientists, economists, and other scholars.[1] Some of the contributors to this book directly address aspects of U.S. governmental foreign policy and its effects in Latin America, the Balkans, Central Asia, Africa, the Middle East, and Southeast Asia. Others focus on the role of social scientists in U.S. imperialist projects. Still others examine connections between "free" trade, corporate power, and the role of military regimes in establishing and maintaining a "New World Order" in the service of multinational corporations.

The anthropologists included in this book are sophisticated in their use of cross-cultural comparison and history, and recognize that cultures are complex and change over time. Most are keenly aware—based on first hand experience—that the analysis of power and control in variegated forms on a global scale is necessary for understanding contemporary realities. The Cold War, economic development programs, and now the "war on terror" have had dramatic effects on people in the "Third World."

In some cases, an anthropologist's repeated efforts to make a prognosis appear clearly as open warnings to policy makers about the possible consequences of government action. Such commentaries are published but more often than not ignored by policy makers—this has especially been true in recent years. When the situation becomes a crisis, the anthropologist writes again, and recommendations once again are not used. After the crisis has come to a head and disaster has occurred, the anthropologist tries to draw a lesson from it, and he or she is sometimes invited in to fix things after the fact.

Lack of response from policy makers to early warnings might partially explain the surge in cultural critiques that have emerged since the attacks of September 11. Literally dozens of anthropologists have written and spoken about multiple aspects of the tragic events and their aftermath, often with tremendous urgency. For this reason, the geographic center of gravity of this collection falls in the Middle East and Central Asia, since the media, government officials, and ordinary Americans have looked upon these areas with interest and concern. Many of the authors counter ethnocentric or stereotypical views of a region's peoples by helping readers understand its cultural complexity and historical connections to Europe and the United States. Confronting persistent ignorance with persistent appeals to reason may lead to change if public opinion can be impacted. Although policy makers may not be quick to use anthropological commentaries, the general public often does a better job. It is to spark citizen thought and action that we write, since without the push and pull of ordinary citizens, there is no democracy.

A publicly engaged anthropology is more necessary now than ever before—not in spite of, but because of, what some call corporate colonialism and what others call free trade. Speaking out and insisting that anthropology play a role in public discussions is especially critical as private interests recruit anthropologists to help promote an expanding multinational corporate dominion by transforming peasants, hunter-gatherers, pastoralists, refugees, and immigrants into mass consumers.

Why Anthropology?

Daily newspapers, evening news programs, and weekly magazines report on a long list of pressing issues. Economic globalization and its contradictory effects, ethnic strife, biotechnology, multiculturalism, fundamentalisms and religious revival, nuclear proliferation, the nature of human intelligence, and the state of the environment frequently make headlines. So do seemingly endless wars on terrorism and drugs.

Topics such as these beg for thoughtful analysis. Many self-described experts, however, often suffer from myopia, ethnocentrism, lack of imagination, and, sometimes, dubious credentials. More and more of them are public relations people posing as independent third parties who conduct scientific research for the highest bidder while concealing conflicts of interest.[2] Others who have been assigned the name "pundits" attempt to speak with authority about topics they often know little about.[3] Some of them speak about culture and civilization as if they had come up with the concepts themselves—and abuse them daily.

Considering this sad state of affairs, anthropologists may be uniquely positioned to speak with knowledge and insight. The anthropological lens focuses on humans holistically and cross-culturally, never losing sight of long-term historical processes. Good anthropology integrates culture, language, biology, and history to answer questions about humans and the societies they have made.

At a time when technical experts are trained to think in reductionistic terms by breaking problems into tinier and tinier pieces, to view issues from an ethnocentric perspective ignorant of other cultures, and to live in the present without remembering the past, many anthropologists still strive to be generalists. This contrasts sharply with the approach of many policy makers in our country, who act under the flawed assumption that human troubles can be bracketed off and separated from history, culture, politics, and the future.

Yet we have learned that humans are not automatons. The human horizon has myriad possibilities: *Homo sapiens* is a creature that sometimes cooperates but just as frequently conflicts, a creature of habit and reflex but also of creativity and innovation, of selfishness but also of altruism. Some of the most persistent and perplexing questions seek to discover how and why groups of people coalesce or break apart—how human relationships hang together or unravel, what changes, what does not. We have long been interested in the question of survival—how, under situations of tremendous ecological, political, or economic pressure, men and women innovate or acquiesce.[4]

Perhaps as importantly, most cultural anthropologists undertake extended fieldwork, living in a different society for a year or more in an effort to understand things "from the native's point of view." We live and talk with real people and piece together complex realties from interviews, observations, documents, and other sources. Anthropologists are interested in streets, barrios, ghettos, villages, and refugee camps as well as airport lobbies, first-class hotels, theaters, and bars.

This wide-angle lens gives us a powerful tool for critiquing contemporary life, since we are at once culturally immersed and detached. With insight, anthropologists have challenged deeply held convictions about affluence and poverty, as when Marshall Sahlins suggested that limited wants—not just the accumulation of material goods—might be an alternative basis for defining wealth.[5] Or about science—as when Bronislaw Malinowski insisted that all peoples have magic, religion, and science.[6] Or about sexual norms—as when Margaret Mead informed us that sexual practices are not universal.[7] Or about "race" —as when Franz Boas demonstrated that biological variation within human populations is much greater than the variation between them— an early critique of biological hierarchies.[8] Time and again, anthropological awareness of alternatives has opened new paths for the future.

Sometimes anthropology has demonstrated an uncanny ability to diagnose problems before they become crises. Anthropological prescience has sometimes foretold events months or years in advance. As we shall see, some anthropologists have very publicly predicted impending political and humanitarian disasters in Iraq, the former Yugoslavia, Somalia, and Afghanistan, to name a few. In the selections in this volume, authors have pointed to specific conditions that signal serious trouble ahead in Central America, Pakistan, the Middle East, and the United States. This work, based upon on-the-ground experience and intimate cultural knowledge, suggests a novel approach towards foreign policy in which anthropologists might take a leading role: a *preventive diplomacy* that aims to forestall (rather than await) future crises by addressing root causes. Current approaches based upon gunboat diplomacy and Realpolitik have proven to be unsustainable in economic and humanitarian terms—or indeed in survival terms.

Speaking Out as a Public Service

On the surface it is peculiar—even bizarre—that U.S. anthropologists don't have an even more public face, especially since so many either work at public institutions of higher learning or directly for government agencies. Taxpayers underwrite much of our work, legislators allocate the funds—but what are they getting in return? Granted, many of us teach, but should this be the extent of our public service? Should service include governmental policy recommendations? Expert testimony before congressional committees? Education of the general public?

We might step back in time, to the period before anthropology in the United States was based in universities. A century ago many of its practitioners were based in museums, public spaces for educating as well as entertaining the public. Some argued that for anthropology to survive, museums had to attract large numbers of laypeople—or else wither away from irrelevance and public indifference. The subject matter was inherently interesting, but the problem, still relevant today, was how to pitch information to the general public in a palatable yet enlightening way.

As more anthropologists became full-time academics in the twentieth century, concern for making knowledge public sometimes lapsed. Activities and publications thought to be nonacademic were seldom useful for attaining tenure (or for promotions), and the gap between academic and nonacademic anthropology widened. Today, the term "journalistic" is sometimes used to stigmatize such work. As a colleague once said, "You have to have two discussions going at the same time—one with the geeks in the department and another with the ordinary folks."

In many cases, university professors have abandoned ordinary folks altogether and are just talking to each other. Kendall Thu of Iowa State observes this when he points out that some cultural anthropologists "have been pursuing trendy issues of postmodernism, blurred genres and identities, hermeneutic interpretation, voices of hegemony, and reflexivity . . . we are making ourselves increasingly irrelevant to contemporary policy and politics."[9] This is not to dismiss postmodern approaches—after all, they have partly inspired critiques of hegemonic discourses, including "Orientalist" discourses that have produced stereotypes of "the East"—but where they are found, introversion and self-absorption have undermined their potential connections to real world affairs. Malaysian anthropologist Wazir Karim argues that much of academic anthropology has isolated itself by refusing to confront pressing political issues such as the use of "Western" knowledge by "Third World" elites for the repression of workers, peasants, women, and indigenous people.[10] And Laura Nader recently noted that "anthropology is presently vastly hampered by both secrecy and self-censorship and in danger of becoming insular to the point of irrelevance except for literary and cultural studies concerns."[11]

In recent decades, anthropologists have become increasingly specialized and consequently fenced into narrow subspecialties and fields. Many are unable to communicate with wider publics. Critics have observed this phenomenon more generally across the social sciences and humanities, while others have commented upon the decline of "public intellectuals" in the United States in the twentieth century. This may be the culmination of historical processes: since at least the 1870s, social scientists who have publicly challenged established structures of power in the United States—particularly corporate power—have often been marginalized, persecuted, or stripped of their positions for allegedly violating the norms of an objective and value-free science.[12] Yet as economist Douglas Dowd once noted, "The alternatives are not 'neutrality' and 'advocacy.' To be uncommitted is not to be neutral, but to be committed—consciously or not—to the status quo."[13] We might take heart in knowing that there are clear exceptions to the rule of intellectual confinement among U.S. academics, as in the case of Edward Said, Patricia J. Williams, Henry Louis Gates, Jr., Cornel West, Juliet Schor, Noam Chomsky, and Saskia Sassen, all of whom communicate with broad publics.

There are more reasons why anthropologists do not reach wider audiences. At the same time that political and critical perspectives have arisen, the corporate media is becoming more restrictive and homogenous. The range of political perspectives has demonstrably narrowed in the last decade, according to media watchdog groups and foreign observers of U.S. conformity.

Factors internal to the discipline may also play a role in anthropologists opting out of communication with wider publics. A host of everyday practices function as barriers between academic anthropologists and nonprofessionals, including the business model of the AAA (and increasingly of academic departments), annual meetings held in luxury hotels, hiring practices and patron-client relationships that tend to exclude women and minorities, and class-based distinctions such as dress, speech, and other practices that reinforce the relatively narrow boundaries of the academic culture.

The need for anthropological input is great. Although many men and women have vast information about the world at their fingertips, never before have so many known so little about it. The acceleration of everyday life, along with passive, seductive, and addictive forms of leisure, block the exchange of knowledge, even easily accessible knowledge. Many ordinary people want to understand how their lives are connected to economic boom and bust, migration, corporate dominion, and war. We have an important role to play in this enterprise, as our predecessors did in the 1920s, the 1940s, and the late 1960s.

A reconnected anthropology might begin by looking at one of the most exotic cultures ever invented—our own. An economic anthropologist from Mars would probably be surprised that in a country where equality is highly valued, the wealthiest 1 percent of the population owns approximately 45 percent of the total assets. In 2001, the average CEO earned 500 times more than the average blue-collar worker, and more than 1,200 times more than the minimum wage worker. Assembly plants continue to close in the Rust Belt, the Deep South, and Silicon Valley, as jobs are exported to Latin America and Southeast Asia where labor costs are cheap and environmental laws are lax or ignored.

If our interplanetary visitor examined politics, he or she might also be intrigued by the collapse of Enron and the apparent contradictions between democracy in theory and in practice. More than half of the members of the House of Representatives and 71 of 100 senators have accepted campaign contributions from Enron, and George W. Bush accepted more than half a million dollars between 1994 and 2001. When eleven congressional committees were scheduled to investigate the company, reports surfaced that of the 248 members of Congress charged with the investigations, no less than 212 received "soft money" campaign contributions from either Enron or its accounting firm, Arthur Anderson.

Undoubtedly fascinated with the contradictory culture of the United States, our extraterrestrial colleague might move on to an analysis of legal systems and find it remarkable that in the present period, certain fundamental guarantees protected by constitutional law have been suspended. The FBI, CIA, and armed forces under the Bush administration have detained more than 1,000 Muslim and Arab people living in the United States in violation of their Constitutional rights, subjected hundreds of millions to greater surveillance, and declared a unilateral "war on terror" in utter disregard of international law. In March 2003 the Bush administration launched a war against Iraq while ignoring the U.N. Security Council.

In times like these, anthropological voices might shed light on cultural contradictions in our own society, the divergence between cultural ideals and realities and what happens as a result, and new possibilities for human action in a democratic society.

This might be a public service and even a civic duty: to observe and comment upon the United States today, the most powerful country on the planet; the relationships between its government officials, military establishment, and multinational corporations; and the effects and consequences of American Empire on the people that we have lived with and learned from in our research.

Anthropologists as Citizen-Scholars

Civic duty can be defined in different ways, and so can civic anthropology. During World War II, many prominent anthropologists in the United States contributed to the war effort. Ruth Benedict wrote her famous study of "culture at a distance," *The Chrysanthemum and the Sword,* to better understand the Japanese; Margaret Mead tried to analyze problems facing American GIs in England; George P. Murdock expanded the Human Relations Area Files with funding from the military; and Clyde Kluckhohn worked with the Office of Strategic Services or OSS (the precursor to the CIA), along with dozens of anthropologists. Others worked directly with Army and Navy intelligence and the Office of War Information (OWI).

These experiences indicate that public engagement does not always result in progressive politics or even humane policies. In fact, cultural knowledge has sometimes been applied during extraordinarily dark chapters in U.S. history. For instance, although anthropologists working for the OWI attempted to "convince the military that they did not have to engage in acts of genocidal annihilation" against Japan to end the war, others working as "community analysts" for the War Relocation Authority enthusiastically advised the government on how to efficiently administer internment camps where approximately 120,000 Japanese and Japanese-Americans were incarcerated on U.S. soil.[14] There are many other examples, including the case of Gregory Bateson, who while working with the OSS "applied his principles of *schismogenesis* to foster disorder among minority populations" in South Asia.[15] Though Bateson would later regret participating in such projects, others did not. Elements of this research were later used in psychological warfare operations and "culture cracking" strategies employed by the CIA in Vietnam and other countries. Our discipline's involvement in World War II reminds us that the application of anthropological knowledge—especially in the direct service of wartime government agencies—is not free of possible contradictions, paradoxes, and ethical dilemmas.

After World War II, anthropologists continued conducting covert operations for the CIA. The American Anthropological Association (AAA) collaborated secretly with the agency in the early 1950s to create a directory of the association's members with information about their research. Eventually, documents revealed that some anthropologists had undertaken clandestine projects with the U.S. military in its war in Southeast Asia in which they provided detailed ethnographic data on peasant communities, prepared surveys and reports on counterinsurgency, and gave information about the region's geography.[16] When word of this became public in the late 1960s and early 1970s, a fact-finding AAA committee headed by Margaret Mead reported no wrongdoing on the part of those involved, to the dismay of many members, particularly younger ones. For some social scientists, clearing the way for public debate on the war in Indochina began to take precedence over informing the CIA, the armed forces, and the military's think tanks. Critical to this shift was a change in notions of accountability: To which constituencies should the anthropologist be accountable? To the federal government and its subcontractors? To the subjects of his or her research? Or directly to the country and the American public?

When anthropologists found that ethnographic information was being used in ways they never intended—for example, to inflict harm upon people such as peasants suspected of being Communist sympathizers—they did not stand helplessly by. They mobilized themselves, rolled up their sleeves, and got to work. It seems clear that by the mid-1960s, a new kind of anthropology was emerging that for some redefined civic responsibility. For this group, civic duty wasn't necessarily unequivocal support for an undeclared U.S. war in Vietnam, or rallying behind the president to support the war. An alternative definition of civic duty might mean protection and promotion of freedom, reason, and equality—even if that conflicted with official government policy.

The painful political lessons of World War II and Vietnam shook our discipline and the academy to their cores. We learned that the military-industrial complex described by President Eisenhower in his 1961 farewell address to the country might undermine America's liberties and democratic processes—and our professional autonomy.

Anthropologists were at the forefront during this transformation.[17] Marshall Sahlins is credited with creating the teach-in at the University of Michigan in 1965, with help from colleagues such as Eric Wolf and, at UC Berkeley, Gerald Berreman. During teach-ins students, professors, and citizens would meet after hours (sometimes in all-night sessions) to read and discuss books and articles about the history and culture of Southeast Asia, Latin America, and areas of the world undergoing upheaval and to talk about current events, especially the war in Vietnam. In 1969 Dell Hymes edited *Reinventing Anthropology*, which among other things called for an anthropology relevant to the times, an awareness of its colonial roots, greater inclusion of minorities in the discipline, and the study of powerful institutions.[18] Others including Laura Nader spoke to community groups such as Kiwanis and Rotary Clubs in order to inform older people about issues concerning young people: free speech, civil rights, women's rights, and Vietnam. Still others insisted that anthropologists be accountable primarily to American principles. Many insisted that the interests of field subjects take precedence over military interests, and succeeded in writing a code of ethics for the American Anthropological Association reflecting this concern—at great risk to their professional careers.[19] (The code of ethics was passed in 1970, but as we shall see in Selection 7, it was diluted in the 1980s.) In different ways these scholars brought universities into the public spotlight, in some cases for the first time in many years, breaking the silence of the McCarthy era.

These scholars shifted their efforts to inform the general public and broaden public debate on issues of war and peace. Others continued informing the generals in the military. Those reaching the general public taught students and laypeople important information useful for carrying out the challenging work of participatory democracy.

Reconnecting Anthropology

What about today? If we focus upon the accelerating expansion of U.S. influence across the globe—and the imminent crises provoked by these new colonial relationships largely invisible to Americans—we find a growing number of examples of a publicly engaged anthropology that communicates directly with the citizenry, independently of official governmental channels. Some are speaking out and living up to the professional and public responsibilities of the discipline—a critical task in the current wartime climate of national fear and uncertainty.[20] Anthropologist David Price has recently suggested that "in times of war we have a fundamental duty as scholars and citizens to counter the limited views of American and allied policy makers . . . efforts in this direction would be most effective if we operate as citizen-scholars outside of governmental agencies." This collection samples such independent scholarship.

It begins with "War, Peace, and Social Responsibility," a section written by anthropologists over a span of eighty years. Franz Boas' letter to the editor of *The Nation,* "Scientists as Spies," is a classic example of how anthropologists have engaged pressing contemporary issues—in this case, the use of social scientists for espionage during World War I. His brief letter aroused so much controversy that it led to his expulsion from the AAA. The next piece is a 1940 article by Boas's student, Margaret Mead, who in "Warfare Is Only an Invention—Not a Biological Necessity" makes an appeal for alternative means of resolving global conflicts. The next selections revisit the Vietnam era. In 1965 Marshall Sahlins shocked readers with an account of psychological torture techniques described to him by U.S. military advisers. Gerald D. Berreman discusses anthropology's lack of accountability following revelations that some of its practitioners had been involved in clandestine counterinsurgency projects. "Two Plus Two Equals Zero," a selection by Laura Nader written in the early 1980s, describes the unplanned, unconscious, and incremental movement toward war in our society at a time of unprecedented growth of the nuclear arsenal. "Dollars That Forge Guatemalan Chains" is a commentary by Beatriz Manz which documents the brutality of the civil war in Guatemala and the U.S. role in supporting the state military in that conflict. David Price's contribution, "Anthropologists as Spies," revisits the topic introduced by Boas in 1919. After examining the espionage cases mentioned by Boas, Price singles out the AAA's long-standing reluctance to issue statements condemning covert research and espionage. He notes that the economic realities of the present era may make spying even more attractive to some: "As increasing numbers of anthropologists find employment in corporations, anthropological research becomes not a quest for scientific truth, as in the days of Boas, but a quest for secret or proprietary data for governmental or corporate sponsors." The section concludes with a commentary by Pierre Bourdieu entitled, "Abuse of Power by the Advocates of Reason," which critiques multinational corporate regimes, the World Bank, and the IMF on the grounds that they are impoverishing entire regions and provoking violent backlash.

The next section, "Prescient Anthropology," zeroes in on the work of anthropologists describing international crises in the making—sometimes years in advance. For example, Robert M. Hayden, who conducted field research in the former Yugoslavia and India, published an early warning in 1991 about the impending threat of ethnic conflict in the post–Cold War era. His words read prophetically, years before the massacres in Rwanda or the former Yugoslavia. Another article by Hayden critiques the unprecedented NATO bombing of Kosovo in 1999. Anna Simons published a series of op-ed pieces for the *Washington Post* on the desperate conditions in Somalia long before *Black Hawk Down*. Her words tell the story of a nation devastated by civil war, famine, and refugees. They also convey concern for lack of media coverage and a poorly informed group of policy "experts." Her words too were visionary; they foretold and then analyzed the botched U.S. mission in Somalia. Other contributors are prescient in their analyses. Articles by Winifred Tate and Lesley Gill critique U.S. military aid to Colombia (specifically, its use in the "war on drugs") and emphasize the necessity for a peaceful resolution to that country's internal conflicts, while Marc Edelman's commentary focuses on the link between free trade policies and famine in Central America. The Israeli occupation of the Gaza Strip and the West Bank and the worsening crisis there are the focus of contributions from a Palestinian anthropologist, Ali Qleibo, and an Israeli anthropologist, Jeff Halper (coordinator of the Israeli Committee against House Demolitions). The section ends with Hugh Gusterson's critique of our government's proposals to dump the comprehensive nuclear test ban treaty.

The section "Prelude to September 11" includes articles and interviews describing grave crises in Central Asia, the Middle East, and Africa. Ashraf Ghani, an anthropologist recently appointed as Afghanistan's finance minister, was by early 1989 warning that abandoning that country could have disastrous consequences over the long term. James Merryman's piece, written following the 1998 attacks on American embassies in Kenya and Tanzania, suggests that aid to the families of hundreds of African victims and a clearer foreign policy might improve our country's standing in those countries. Robert Fernea and Barbara Nimri Aziz focus on various aspects of the first Gulf War and the aftermath of the economic embargo. Fadwa El Guindi, writing years before most Americans had heard of the Taliban, published an op-ed piece describing the plight of women in Algeria, Afghanistan, and several other predominantly Muslim societies. An interview with Zieba Shorish-Shamley describes different aspects of the Taliban's repression of women. The section concludes with William O. Beeman's 1998 analysis of the "mess in Afghanistan" and the role of oil corporations seeking to secure a route to the petroleum reserves of the Caspian Sea.

The attacks on the World Trade Center and the Pentagon inspired a great many responses from academics, and the section "Anthropological Interpretations of September 11" presents some of the most thoughtful and well articulated. Catherine Lutz, who has recently focused her career on the relationship between society and the military in the United States, writes that our country has been in "a permanent state of war" since the late 1930s but that for many Americans this has not been visible because conflict has been "outsourced to the global south." David Harvey, Talal Asad, and colleagues from the CUNY Graduate Center strongly condemn the attacks and then make an impassioned appeal for the United States to refrain from the "intensification of erroneous policies and practices" overseas. William O. Beeman's article focuses on the dangers of engaging bin Laden and his allies in a shortsighted war of revenge. In separate articles, Janet McIntosh and Wade Davis critique the inability or unwillingness of our leaders to come to terms with the role of the United States in creating the conditions that led to the attacks of September 11.

The next section is "On Afghanistan, Central Asia, and the Middle East." Robert Canfield's piece emphasizes the complexity of Afghanistan and painstakingly outlines the relationships between the Taliban, mujahedeen, "Arab-Afghans" (including bin Laden), and different ethnic groups within Afghanistan. Ashraf Ghani's contribution examines the complexity of the political situation in Afghanistan and the possible risks of quick military action there by our armed forces. Nazif Shahrani counsels the eventual formation of a new Afghanistan based on the stability of past models: "The international community should encourage the creation of a government that recognizes the crucial role of the local and regional communities in self-governance, as existed in earlier eras in Afghanistan." The next selection is an interview with Zieba Shorish-Shamley at meetings in Brussels, Belgium, in which Afghan women's groups were creating a common set of demands. She emphasizes the need for women to be fairly represented in Afghanistan's new government. David Edwards and Shahmahmood Miakhel stress the importance of enlisting the aid of ordinary Afghans in confronting the Taliban regime. Kamran Asdar Ali focuses on the dilemmas faced by Pakistan following the events of September 11, specifically the tensions faced by its leaders in the face of mounting domestic criticism for cooperation with the United States. Finally, an article based on interviews with Sergei Arutyunov and Ian Chesnov describes how the Russian war on Chechnya has destroyed kinship structures that formed the basis of social life. According to the report, "Chechnya's younger people . . . are disoriented, and are now looking for new authority figures—a search that in many instances leads them to the radical Wahhabi Islamic sect or leaders of criminal rings."

In the next section, "Examining Militarism and the 'War on Terror,'" anthropologists explore several pressing issues after September 11. William O. Beeman's commentary challenges the assumptions of U.S. leaders proclaiming anti-terrorist messages by delving into the centuries-old patterns of Western exploitation of societies in the Middle East. David Price notes that the vague definition and use of the word "terrorism" as a catchall phrase has led to its rapid adoption by Russian leaders to describe Chechnya's separatists, by Chinese leaders to describe Uighur separatists, and by others. Consequently, the "war on terror" poses a threat to native peoples and ethnic minorities throughout the world. In separate commentaries, John Burdick and Roberto J. González argue that U.S. bombing raids over Afghanistan—and the resulting civilian casualties—are making future terrorist attacks on the United States more, not less, likely to occur. Dale F. Eickelman's contribution makes a critical point: that new media technologies including video and satellite images, computers, and advanced telecommunications are a part of daily life in the Arab-speaking world. Mahmood Mamdani makes an impassioned plea for U.S. policy makers not to allow the "war on terror" to permit U.S.-African relations to slide back to the Cold War era. The section closes with a Thomas McKenna interview which explores the historical roots of Muslim separatism in the Philippines. The wide-ranging interview touches upon the effects of Spanish and U.S. colonialism on Muslim identity, as well as more recent developments.

The final section, "Academic Freedom and Civil Liberties," analyzes attacks on constitutional guarantees within the United States. Roberto J. González and David Price examine the implications of a document circulated by the American Council of Trustees and Alumni in late 2001, which singles out dozens of academics for allegedly being "short on patriotism," while Hugh Gusterson—the first scholar named in the report—takes issue with the way in which its authors take statements out of context. More importantly, he also describes how this fits a long historical pattern of scapegoating that tends to occur in our country during times of war. Laura Nader's article, published two months before the attacks on the World Trade Center and the Pentagon, is about "coercive harmony"—imposed social harmony—and its consequences. The concept's relevance in the post–September 11 period is clear, as many Americans feel pressure to fall into line with the dictates of the Bush administration's policies. She writes: "Coercive harmony can stifle dissent for a while. But if dissent is too tightly bottled up, it will explode . . . Academics should not be party to establishing an ideology of consensus on our increasingly corporatized campuses. Instead, we have a duty to investigate the dangers of coercive harmony and to expose repression when it poses as consensus."

Taken as a whole, the collection makes a strong case for the relevance of anthropology to the contemporary world, as well as for the strength and vitality of tried and true techniques used by its practitioners.

An Argument for Public Anthropology

Many academics have been trained to think that writing for the public is not worth doing because it is perceived as politically risky. But is there any truth to this assertion? Is anthropology perceived as a subversive activity?

On the surface, these appear to be challenging times for academic freedom. In October 2001, a Washington, D.C.–based group called the American Council of Trustees and Alumni published a report titled *Defending Civilization: How Our Universities Are Failing America.* It documented 117 campus incidents as "evidence" of academic anti-Americanism and was distributed to university regents, trustees, and administrators. Of the forty-five scholars cited in the report, five were anthropologists. More anthropologists were included than scholars of any other discipline.

It seems that anthropologists were highly visible on the list because ours is a field that contextualizes and integrates multiple points of view —social, political, economic, and historical—and of course because many of us do this kind of work in foreign countries. What has changed radically is not anthropology but the time in which we are living. Today, some view contextual, historical knowledge about other cultures as subversive, unpatriotic, and possibly un-American!

But fortunately, they appear to be on the margins. The response to the ACTA report was dramatic and critics on the right and the left protested. Lynne Cheney and Joseph Lieberman, who co-founded ACTA in 1995, distanced themselves from the report.

Because of a surge in publicly engaged anthropology since September 11—including participation in campus rallies and teach-ins—it is clear that anthropologists have an important job ahead. Threats and blacklists are a sign that we are following in the footsteps of Boas, Mead, Montagu, and others who spoke up and were harshly criticized for their views by some and lauded by others.

The rewards of participating in a publicly engaged anthropology more than compensate for the challenges. Writing for and speaking with the general public is intellectually challenging, politically satisfying—and exhilarating.

Such work is intellectually challenging because it encourages the translation and distillation of complex ideas into a language that non-specialists can understand. (Imagine explaining the meaning of cultural relativism or social solidarity or the significance of clans to a person who has never taken an anthropology course or read a book on the topic.) The limitations are severe—the typical op-ed piece is limited to 750 words. This is a focused kind of writing and speaking that takes time, effort, and verbal economy. It promotes the use of appropriate metaphors, logical argumentation, precise timing, and conciseness.

Politically, this work can be satisfying because it connects us to our civic duties and provides a public service: citizen education. By articulating thoughtful, informed perspectives for a wide audience, we are providing interested people with viewpoints that might otherwise go unmentioned, particularly in the current climate of self-censorship on the part of the corporate media and the public at large. We might even think of this work as democratic outreach, or social science in the service of society, or even civic anthropology for the twenty-first century. Perhaps a clearer articulation of the vital role played by citizen-scholars would lead to a new valuation of intellectual work in the public interest and recognition of this work in tenure reviews. In this regard, the U.S. case is almost unique. In most countries of the world, intellectuals are *expected* to be participants in citizen causes and do so, sometimes at the risk of being jailed—or worse.

Finally, writing and speaking with the general public can be exhilarating. Letters or phone calls in response to an op-ed piece can be educational and used as tools for reflection. They may lead to connections with community groups, activists, policy makers, or invitations to write and speak publicly. And not least of all, communication with the public dramatically demonstrates to students that anthropology does indeed have a public face and relevance in the contemporary world.

Recently Robert Borofsky asked Norwegian anthropologist Fredrik Barth what steps might be taken to draw more anthropologists into public engagements. He answered: "The image that comes to mind is of American anthropologists, like penguins on the edge of an ice sheet afraid that something in the water will eat them. They stand on the ice and push and push each other until one falls in, and then they see what happens to him. If nothing bad happens, then they might be willing to dive in, too."[21]

The contributors to this collection are jumping into chilly waters. The experience can be startling, refreshing, and exhilarating. Others have taken the plunge as well: the extraordinary and inspiring efforts of Cultural Survival and Living Beyond Culture exemplify a kind of public engagement being carried out by valiant anthropologists whose work is deeply rooted in indigenous and local struggles. As more and more anthropologists and students embark upon such adventures, they are sure to find strength in numbers. We have much to contribute, and even more to gain.

NOTES

1. See Chalmers A. Johnson, *Blowback: The Costs and Consequences of American Empire* (New York: Metropolitan Books, 2000); Paul Kennedy, *The Rise and Fall of the Great Powers: Economic Change and Military Conflict from 1500 to 2000* (New York: Vintage Books, 1989); Paul Sweezy, Harry Magdoff, John Bellamy Foster, and Robert McChesney, "U.S. Military Bases and Empire," *Monthly Review*, March 2002, pp. 1–16.

2. This trend is described in Sheldon Rampton and John Stauber, *Trust Us, We're Experts!* (New York: Tarcher Putnam, 2001).

3. The term "pundit" is derived from the Hindi term *pandit*, meaning "religious scholar," and was adopted by British colonists in India in 1816 as a term meaning "learned person." Today the word preserves a bit of irony and questioning of the person's authority.

4. See Laura Nader, "Anthropology!" *American Anthropologist* 103, no. 3 (September 2001): 1–12.

5. See Marshall Sahlins, *Stone Age Economics* (Chicago: Aldine, 1972), pp. 1–39.

6. See Bronislaw Malinowski, *Magic, Science, Religion, and Other Essays* (Garden City, N.J.: Anchor Doubleday, 1948 [1925]).

7. See Margaret Mead, *Coming of Age in Samoa* (Washington, D.C.: American Museum of Natural History, 1928).

8. See Franz Boas, *Race, Language, and Culture* (New York: Macmillan, 1940).

9. See Kendall M. Thu, "Anthropologists Should Return to the Roots of Their Discipline," *Chronicle of Higher Education* (April 30, 1999): A56.

10. See Wazir Karim, "Anthropology without Tears: How a 'Local' Sees the 'Local' and the 'Global,'" in Henrietta Moore, ed., *The Future of Anthropological Knowledge* (London: Routledge, 1996), pp. 115–138.

11. Quoted March 29, 1999, in a symposium of the American Association for the Advancement of Science titled "Secrecy in Science" at the Massachusetts Institute of Technology. Accessed from the electronic text of her comments, as posted at <http://www.aaas.org/spp/secrecy/Presents/nader.htm>.

12. See Mary O. Furner, *Advocacy and Objectivity: A Crisis in the Professionalization of American Social Science, 1865–1905* (Lexington: University Press of Kentucky, 1975). For one account of the decline of public intellectuals in the twentieth century, see Russell Jacoby, *The Last Intellectuals* (New York: Basic Books, 1987).

13. See Douglas Dowd, "Thorstein Veblen and C. Wright Mills: Social Science and Social Criticism," in Irving Horowitz, ed., *The New Sociology* (New York: Oxford University Press, 1964), pp. 54–66.

14. David Price, "Lessons from Second World War Anthropology," *Anthropology Today* 18, no. 3 (June 2002): 18. See also Orin Starn, "Engineering Internment: Anthropologists and the War Relocation Authority," *American Ethnologist* 13, no. 4 (December 1996): 700–720.

15. See David Price, "Past Wars, Present Dangers, Future Anthropologies," *Anthropology Today* 18, no. 1 (March 2002): 3–5.

16. See Eric R. Wolf and Joseph G. Jorgensen, "Anthropology on the Warpath in Thailand," *New York Review of Books*, November 19, 1970, pp. 26–35.

17. See Laura Nader, "The Phantom Factor: Impact of the Cold War on Anthropology," in Noam Chomsky, ed., *The Cold War & the University* (New York: New Press, 1997), pp. 107–146.

18. See Dell Hymes, ed., *Reinventing Anthropology* (New York: Vintage, 1969). The contributions by Gerald D. Berreman, William S. Willis, Jr., Eric Wolf, and Laura Nader are especially relevant.

19. See Eric Wakin, *Anthropology Goes to War: Professional Ethics and Counterinsurgency in Thailand* (Madison: University of Wisconsin Center for Asian Studies, 1992).

20. See Laura Nader, "Breaking the Silence—Politics and Professional Autonomy." *Anthropological Quarterly* (winter 2001): 155–163.

21. Quoted in "Envisioning a More Public Anthropology: An Interview with Fredrik Barth," April 18, 2001. Accessed from electronic text posted at <http://www.publicanthropology.org/Journals/Engaging-Ideas/barth.htm.>

PART I

WAR, PEACE, AND SOCIAL RESPONSIBILITY

CHAPTER 1

SCIENTISTS AS SPIES

The Nation, October 16, 1919

FRANZ BOAS   Franz Boas (1858–1942), who founded the first American academic department of anthropology at Columbia University in 1898, wrote many popular articles in the early 1900s on issues including race problems, immigration, and U.S. involvement in World War I. He profoundly believed that scientific knowledge widely disseminated could potentially lead to popular enlightenment and social reform.[1]

In the following article, Boas condemns anthropologists recruited by the U.S. government for espionage during World War I. He was especially outraged to learn that two of the spies had used contacts that he had provided to them for research purposes. When the issue came before the American Anthropological Association in 1920, Boas was censured and removed from office.

Boas had become an American citizen in 1891, yet remained sympathetic to his native Germany. He publicly opposed U.S. entry into World War I. These circumstances undoubtedly made him even more sensitive to the idea of his fellow anthropologists engaging in espionage for the American side.

In an eloquent letter to the editor published in the *New York Times* on January 8, 1916, Boas revealed his own changing attitudes about U.S. foreign policy in the context of a rapidly expanding American Empire: "At the time of my arrival more than thirty years ago, I was filled with admiration of American political ideals . . . I thought of it as a country that would not tolerate interference with its own interests, but that would also refrain from oppression of unwilling subjects . . . A rude awakening came in 1898, when the aggressive imperialism of that period [in Cuba, the Philippines, etc.] showed that the ideal had been a dream . . . The America that had stood for right, and right only, seemed dead; and in its place stood a young giant, eager to grow at the expense of others."[2]

To the Editor of *The Nation:*

Sir: In his war address to Congress, President Wilson dwelt at great length on the theory that only autocracies maintain spies; that these are not needed in democracies. At the time that the President made this statement, the Government of the United States had in its employ several spies of unknown number. I am not concerned here with the familiar discrepancies between the President's words and the actual facts, although we may perhaps have to accept his statement as meaning correctly that we live under an autocracy; that our democracy is a fiction. The point against which I wish to enter a vigorous protest is that a number of men who follow science as their profession, men whom I refuse to designate any longer as scientists, have prostituted science by using it as a cover for their activities as spies.

A soldier whose business is murder as a fine art, a diplomat whose calling is based on deception and secretiveness, a politician whose very life consists in compromises with his conscience, a business man whose aim is personal profit within the limits allowed by a lenient law—such may be excused if they set patriotic devotion above common everyday decency and perform services as spies. They merely accept the code of morality to which modern society still conforms. Not so the scientist. The very essence of his life is the service of truth. We all know scientists who in private life do not come up to the standard of truthfulness, but who, nevertheless, would not consciously falsify the results of their researches. It is bad enough if we have to put up with these, because they reveal a lack of strength of character that is liable to distort the results of their work. A person, however, who uses science as a cover for political spying, who demeans himself to pose before a foreign government as an investigator and asks for assistance in his alleged researches in order to carry on, under this cloak, his political machinations, prostitutes science in an unpardonable way and forfeits the right to be classed as a scientist.

By accident, incontrovertible proof has come to my hands that at least four men who carry on anthropological work, while employed as government agents, introduced themselves to foreign governments as representatives of scientific institutions in the United States, and as sent out for the purpose of carrying on scientific researches. They have not only shaken the belief in the truthfulness of science, but they have also done the greatest possible disservice to scientific inquiry. In consequence of their acts every nation will look with distrust upon the visiting foreign investigator who wants to do honest work, suspecting sinister designs. Such action has raised a new barrier against the development of international friendly cooperation.

EDITOR'S NOTES

1. See George W. Stocking Jr., "Anthropology and Society," in Franz Boas, *A Franz Boas Reader* (Chicago: University of Chicago Press, 1975), pp. 307–309. Following the German sociological tradition of Max Weber, Boas assumed that as scientists, anthropologists should hold themselves to a high standard of objectivity—even when they produced truths threatening powerful interests. This was clearly exemplified in Boas' attacks on racism: since racial hierarchies were based upon faulty science, racist policies had no rational justification.

2. Ibid., pp. 331–332.

SUGGESTIONS FOR FURTHER READING

Boas, Franz
    1940   *Race, Culture, and Language.* New York: Macmillan.
    1974   *A Franz Boas Reader.* Edited by George W. Stocking Jr. Chicago: University of Chicago Press.

CHAPTER 2

WARFARE IS ONLY AN INVENTION—NOT A BIOLOGICAL NECESSITY

Asia, 1940

MARGARET
MEAD

Margaret Mead (1901–1978) was among Boas' most renowned students. Like her mentor, she made anthropological knowledge accessible to the general public and frequently critiqued aspects of American culture.

Along with dozens of anthropologists, Mead served as a government adviser during World War II. Together with Ruth Benedict she founded the Columbia University Research in Contemporary Cultures project, which was under the auspices of the U.S. Office of Naval Research and analyzed the cultures of America's enemies and allies, including Germany, Japan, England, France, and the Soviet Union.

Mead was profoundly affected by the advent of a nuclear age, after U.S. planes bombed Hiroshima and Nagasaki. Throughout her career, she publicly expressed opposition to war as a means of resolving conflict—perhaps a contradictory stance in light of her involvement with U.S. military and intelligence efforts. She once said, "Those who still cling to the old, simple definition of patriotism have not yet recognized that since Hiroshima there cannot be winners and losers in a war, but only losers. And they are vocal out of desperation about a world they do not understand."[1]

The following article was published in 1940, as Nazi Germany invaded Europe and the Japanese swept across Asia. Mead's argument is lucid and powerful: that war is a cultural phenomenon, not a biological one. It still stands as a thought-provoking counterpoint to those who assert that warfare is a part of human nature. Readers should be aware of the occasional use of outdated terminology such as "simple peoples," which reflects the persistence of elements of Victorian-era social evolutionism in American anthropology as late as the 1940s.

Mead has had many critics over the years. Perhaps the sharpest rebukes have come from those critical of the contradictions between her public antiwar statements and writings and her tacit support of U.S. foreign policy.

Anthropologist Peter Worsely notes, "Mead's political stance . . . [and] her criticisms of Western institutions [are] always vitiated by her commitment to U.S. foreign policy . . . Mead's theoretical posture of concern about the danger of global war never prevented her continuing in the service of the U.S. State Department and the military long after World War II."[2]

Is war a biological necessity, a sociological inevitability, or just a bad invention? Those who argue for the first view endow man with such pugnacious instincts that some outlet in aggressive behavior is necessary if man is to reach full human stature. It was this point of view which lay behind William James's famous essay, "The Moral Equivalent of War," in which he tried to retain the warlike virtues and channel them in new directions. A similar point of view has lain behind the Soviet Union's attempt to make competition between groups rather than between individuals. A basic, competitive, aggressive, warring human nature is assumed, and those who wish to outlaw war or outlaw competitiveness merely try to find new and less socially destructive ways in which these biologically given aspects of man's nature can find expression. Then there are those who take the second view: warfare is the inevitable concomitant of the development of the state, the struggle for land and natural resources, of class societies springing not from the nature of man, but, from the nature of history. War is nevertheless inevitable unless we change our social system and outlaw classes, the struggle for power, and possessions; and in the event of our success warfare would disappear, as a symptom vanishes when the disease is cured.

One may hold a sort of compromise position between these two extremes; one may claim that all aggression springs from the frustration of man's biologically determined drives and that, since all forms of culture are frustrating, it is certain each new generation will be aggressive and the aggression will find its natural and inevitable expression in race war, class war, nationalistic war, and so on. All three of these positions are very popular today among those who think seriously about the problems of war and its possible prevention, but I wish to urge another point of view, less defeatist, perhaps, than the first and third and more accurate than the second: that is, that warfare, by which I mean recognized conflict between two groups as groups, in which each group puts an army (even if the army is only fifteen pygmies) into the field to fight and kill, if possible, some of the members of the army of the other group—that warfare of this sort is an invention like any other of the inventions in terms of which we order our lives, such as writing, marriage, cooking our food instead of eating it raw, trial by jury, or burial of the dead, and so on. Some of this list anyone will grant are inventions: trial by jury is confined to very limited portions of the globe; we know that there are tribes that do not bury their dead but instead expose or cremate them; and we know that only part of the human race has had the knowledge of writing as its cultural inheritance. But, whenever a way of doing things is found universally, such as the use of fire or the practice of some form of marriage, we tend to think at once that it is not an invention at all but an attribute of humanity itself. And yet even such universals as marriage and the use of fire are inventions like the rest, very basic ones, inventions which were, perhaps, necessary if human history was to take the turn that it has taken, but nevertheless inventions. At some point in his social development man was undoubtedly without the institution of marriage or the knowledge of the use of fire.

The case for warfare is much clearer because there are peoples even today who have no warfare. Of these the Eskimos are perhaps the most conspicuous examples, but the Lepchas of Sikkim described by Geoffrey Gorer in *Himalayan Village* are as good. Neither of these peoples understands war, not even defensive warfare. The idea of warfare is lacking, and this idea is as essential to really carrying on war as an alphabet or a syllabary is to writing. But, whereas the Lepchas are a gentle, unquarrelsome people, and the advocates of other points of view might argue that they are not full human beings or that they had never been frustrated and so had no aggression to expend in warfare, the Eskimo case gives no such possibility of interpretation. The Eskimos are not a mild and meek people; many of them are turbulent and troublesome. Fights, theft of wives, murder, cannibalism, occur among them—all outbursts of passionate men goaded by desire or intolerable circumstance. Here are men faced with hunger, men faced with loss of their wives, men faced with the threat of extermination by other men, and here are orphan children, growing up miserably with no one to care for them, mocked and neglected by those about them. The personality necessary for war, the circumstances necessary to goad men to desperation are present, but there is no war. When a traveling Eskimo entered a settlement, he might have had to fight the strongest man in the settlement to establish his position among them, but this was a test of strength and bravery, not war. The idea of warfare, of one group organizing against another group to maim and wound and kill them was absent. And, without that idea, passions might rage but there was no war.

But, it may be argued, is not this because the Eskimos have such a low and undeveloped form of social organization? They own no land, they move from place to place, camping, it is true, season after season on the same site, but this is not something to fight for as the modern nations of the world fight for land and raw materials. They have no permanent possessions that can be looted, no towns that can be burned. They have no social classes to produce stress and strains within the society which might force it to go to war outside. Does not the absence of war among the Eskimos, while disproving the biological necessity of war, just go to confirm the point that it is the state of development of the society which accounts for war and nothing else?

We find the answer among the pygmy peoples of the Andaman Islands in the Bay of Bengal. The Andamans also represent an exceedingly low level of society; they are a hunting and food-gathering people; they live in tiny hordes without any class stratification; their houses are simpler than the snow houses of the Eskimo. But they knew about warfare. The army might contain only fifteen determined pygmies marching in a straight line, but it was the real thing nonetheless. Tiny army met tiny army in open battle, blows were exchanged, casualties suffered, and the state of warfare could only be concluded by a peacemaking ceremony.

Similarly, among the Australian aborigines, who built no permanent dwellings but wandered from water hole to water hole over their almost desert country, warfare—and rules of "international law"—were highly developed. The student of social evolution will seek in vain for his obvious causes of war—struggle for lands, struggle for power of one group over another, expansion of population, need to divert the minds of a populace restive under tyranny, or even the ambition of a successful leader to enhance his own prestige. All are absent, but warfare as a practice remained, and men engaged in it and killed one another in the course of a war because killing is what is done in wars.

From instances like these it becomes apparent that an inquiry into the causes of war misses the fundamental point as completely as does an insistence upon the biological necessity of war. If a people have an idea of going to war and the idea that war is the way in which certain situations, defined within their society, are to be handled, they will sometimes go to war. If they are a mild and unaggressive people, like the Pueblo Indians, they may limit themselves to defensive warfare, but they will be forced to think in terms of war because there are peoples near them who have warfare as a pattern, and offensive, raiding, pillaging warfare at that. When the pattern of warfare is known, people like the Pueblo Indians will defend themselves, taking advantage of the natural defenses of their mesa village site, and people like the Lepchas, having no natural defenses and no idea of warfare, will merely submit to the invader. But the essential point remains the same. There is a way of behaving which is known to a given people and labeled as an appropriate form of behavior; a bold and warlike people like the Sioux or the Maori may label warfare as desirable as well as possible, a mild people like the Pueblo Indians may label warfare as undesirable, but to the minds of both peoples the possibility of warfare is present. Their thoughts, their hopes, their plans are oriented about this idea— that warfare may be selected as the way to meet some situation.

So simple peoples and civilized peoples, mild peoples and violent, assertive peoples, will all go to war if they have the invention, just as those peoples who have the custom of dueling will have duels and peoples who have the pattern of vendetta will indulge in vendetta. And, conversely, peoples who do not know of dueling will not fight duels, even though their wives are seduced and their daughters ravished; they may on occasion commit murder but they will not fight duels. Cultures which lack the idea of the vendetta will not meet every quarrel in this way. A people can use only the forms it has. So the Balinese have their special way of dealing with a quarrel between two individuals: if the two feel that the causes of quarrel are heavy, they may go and register their quarrel in the temple before the gods, and, making offerings, they may swear never to have anything to do with each other again. But in other societies, although individuals might feel as full of animosity and as unwilling to have any further contact as do the Balinese, they cannot register their quarrel with the gods and go on quietly about their business because registering quarrels with the gods is not an invention of which they know.

Yet, if it be granted that warfare is, after all, an invention, it may nevertheless be an invention that lends itself to certain types of personality, to the exigent needs of autocrats, to the expansionist desires of crowded peoples, to the desire for plunder and rape and loot which is engendered by a dull and frustrating life. What, then, can we say of this congruence between warfare and its uses? If it is a form which fits so well, is not this congruence the essential point? But even here the primitive material causes us to wonder, because there are tribes who go to war merely for glory, having no quarrel with the enemy, suffering from no tyrant within their boundaries, anxious neither for land nor loot nor women, but merely anxious to win prestige which within that tribe has been declared obtainable only by war and without which no young man can hope to win his sweetheart's smile of approval. But if, as was the case with the Bush Negroes of Dutch Guiana, it is artistic ability which is necessary to win a girl's approval, the same young man would have to be carving rather than going out on a war party.

In many parts of the world, war is a game in which the individual can win counters—counters which bring him prestige in the eyes of his own sex or of the opposite sex; he plays for these counters as he might, in our society, strive for a tennis championship. Warfare is a frame for such prestige-seeking merely because it calls for the display of certain skills and certain virtues; all of these skills—riding straight, shooting straight, dodging the missiles of the enemy and sending one's own straight to the mark—can be equally well exercised in some other framework and, equally, the virtues—endurance, bravery, loyalty, steadfastness—can be displayed in other contexts. The tie-up between proving oneself a man and proving this by a success in organized killing is due to a definition which many societies have made of manliness. And often, even in those societies which counted success in warfare a proof of human worth, strange turns were given to the idea, as when the Plains Indians gave their highest awards to the man who touched a live enemy rather than to the man who brought in a scalp—from a dead enemy—because the latter was less risky. Warfare is just an invention known to the majority of human societies by which they permit their young men either to accumulate prestige or avenge their honor or acquire loot or wives or slaves or sago lands or cattle or appease the blood lust of their gods or the restless souls of the recently dead. It is just an invention, older and more widespread than the jury system, but nonetheless an invention.

But, once we have said this, have we said anything at all? Despite a few instances, dear to the hearts of controversialists, of the loss of the useful arts, once an invention is made which proves congruent with human needs or social forms, it tends to persist. Grant that war is an invention, that it is not a biological necessity nor the outcome of certain special types of social forms, still once the invention is made, what are we to do about it? The Indian who had been subsisting on the buffalo for generations because with his primitive weapons he could slaughter only a limited number of buffalo did not return to his primitive weapons when he saw that the white man's more efficient weapons were exterminating the buffalo. A desire for the white man's cloth may mortgage the South Sea Islander to the white man's plantation, but he does not return to making bark cloth, which would have left him free. Once an invention is known and accepted, men do not easily relinquish it. The skilled workers may smash the first steam looms which they feel are to be their undoing, but they accept them in the end, and no movement which has insisted upon the mere abandonment of usable inventions has ever had much success. Warfare is here, as part of our thought; the deeds of warriors are immortalized in the words of our poets, the toys of our children are modeled upon the weapons of the soldier, the frame of reference within which our statesmen and our diplomats work always contains war. If we know that it is not inevitable, that it is due to historical accident that warfare is one of the ways in which we think of behaving, are we given any hope by that? What hope is there of persuading nations to abandon war, nations so thoroughly imbued with the idea that resort to war is, if not actually desirable and noble, at least inevitable whenever certain defined circumstances arise?

In answer to this question I think we might turn to the history of other social inventions, and inventions which must once have seemed as finally entrenched as warfare. Take the methods of trial which preceded the jury system: ordeal and trial by combat. Unfair, capricious, alien as they are to our feeling today, they were once the only methods open to individuals accused of some offense. The invention of trial by jury gradually replaced these methods until only witches, and finally not even witches, had to resort to the ordeal. And for a long time the jury system seemed the best and finest method of settling legal disputes, but today new inventions, trial before judges only or before commissions, are replacing the jury system. In each case the old method was replaced by a new social invention. The ordeal did not go out because people thought it unjust or wrong; it went out because a method more congruent with the institutions and feelings of the period was invented. And, if we despair over the way in which war seems such an ingrained habit of most of the human race, we can take comfort from the fact that a poor invention will usually give place to a better invention.

For this, two conditions, at least, are necessary. The people must recognize the defects of the old invention, and someone must make a new one. Propaganda against warfare, documentation of its terrible cost in human suffering and social waste, these prepare the ground by teaching people to feel that warfare is a defective social institution. There is further needed a belief that social invention is possible and the invention of new methods which will render warfare as out of date as the tractor is making the plough, or the motor car the horse and buggy. A form of behavior becomes out of date only when something else takes its place, and, in order to invent forms of behavior which will make war obsolete, it is a first requirement to believe that an invention is possible.

EDITOR'S NOTES

1. Quoted in William O. Beeman, "Postscript to September 11: What Would Margaret Mead Say?" *Pacific News Service*, November 27, 2001.

2. See Lenora Foerstel and Angela Gilliam, eds., *Confronting the Margaret Mead Legacy: Scholarship, Empire, and the South Pacific.* (Philadelphia: Temple University Press, 1992).

SUGGESTIONS FOR FURTHER READING

Mead, Margaret
1942 *And Keep Your Powder Dry: An Anthropologist Looks at America.* New York: W. Morrow and Co.
1975 *World Enough: Rethinking the Future.* Boston: Little, Brown and Co.
Mead, Margaret, and Rhoda Metraux, eds.
2000 [1953] *The Study of Culture at a Distance.* London: Bergahn Books.

CHAPTER 3

"ONCE YOU'VE BROKEN HIM DOWN . . ."

The Nation, October 25, 1965

MARSHALL
SAHLINS

For some anthropologists, public engagement has meant organizing public forums for open discussion of critical events. In the spring of 1965, a handful of professors at the University of Michigan initiated a series of such meetings when they canceled classes and held public lectures (or "teach-ins") on the Vietnam War to protest the government's escalation of the conflict. (The term "teach-in" was derived from the sit-ins in which African Americans and their sympathizers challenged segregation practices by engaging in civil disobedience during the late 1950s and early 1960s.) Among those who coordinated the first teach-in was Marshall Sahlins, a young anthropology professor credited with conceiving the idea. Weeks later, the organizers challenged U.S. government officials to a public debate in Washington, D.C. which was called the National Teach-In. It received national and international media attention.[1]

In August 1965, Sahlins went to Vietnam on a fact-finding mission as a representative of the Inter-University Committee (the sponsors of the National Teach-In). The following article, written by Sahlins for *The Nation* shortly after his visit, consists of a gripping and revelatory interview he conducted with two U.S. military advisers in the Mekong Delta after accompanying them on a nighttime patrol at the Cambodian border. It reveals the use of psychological torture by American personnel.

Recent events suggest that such tactics may once again be part of our military's arsenal. A December 26, 2002, report published in the *Washington Post* described how U.S. intelligence officials were subjecting suspected Al Qaeda and Taliban forces to "stress and duress" techniques, as well as transporting them to third countries (with poor human rights records) for interrogation.[2]

Advanced anti-communism trades places with the enemy. It becomes opposite-communism, and "opposites" are things alike in every respect save one. The final stages of American dissolution in Vietnam will be marked by imitation of the enemy's techniques. I have heard it foreshadowed in the talk of Saigon officialdom: *discipline,* a senior American civilian officer told me, is what the South Vietnamese government needs; *power,* he said, is the only thing the Chinese can understand; *history,* he said, will prove us right. In a remote provincial outpost I found two Americans who had appropriated as their own draconian Chinese methods of interrogation and indoctrination ("motivation" is the American newspeak). The forced destruction of people's beliefs is no longer properly described as something "they" do. Torturously exacted confession and conversion are no longer things we fight against: these are now part of our own arsenal, weapons of our own struggle.

The two Americans were leaders of a "motivation" team working among Vietnamese Popular Forces.[3] The team included four Vietnamese instructor-cadres, two of these ex-Vietcong. The dominant of the two Americans was a field representative of a civilian agency; he was assisted by a Special Forces officer. Both were highly qualified, competent in Vietnamese language and custom, and dedicated to Vietnam and their vision of its future. Their program was anticommunist revolution: they were training Popular Forces as revolutionary cadres. The texts were classic communist handbooks on revolutionary warfare, books these Americans studied and clearly admired; it does not go too far to say they were disciples, or at least revisionist disciples, of Mao Zedong, Ho Chi Minh, and Che Guevara.

I lived in with them for a night and a good part of a day. They briefed me and allowed me to see the work for myself. But it is not of this guerrilla program that I write. It is of a discussion I had with the Americans about torture and the transformation of Vietcong prisoners to anticommunism. The two Americans allowed they had some experience with it, and some ideas of how it is properly done.

The interrogation methods the Americans described are copied from those used most effectively by the Chinese, as they themselves explained. (Of course, there are precedents—for example, the Inquisition.) The treatment seems a compressed and abbreviated version of the procedures used on American POWs during the Korean War. The interrogator has at most four or five days before he must send the prisoner on. Physical torture is precluded. A special type of "mental torture" (their term) is instead inflicted. But it aims not merely at eliciting

THE OTHER ASCENT INTO THE UNKNOWN

VIET-NAM

©1965 HERBLOCK
THE WASHINGTON POST

military information. The prisoner's disclosures are at the same time a betrayal of his cause and a confession of his errors, a renunciation of belief.

If the technique really is effective, and the Americans claim it is, I think it must be because of some rather special qualities of revolutionary warfare and warriors. It has to be understood that a Vietcong prisoner comes in with certain comprehensions and expectations that are deeply entwined with his revolutionary ("communist") commitment. A guerrilla movement depends decisively on secrecy. Its members are visible daily to the enemy but must be unknown to him; they maintain a hinterland conspiracy of silence; a single traitor wrecks the organization of a whole village, perhaps a district. The guerrilla thus understands that secrecy is a first principle of the revolution. But, by the same token, intelligence becomes a first principle of the counterrevolution. The prisoner, therefore, expects to be tortured for information and ultimately killed if he remains steadfast. He meets his interrogators prepared to resist the worst: it is a test of his revolutionary soul.

Something must be said as well of the two Americans who described the interrogation methods to me. First—and it is a thing seriously to consider—these men are not strangers, not people who have been metamorphosed by some satanic forces to a point beyond our understanding or recognition. Met on a college campus or in a business office, they would not attract unusual attention. Their attitudes toward Vietnam are indeed more scholarly than demonic. They want to involve themselves in the country. They profess with sincerity their respect for the people—so much that they actively wish them a better fate. And now consider this interview, what they said and what they revealed of themselves. After I left them I had the sickening feeling of "there but for the grace of God . . ."

The main protagonist—identified as "Mr. X"—describes himself as an "agnostic atheist," but clearly he believes in the Devil if not in God. In fact, his is a holy work: to exorcise the Communist devils possessing Vietcong. He undertakes the prisoner's "conversion" for the prisoner's own good: he is "helping" the man, saving him. I ask, "What gives you the right?" "Your belief," he answers. It gives him the right to "proselytize."

And now consider this interview, what they said and what they revealed of themselves. What follow are excerpts from a tape recording I made of our conversation. Three asterisks in the transcript indicate that a portion of the interview is skipped over; three dots, that a portion of an answer is elided; and a word in parenthesis followed by a question mark indicates an imperfect rendering on the tape and my guess of the word involved.

MR. X: At this time [the prisoner] kind of feels an emotional dependence upon you because for two days you've been protecting him from the big, outside ugly world that he doesn't understand: feeding him good chow, talking with him, calling him a [*kambelo?*] of the NLF, not the derogatory term of Vietcong . . . Then you indicate that this nice treatment that he's had so far [has] not been disinterested good treatment, that we expect his cooperation. This again reintroduces the whole issue of the big, ugly outside world. What's going to happen to him now? Well, he might tell you a couple of things, beginning with rather innocuous things. Well, you can imply that you knew that already, what you're really after are better things and this might rather [uncalm?] him. Then you might say, "Jeez, that scrape you got on your shoulder . . . it obviously needs attention; we'll have to give you some penicillin." And while you're giving him the penicillin, you're telling him that, "You know, there are these other types of people who just . . ."

* * *

MR. X: Actually again, this is the technique that Captain [Y] . . . and myself have been trying to promote in an advisory relationship. Again, it's a technique that's been used most effectively by the Chinese, in which you've pulled the man out of his familiar environment: he's dependent . . . upon you for his continual well-being. And even though the prisoner may [resist?], it's kind of an emotional interdependence that's created, and what you try and do is [use?] this emotional interdependence in such a way that he comes to the point where he must tell you what he knows.

SAHLINS: It's in effect brainwashing—is that the point of this?

MR. X: No, what it is, is breaking him down. But . . . once you've broken him down, it comes to the point where he wakes up in a sweat one morning and tells you, "All right." Then he tells you the names of the two people in his cell; or, he gives you the location of the camp that he just recently came from. Then you're through with him, in practical terms. You've got what you needed to continue operating. But at this point, if you really believe in anything yourself, what you've got to do is give him something to hope for before you send him back for further processing. Because you have just brought this individual to the lowest point in his life in terms of human meaning and existence. So at that point, that's when you've got to stress that, "Well now we're releasing you for further processing. But for you, what you've just told us is the beginning of a positive affirmation. We just can't process you right into our unit now; because you don't know what we stand for and what we're fighting for, but we hope that someday you will be joining us." See, we don't have time to get any brainwashing. The Chinese can do that because they have POWs for months and months and months. If we get a guy, we've got him for two to five days, and then he's out of our hands. In that two to five days, we've got to get the information we need. But we will not get the information we need by physical torture. We've got to get it by an emotional and mental torture. And you can do that because that's what they're least adequately prepared for. It's what Americans are least adequately prepared for when they find themselves in the other side's hands.

*   *   *

SAHLINS: What kind of control do you have over Arvin [Vietnam army] types of interrogation [i.e., physical torture]?

MR. X: Well again, that's an advisory function. And what you're trying to do is—this is just a traditional, feudal Asian society, mainland style—and what you're trying to do is change the course of warfare in Asia. To some extent this has been done: the Chinese People's Liberation Army; it's happened probably in the Japanese army, the Japanese Self-Defense and Home Defense Armies. But until the end of World War II, we always thought of the Japanese army as a real cruel, vindictive bunch of cutthroats. Well, it turned out in post–World War II analysis that the Bataan Death March was something that they handled to the best of their ability, given the available transport and the way that they would have handled their own prisoners. They just moved them, and they moved them as fast as they could. People who couldn't keep up the pace in some cases were helped and in some other cases—just according to the individual guard—were bashed and thrown aside. Vietnamese to our eyes seem rather cruel sometimes to prisoners, but they're not doing this with any ideological vengeance. They're doing that because that's just been the bent of warfare in Mainland Asia for a thousand years, and what we have got to try to do is sophisticate it, and tell them, "Look, that's just not the way." It's a slow process; we're attempting a reformation of a whole society.

SAHLINS: What practical is being done to discourage this kind of thing?

MR. X: Well, guidance on the spot—

CAPTAIN D (Sahlins' escort): It's up to the individual advisers—

MR. X: The individual adviser giving guidance on the spot.

CAPTAIN D: Sometimes it's successful, sometimes not—

CAPTAIN Y: In most cases, it's not.

SAHLINS: From what you say about mental torture, you wouldn't make any distinction in the morality of either kind [i.e., physical versus mental torture]?

MR. X: Hell, no! I don't make any distinction in morality at all: torture is torture, and when you fuck around with a guy's mind and his whole basic raison d'être, you're really hurting him—especially when he's prepared mentally, spiritually, for the physical torture.

SAHLINS: Then the attempt to discourage Vietnamese water torture . . . is just because the other type [mental torture] doesn't offend American sensibilities as much?

MR. X: No, it's not because of that. Because we don't concern ourselves here with American sensibilities. We concern ourselves with what will work.

CAPTAIN Y: It's relatively ineffective.

MR. X: It's ineffective. It may sound hard-boiled to say that we don't concern ourselves with American sensibilities—but we don't. We're concerning ourselves with Vietnamese sensibilities.

SAHLINS: What about the sensibilities of the Americans who are involved . . . the person who's torturing?

MR. X: To most of the Americans, to most of the simple-minded Americans who get involved in Vietnam—that's all the *Boobus americanus* that H. L. Mencken spoke about—undoubtedly they think that the mental and emotional torture we're talking about is the least objectionable, because they've never really paused to seriously reflect about it themselves; or perhaps they did not go through the experience of being a POW in the Korean Conflict themselves. And they can probably tell you, "Oh, Jesus, I'd try and stop that physical torture, because I know it's just wrong"— you know. But we think that we're looking into it a little more deeply, and we see that the mental and spiritual torture that we bring a man through to the point where he voluntarily gives you the information is pretty rough stuff to get involved in too. But it works.

SAHLINS: How do you offset the damage to yourself?

MR. X: Your belief. Your belief: you have to sincerely believe that in the long run you're helping this man. It's like an AA cure. If you're just breaking the guy down for the sake of getting a poor helpless alcoholic who's hipped on NLF propaganda to admit that he was wrong and give you the information, then you're going to send him out in the street a crushed derelict, then there's something wrong with you. But you have to really believe, as we do—although we get discouraged sometimes by our [Vietnamese] counterparts—you have to really believe that you're *helping* this guy to something better.

SAHLINS: Conversion from communism is involved in the torture.

MR. X: Conversion from anything to anything involves a certain degree of self-torture. We just accelerated the process because we need that fucking information.

SAHLINS: This is better for him?

MR. X: He's alive, and you can still help him . . .

*   *   *

MR. X: Most Americans, unfortunately, don't bother to think deeply about the stuff they get involved in and they make superficial judgments: "Well, it's wrong to torture this guy physically because we're all part of the same (background?)"—

CAPTAIN Y: If you ask you'll get probably 80 percent of the people [U.S. military] will say, "Well, I didn't get involved in it. When they capture them, when they capture the Vietnamese communists, I just turn my back and go and have a cigarette."

MR. X: They take a drink from their canteen and light up a cigarette. And that's discouraging . . . I'd rather get—not get involved in it, not in the actual physical torture myself—but I'd rather be right there and see it done, and then laugh like a horse when it doesn't work and they don't get the information. And then in the long run you're affecting the situation when you just laugh at this guy and say: "Look, you think he's gonna break? So you cut up his stomach a little bit and his insides fell out . . . He got the last laugh on you, because he didn't talk a bit." And maybe it'll make the guy think, you know, and ten times later, after ten more people have faded out because he physically tortured them, maybe he'll say: "Okay, wise American adviser, what would you do?" . . . We have a moral responsibility, it seems to me, once we've stepped into this country, to involve ourselves in the complete fabric of the country and to understand it, and then try and help the Vietnamese to look at some different alternatives . . . We should be acting as a catalyst, as a thinking catalyst in Vietnam. But you cannot be a catalyst unless you know the entire fabric of the thing. And lighting up a cigarette when they bring a prisoner in for questioning is—well, that's an immoral—

CAPTAIN Y: It's just like saying, "It doesn't happen."

MR. X: That's just about the height of immorality, I think. To think that you can just absolve yourself. That's saying that every man *is* an island; or at least when it is comfortable, when it's comfortable for me to be an island unto myself, then I am; and the bell's tolling for that poor fucker under the knife, not me. That's real bad. And again, it's a simple-minded approach.

*   *   *

[Mr. X had mentioned that one of the rules imparted to the cadres in training was "be kind to prisoners." I asked if that wasn't a rule he disobeyed.]

MR. X: Well, if the final result of it is—it's a cruel process—but the result of bringing him closer to you, of conversion—it's a tortuous process of conversion—but the result is a kind one . . . If you believe in your program, this is what you do . . .

SAHLINS: Do you believe in breaking people down so they agree with your program? And breaking them down justifies the end?

MR. X: No . . . That's why we would not take a guy who's been broken directly into our unit at this time . . .

SAHLINS: Either you will rehabilitate him by converting him to your belief or you're going to leave him a mental wreck . . . Can your ends be so God-given as to give you this right among humanity to do this?

MR. X: I don't know. I don't really believe anybody's hands are God-given. I'm an agnostic atheist.

SAHLINS: No, your ends. I'm not asking you for religious beliefs. What I'm asking is, do you believe you have the right to impose by this method—

MR. X: I think I've got the right to try. Nobody's got the right to succeed—guaranteed. But everybody's got the right to promote and proselytize what they believe.

*   *   *

CAPTAIN Y: If we do not break this guy, if we do not attempt to change his ideas, then in essence what have we done? We've said that basically he's right!

SAHLINS: No, that isn't so. One agrees to disagree as a matter of principle in a democratic system.

MR. X: Oh wait, this is [where] we began . . . I've had some tremendous conversations with these guys, and we begin by agreeing to disagree. But you can soon get this guy so flustered and so shaken up that before he knows it, he's agreeing with you—because his assumptions to begin with were rather vulnerable.

SAHLINS: But that isn't the issue here. The issue here is whether you will impose your will by this technique, which is—

MR. X: We don't know what our will is yet.

SAHLINS: You will impose your ideas by this technique—

MR. X: What ideas?

*   *   *

SAHLINS: . . . I asked the question, how do you justify the effect upon yourself of acting in this way? And you said you're doing the guy a service. Now, I'm asking you, do you believe you have the right to impose your will on somebody, impose what you believe—

MR. X: We are not imposing our will. We are not imposing will. Even after you've broken him and gotten the information, he's still a free agent.

*   *   *

MR. X: Not impose will—if he fails to accept . . . an alternative. And not *our* alternative; there are a number of alternatives. Because in essence that's what we're trying to show him.

*   *   *

SAHLINS: So as a matter of fact by this process you either transform him from that belief into one of a range of acceptable beliefs, or you will leave him a mental wreck—

MR. X: But we don't leave him this way. We have brought him to a point where he realizes that the faith he placed in his previous system was essentially not powerful. He has volunteered the information. At this point he's got to find a new way. He's got to have a way out of his dilemma, and the people at the training centers should be skillful enough to point out to him a number of alternatives.

SAHLINS: We come back to the question: whether you have the

right—by these techniques, which are external to him—to deny
him [the] belief that he came in with in his hand and only accept
a set of alternatives which you propose?

* * *

MR. X: Listen, I've met guys . . . We had a guy in Phu Yen Province in
the summer of '63 who was the Propaganda Director for the NLF
in that province; and boy, we just worked ourselves literally ragged
in four days trying to bring that guy to the point where he'd tell us
a few things, and he was tremendous—just tremendous. Didn't tell
us a thing.

SAHLINS: You admire this guy?

MR. X: Tremendous—tremendous.

SAHLINS: So you admire more a person who will not acquiesce to
the thing that you say is right than one who does?

MR. X: No, not true. I didn't say that at all. I admire a guy who will
tortuously admit—if he really believes—that, "Oh Jesus, I never
thought about that before. Those guys [NLF] they told me something else; and you're really doing something else." A guy like that
who will examine his previously arrived conclusions and change
his mind, I admire that—

SAHLINS: That's very admirable, but it doesn't describe the process
you went through, which was to leave him in a situation where
either he takes his set of alternatives which you give him or he is a
mental wreck.

MR. X: Remember, this was an act of *affirmation* on his part, where
he yields the information voluntarily. But it's only a beginning; it's
only a beginning; and it's not fair to leave him at the point where
he's just made the beginning.

* * *

MR. X: It's just like an alcoholic. An alcoholic can attend the meetings and he can see everybody else get embarrassed; and if he
doesn't want to join them he can just back out again. But once a
guy begins to join this little society of alcoholics—

CAPTAIN Y: These cadres we have [as instructors]—these ex-VCs,
ex-NLF, ex-Viet Minh—they all in some way or another gave
up something in their own mind when they turned, came to the
government.

* * *

MR. X: . . . what we're trying to show these guys when we're in-
terrogating them, through this tortuous process, is that you're not

better [off] under the NLF. "Your whole series of assumptions has got to be re-examined here, and we're here to help you re-examine them. And, Jesus, there's some guys here have got some more basic ideas of how they'd like to examine you, but we're just holding these guys off . . . and we'll take good care of you." That's the kind of a dirty trick—[but] when you've only got four days . . .

SAHLINS: Have you done this with Vietcong?

MR. X: We don't do anything because we're advisers—in every sense.

EDITOR'S NOTES

1. See Elinor Langer, "National Teach-In," *Science* (May 21, 1965): 1075–1077; see also Marshall Sahlins, "The Future of the National Teach-In: A History," in Marshall Sahlins, *Culture in Practice: Selected Essays* (New York: Zone Books, 2000), pp. 209–218.

2. See Dana Priest and Barton Gellman, "'Stress and Duress' Tactics Used on Terrorism Suspects Held in Secret Overseas Facilities," *Washington Post*, December 26, 2002, p. A1.

3. The Vietnamese Popular Forces were anticommunist troops. The Vietcong, referred to later in this article as the National Liberation Forces (NLF), were Communist.

SUGGESTION FOR FURTHER READING

Sahlins, Marshall
    2000   *Culture in Practice: Selected Essays.* New York: Zone Books.

CHAPTER 4

CONTEMPORARY ANTHROPOLOGY AND MORAL ACCOUNTABILITY

Thomas Weaver, ed., *To See Ourselves*, 1973

GERALD D. BERREMAN   By 1970 documentary evidence surfaced which implicated the involvement of American anthropologists and other social scientists in clandestine counterinsurgency work from 1965 to 1969. In 1965, anthropologists were reported to have participated in Project Camelot, a CIA-supported counterinsurgency program in Latin America. And during the American wars in Indochina, documents taken from the office of a UCLA anthropologist revealed that several anthropologists had secretly assisted the war effort by providing information about Thai culture and communities to the U.S. military.[1]

In this article (first delivered as a talk in 1967), Gerald D. Berreman critiques the notion of a "value-free" social science. He notes that clandestine anthropological activities sponsored by the Department of Defense and other parts of the U.S. military establishment can have disastrous political, professional, and ethical consequences.[2] Berreman has consistently sought to keep anthropological research in the public domain, available to anyone.

Berreman's contribution to ethics in anthropology included a leading role in the American Anthropological Association's standing Committee on Ethics. In November 1970, he and the other committee members formulated the "Principles of Professional Responsibility," which the association adopted in May 1971. The document states that the "anthropologist's paramount responsibility is to those he [or she] studies. When there is a conflict of interest, these individuals must come first."[3]

The notion that contemporary world events are irrelevant to the professional concerns of anthropologists was laid neatly to rest at the 1966 meeting of the American Anthropological Association when Dr. Michael Harner rose to challenge the ruling of the president-elect that a resolution condemning the United States' role in the war in Vietnam was out of order because it did not "advance the science of anthropology" or "further the professional interests of anthropologists." Dr. Harner suggested that "genocide is not in the professional interests of anthropologists." With that, the chair was voted down.

The dogma that public issues are beyond the interests or competence of those who study and teach about man comprises myopic and sterile professionalism, and a fear of commitment which is both irresponsible and irrelevant. Its result is to dehumanize "the most humanist of the sciences," as Eric Wolf has called our discipline; to betray utterly the opportunity and obligation which he has claimed for anthropology, namely: "the creation of an image of man that will be adequate to the experience of our time."

That neutrality in science is illusory is a point which has been made often and well.

The famous anthropologist Franz Boas was alert to startlingly similar problems in the uses of anthropology and anthropologists during World War I, and deplored them publicly. "A number of men who follow science as their profession [including 'at least four men who carry on anthropological work'] . . . have prostituted science by using it as a cover for their activities as spies," he wrote in 1919.

If science has no responsibility, scientists do. Scientists are people. They cannot escape values in the choices they make nor in the consequences of their acts.

If anthropologists choose to collect their data and make their analyses without regard to their use—leaving that choice to others—they may believe that they are adhering to the most rigorous scientific canons. But to say *nothing* is not to be neutral. To say nothing is as much a significant act as to say *something*. Douglas Dowd noted that "the alternatives are not 'neutrality' and 'advocacy.' To be uncommitted is not to be neutral, but to be committed—consciously or not—to the *status quo*; it is, in C. Wright Mills' phrase, 'to celebrate the present.'"

Silence permits others in the society who are less reticent, perhaps less scrupulous, almost certainly less informed, to make their own use of scientific findings. It leaves to politicians and journalists, to entrepreneurs, scoundrels, and madmen, as well as to statesmen and benefactors—but especially to the powerful—the interpretation and manipulation of matters about which they frequently know little, and of whose implications they know less, and nearly always far less than those who collected the material or made the analyses. It is therefore wishful thinking of the most elemental sort to assume that anthropological work can be put before the public without context or interpretation, there to be judged freely and intelligently on its merits without prejudice or manipulation, and to be acted upon accordingly. To assume *that* is to contribute to misuse born of ignorance or worse. Scientists cannot divorce themselves from the consequences of their scientific acts any more than they can from those of any of their other acts as human beings. This is a fact of existence in human society and it is a tenet of democracy.

Science—even social science—has finally arrived in our society. The rewards to be obtained for supplying social science data and social science interpretations of the right kinds and in the right places are generous. The intellectual today can join the hired myth-makers and apologists of Madison Avenue and Washington. On campus he can be the paid consultant or the academic entrepreneur and grantsman. As Irving Howe has remarked, "For once, the carrots are real." In this context, the prevalence of social scientists whose eyes are on the main chance rather than on the condition of man should not be surprising. This is the context within which we find social scientists whose "ideology of non-involvement in the social effects of scientific research," Sidney Willhelm noted, simply frees them from social responsibility, creating an "unaccountable scientific aristocracy," closely allied to the governmental, military, and corporate elites who buy their services and validate their heady status. As Noam Chomsky has written, "The problems with which research is concerned are those posed by the Pentagon or the great corporations, not, say, by the revolutionaries of Northeast Brazil or by SNCC [the Student Nonviolent Coordinating Committee]. Nor am I aware of a research project devoted to the problem of how poorly armed guerrillas might more effectively resist a brutal and devastating military technology." Yet such alternative problems would be likely to interest at least some social scientists.

The rationale which supports this scientific unaccountability among moral men is the myth of a value-free social science. This myth has been exposed to all but its most avid beneficiaries and the most credulous in its audience, as we have seen in this section. Yet it still serves to maintain a whole segment of the profession—or at least to sustain the symbiotic relationship between that segment of social scientists and the corporate foundations and governmental agencies who buy its findings, using them only as and if they see fit. It was Alexander Leighton who said that administrators use the findings of social scientists as a drunk uses a lamp post—for support rather than illumination. It is not important what social scientists say so much as how what they say is used. That depends upon how amenable it is to use and *that* is where the myth of freedom from values is crucial, and where the social responsibility of the social scientist lies.

The myth of value-freedom in physical science disappeared in the atomic cloud. In social science it is fading, as we have seen, in the dust of Camelot, the blood of Vietnam, and the duplicity of the CIA.

Today, if scientific truth is to be understood and acted upon, those who discover and know it must forcefully announce not only their knowledge, but its implications and consequences. As Winetrout says in the closing paragraph of his essay honoring the courageous [sociologist C. Wright] Mills: "In our present-day world, it is not enough to be scholarly; one must be concerned and angry enough to shout. It is not enough to understand the world; one must seek to change it."

No doubt, the world will change; no doubt, the social scientist's knowledge will contribute to that change. His responsibility is to see that this knowledge is used for humane changes. Simply, scientists must be responsible for what they do.

Thirty years ago, Robert Lynd maintained that "either the social sciences know more than do . . . *de facto* leaders of the culture as to what the findings of research mean, as to the options the institutional system presents, as to what human personalities want, why they want them, and how desirable changes can be effected, *or* the vast current industry of social science is an empty facade." To repeat Kathleen Gough's question, "Who is to evaluate and suggest guidelines for human society, if not those who study it?"

Our positive responsibility as scientists is to present what we know and what inferences we draw from our knowledge as clearly, thoughtfully, and responsibly as we can. This is a value position with practical and humane consequences. We have already heard from C. Wright Mills. In another work, he decried the "divorce of knowledge from power," and wrote:

> As a type of social man, the intellectual does not have any one political direction, but the work of any man of knowledge, if he is the genuine article, does have a distinct kind of political relevance: His politics, in the first instance, are the politics of truth, for his job is the maintenance of an adequate definition of reality. Insofar as he is politically adroit, the main tenet of his politics is to find out as much of the truth as he can, and to tell it to the right people,

at the right time, and in the right way. Or, stated negatively: to deny publicly what he knows to be false, whenever it appears in the assertions of no matter whom; and whether it be by virtue of official secret or an honest error. The intellectual ought to be the moral conscience of his society, at least with reference to the value of truth, for in the defining instance, that *is* his politics. And he ought also to be a man absorbed in the attempt to know what is real and what is unreal.[4]

I know of no statement which speaks to the responsibility of social scientists in our time as cogently as that one.

Douglas Dowd identifies the focal point of opposition by the young and by intellectuals in the word hypocrisy—hypocrisy in American deeds versus American words. This is where we as scientists and as teachers have a major responsibility: to speak the truth; to provide "an adequate definition of reality." Candor is a major precondition for trust and for rational action, and this is what is lacking or threatened in our society—in foreign policy, in race relations, in poverty programs, in support of scholarship and research, in university administration, in virtually every sphere of our national life.

The reaction of many anthropologists is to say and do nothing about the problems of the day; to retreat into research, administration, or teaching. Lulled by activity into a sense of purpose, accomplishment, and virtue, they hope that things will somehow work out. Do we need Edmund Burke to remind us that "the only thing necessary for the triumph of evil is for good men [and, I might add, informed men] to do nothing"?

Anthropologists have not lacked outspoken champions of truth— truth about race, about poverty, about professional ethics, about the heavy hands of government and private capital in formulating research, about war, and especially about the war in Indo-China. Probably anthropologists have more of them in proportion to their numbers than any other academic discipline and any other profession. But we need to emphasize and value these contributions in order to counteract the powerful and irresponsible professionalism which belittles or condemns these humane endeavors in favor of the mindless and trivial successes obtained under the illusion of freedom from responsibility for one's self and one's work.

In a world where anything scientists learn is likely to be put to immediate and effective use for ends beyond their control and antithetical to their values, anthropologists must choose their research undertakings with an eye to their implications. They must demand the right to have a hand or at least a say in the use of what they do as a condition for doing it.

We anthropologists must seek to apply our knowledge and skills to real problems, defined by us and not simply accepted from the sources which provide our funds. We must ask questions which address the problems of our time rather than merely those which minimize or obscure them. Nor does the incompleteness of our knowledge disqualify us scientifically, rationally, or morally from asserting what we know. Mills pointed out 20 years ago that "if one half of the relevant knowledge which we now possess were really put into the service of the ideals which leaders mouth, these ideals could be realized in short order." Gouldner has followed logically with the statement: "The issue . . . is not whether we know enough; the real questions are whether we have the courage to say and use what we know." This is why we must not be timid in asserting ourselves individually and collectively wherever we can. This is why our professional association should not now be chary to express views on matters of public policy just as we have not been in the past (as you have seen in the Resolutions) and just as other such groups express views on such matters. For students of human behavior to decline comment on human behavior is irresponsibility in a democracy, no matter how controversial the issues.

EDITOR'S NOTES

1. See Irving Horowitz, ed., *The Rise and Fall of Project Camelot* (Cambridge: MIT Press, 1968); see also Eric R. Wolf and Joseph G. Jorgenson, "Anthropology on the Warpath in Thailand," *New York Review of Books*, November 19, 1970, pp. 26–35.

2. See also Gerald D. Berreman, "Academic Colonialism—Not So Innocent Abroad," *The Nation*, November 10, 1969, pp. 505–508.

3. The code of ethics was published in the *Newsletter of the American Anthropological Association*, November 1970, pp. 15–16.

4. "On Knowledge and Power," in Irving Horowitz, ed. *Power, Politics, and People* (New York: Ballantine Books, 1964), p. 611.

SUGGESTION FOR FURTHER READING

Berreman, Gerald D.
    1981   *The Politics of Truth: Essays in Critical Anthropology.* New Delhi: South Asian Publishers.

CHAPTER 5

TWO PLUS TWO EQUALS ZERO—WAR AND PEACE RECONSIDERED

Radcliffe Quarterly, March 1983

LAURA NADER   In the 1980s, many Americans expressed a growing concern over the escalation of the nuclear arms race between the United States and the Soviet Union. Laura Nader took a strong public stand against pro-nuclear policies throughout this period, and used anthropological ideas about group dynamics and cultural control to inform her critiques. As early as 1969, she recommended that anthropologists begin to "study up"—that is, research powerful institutions and bureaucracies— and her work among nuclear physicists demonstrates how social scientists can shed light on the practices of high-tech cultures.

In this article, Nader examines the drift toward war in a nuclear age. She argues that institutionalized insanity, organizational survival, and short-term self-interest on the part of policy makers and the military-industrial complex may jeopardize the long-term survival of humanity.

The people responsible for the current nuclear arms policies are a small number of men who circulate between government laboratories, universities, the defense and military establishment, and defense contracting industries. These people promote the belief that we need nuclear capabilities, that we can win a nuclear war or keep the peace through nuclear buildup. They promulgate refined distinctions that make it appear that there are serious internal debates on nuclear arms. As the nuclear debate expands, I am increasingly hearing people say that Americans are being led down the path to a national Jonestown and that other governments may be performing the same function for their people.

Actually the analogy to Jonestown does not quite hold: Jones needed followers to have a Jonestown. Yet there is some similarity. While

Americans are not actively following, perhaps they trust that some-where in the government different sides of the arguments surrounding the nuclear arms race are being openly debated. Open debate will only happen, however, if citizens themselves broaden the debate and question official "wisdom," a process that is beginning to occur.

Among well-known citizens who have helped broaden and deepen the debate are individuals who are or who have been insiders to nuclear research. Scientists like Hans Bethe, Herbert York, Robert Wilson, and the late George Kistiakovsky, who were involved as division heads or group leaders in the Manhattan Project or as government laboratory leaders since World War II, have defected from a group-think mentality. The merging of interest between such scientists and the grass-roots peace movements concerned about the wisdom of a $222 billion defense program that could lead to global annihilation has added a new dimension to the peace movement. And just plain people are more often making the observations that could be useful reminders to in-sulated minds. One such observation appeared in a letter-to-the-editor section of a major newspaper noting that President Reagan's naming the MX [missile] a "Peacekeeper" is like "Robespierre describing the guillotine as a headache remedy." Another letter discusses the Orwell-ian "war is peace" thesis in which a constant state of war allowed the superpowers to control populations and maintain a war economy. As insiders and outsiders join forces, the dangers, the hoax, and the pros-pects of a different future will become more specified.

The dangers have become policy under the present administration. Although defense and detente were central ideas in earlier debates, in-creasingly we hear about first strike and winning a protracted nuclear war. Nuclear suicide is being contemplated as a way to preserve our Western civilization and our American democracy. Peaceful coexis-tence with the Soviets is no longer a goal; rather, we hear talk about radically altering the nature of Soviet society through confrontation. This becomes abundantly clear in Robert Scheer's new book *With Enough Shovels* (1982), and there is among some an obsession that a postnuclear victory (sic) would ensure destruction of Soviet political authority and cause "the emergence of a postwar world order compat-ible with Western values." The notion that the Soviets are responsible for general world unrest goes unqualified in these circles.

There are three concepts that have influenced my thinking about war over the past decade. They are institutionalized insanity, organiza-tional survival, and short-term self-interest. Institutionalized insanity operates in groups, has immunity from the forces of society that would come down hard on insane individuals, and has not been widely recognized as a social problem, even though insanity in groups exhibits many of the same qualities as insanity in individuals. Herb York refers to the problem of insanity in his interview with Mr. Scheer: "What's going on right now is that the crazier analysts have risen to higher positions than is normally the case." Senator Alan Cranston refers to an interview that Scheer had with [Undersecretary of Defense] T. K. Jones that went "far beyond the bounds of reasonable, rational, responsible thinking," when the latter made the now infamous suggestion: If there are enough shovels to go around, everybody's going to make it. The Reagan reference to Russians as "godless" monsters is additional proof of the thinking that leads to messianic planning to defend presumed U.S. vulnerabilities. I say presumed, because both inside and outside the administration deficiencies in nuclear arms arguments have been challenged or qualified by Hans Bethe, Admiral Hyman Rickover ([author of] *No Holds Barred*, 1982), and many others.[1]

The architects of the present administration are said to be intellectuals, people who in the words of Mr. Scheer can separate their rhetoric from the consequences of what they advocate. Another view was revealed to me recently by a man who had worked in the Pentagon for more than 25 years. When I asked him if the Pentagon were studying the problem of depressed white middle-aged men in positions of power and responsibility, he added, "and who are being advised by depressed men."

Organizational Survival

The concept of organizational survival has been used to understand organizational behavior. For no matter what the explicit goals of an organization are, its most central, albeit usually implicit goal, is its own survival. An organization takes on a life of its own. Although both institutionalized insanity and organizational survival are ubiquitous, they are of particular importance in the nuclear arms race. If institutionalized insanity operates among military and defense people, behavior in their circles that outsiders might think crazy (like the idea that somebody can win a nuclear war) goes undetected and undebated. This situation can persist for a long enough period to ensure that many organizations have invested so much in policies arising from this insanity that organizational survival begins to take precedence over national or even personal survival. Ideologies and rationales are developed within these groups to defend the plan of action. These defenses are reinforced by actual or perceived outside criticism, and become so strong that the insanity is further strengthened. Ideological obsessions among bureaucrats may more often be the result of powerlessness than the political persuasion of the government.

Permanent War Economy

The defense industry is self-interested and profit motivated, as Admiral Rickover made abundantly clear in his last testimony before Congress. World War II heralded the beginning of close ties between industry and defense. In fact, Washington was such a soft touch that, according to Richard Barnet's *Roots of War* (1972), Charles E. Wilson of General Electric, who recognized the profitability of the emerging defense industry, talked of "building a permanent war economy." During the Eisenhower years, the theory developed among liberal politicians, economists, and business that high military spending would stimulate the economy. This theory was put into practice during the Kennedy administration through an enormous increase in military spending. Due to government sponsorship, defense industries profit from the benefits of long-term contracts, interest-free loans, payment by government of most plant and capital equipment, and government willingness to pay prices subjected to continuous upward renegotiation. These industries are among the biggest, most powerful, technologically advanced units of economic power in the country, and U.S. National Security policy is directed by elite groups largely recruited from business. Critics of government-industry relations have argued that exorbitant prices for poor quality products, and rampant fraud should encourage the government to produce its own products. While Admiral Rickover has been very specific about the fraud problem, others have argued that high-level military spending is having an adverse effect on the civilian economy. Increased military spending has weakened the U.S. position in the international marketplace and increased inflation at home.

I would suggest that we examine the rational and nonrational aspects of the arms race when considering what we should do. The nuclear freeze is a first step, one that if implemented, could give us time to address more fundamental societal questions. There may be something about the way our society has changed since the 1930s that is legitimizing the drift to war. I remember my father saying years ago that we had never found a civilian economic solution to the Great Depression, we simply postponed solutions by going to war. In fact, preparing for war has become endemic to the superpowers. There may be internal structural reasons beyond opposing ideologies that are behind this pattern.

Danger and Opportunity

When we despair, we need to remember that these are times of danger and opportunity. The antinuclear movement is wise to plan its actions in steps beginning with the nuclear freeze and no-first-use declarations. At the same time, we need to develop positive economies and futures for nation-state societies that are not dependent on war for continued existence. To achieve these goals, those concerned with the arms race might well link up with the environmental movements and with healthy alternatives being worked on by the women's movements. There will be specific recommendations for getting out of this drift toward nuclear war that follow patterns of logical reasoning, i.e., "Nuclear war is not good for your health, and here are a series of paths that lead to exit." What we also need are plans for drawing people away from nuclear drift and toward positive goals. In addition to *Nuclear Nightmares* by Nigel Calder (1980) we need to visualize peaceful worlds, a world bent on creation versus destruction, on communication rather than distrust between nations. The role of citizen will be crucial in this process: our voices will not be hindered by bureaucracies. In *Our Depleted Society* (1965), Seymour Melman has written on what we could do with our $222 billion if the emphasis on the arms race were reduced. There has been talk about the economic successes of Japan and West Germany. Why can't we imagine what the economies of the U.S. and the USSR might be without the arms race? Can we find solutions for the Great Depression that do not include warfare and use these solutions as a positive enticement away from nuclear war? Can we address the very serious problem of personal powerlessness among top-level officials in countries like the U.S. or the USSR?

I am arguing that we recognize the limits placed upon our leaders, both military and civilian, and that we realize the role we need to play in generating the necessary optimism to empower people to become active. Under such conditions we could think about developing economies appropriate to the conditions of peace and force ourselves to recognize the differences between wasteful versus adequate defense spending. National security may be best guaranteed by a healthy society. We need to lead the contest between nations into other areas such as peace-time high technology. This will require us to heed Admiral Rickover's advice, which has been echoed elsewhere: "Look at how our society is put together—political and economic power is increasingly being concentrated among a few large corporations and their officers." This is not the American dream, not what Jefferson contemplated. This is not what we would fight a war to preserve, but it may be what some might fight a war to obliterate when we can no longer tolerate the gap between what we would like to be and what we are.

EDITOR'S NOTE

1. Dr. Hans Bethe, physicist, led the theoretical division of the Manhattan Project and won the 1967 Nobel Prize in Physics. Admiral Hyman Rickover (1900–1986) was a longtime U.S. naval officer and engineer who developed the world's first nuclear-powered engines and the first atomic-powered submarine, the USS *Nautilus*, launched in 1954.

SUGGESTIONS FOR FURTHER READING

Nader, Laura
    1969   "Up the Anthropologist—Perspectives Gained from Studying Up." In *Reinventing Anthropology*, edited by Dell Hymes. New York: Vintage.
    1981   "Barriers to Thinking New About Energy," *Physics Today* 34, no. 3: 9, 99–102.
    1986   "The Drift to War." In *Peace and War: Cross-Cultural Perspectives*, edited by Mary LeCron Foster and Robert A. Rubenstein, pp. 185–192. New Brunswick, N.J.: Transaction Books.

CHAPTER 6

DOLLARS THAT FORGE GUATEMALAN CHAINS

New York Times, March 18, 1985

BEATRIZ
MANZ

The specter of nuclear holocaust haunted Americans during the Cold War era, but conventional wars also raged abroad in the 1970s and 1980s, often with U.S. support. The twentieth-century history of Guatemala was extraordinarily bloody. Since the colonial era, a small elite has controlled most of the country's land and indigenous farmers have been forced to work their plantations. In the 1900s many plantations were owned and operated by U.S. corporations such as United Fruit Company. In 1951, Jacobo Arbenz was elected president on a platform of land reform and soon began expropriating fields for redistribution to peasants. But in 1954, the CIA engineered a coup which left Guatemala in the hands of a military dictatorship. Over the next forty years, approximately two hundred thousand people—mostly Mayans—were killed by armed groups openly funded by the United States in the name of halting communism. Guatemala is among the clearest examples of U.S.-sponsored state terror in recent history.

In this article, Beatriz Manz describes the scale of Guatemalan violence and the continuing role of the United States in perpetuating the terror. But the bloodshed did not end, and was not directed solely at Mayan peasants. In 1990, assassins killed Guatemalan anthropologist Myrna Mack; her murder was almost certainly politically motivated. Not until 1996 did the government and the opposition sign U.N.-sponsored peace accords, formally ending the thirty-year civil war.

Freedom of Information Act documents released in 1999 confirm that as early as the 1960s U.S. officials helped to implement a counterinsurgency strategy relying upon death squads (consisting of plainclothes Guatemalan military agents) to eliminate suspected "subversives." During a visit to Central America in March 1999, President Clinton apologized for U.S. involvement in Guatemala's civil war.

The Administration is proposing a major increase, from $13 million to $35 million, in security assistance to Guatemala based on a dual deception—that human rights have improved under General Oscar Humberto Mejía Victores and that the military will soon turn over power to an elected civilian government.

In contrast to virtually every independent human rights organization, a State Department report on Guatemala issued last month maintained that "overall human rights conditions improved in 1984." In fact, ghastly violence—beatings, rape, torture, mutilations, and assassinations—has become a normal state of affairs. Nor is it a secret war: hundreds of people have been publicly abducted, and mutilated corpses are strewn throughout the countryside. More than 150 articles have appeared in the Guatemalan press detailing killings, disappearances, and gruesome atrocities in the last three months alone.

The military has come to rely on terror as the centerpiece of a counterinsurgency campaign designed to smash the guerrillas' base of support—to disrupt life among hundreds of thousands of ordinary Guatemalan villagers. The results of this campaign are staggering even by the bloody standards of Guatemala. Some 100,000 children are said to have lost one or both parents to political violence. Of the one million inhabitants in the northwestern part of the country, the center of army activity, 150,000 have fled to Mexico and 250,000 have been displaced or had their lives severely disrupted. In one highland municipality, 46 villages were abandoned. One of these villages, Finca San Francisco Nentón, was the site of a military massacre of 302 men, women, and children, on July 17, 1982.

In the years since then, selective killings and abductions have more or less replaced large-scale massacres, but the architects of yesterday's slaughter are still designing policy. In fact, many of those responsible for atrocities have been promoted rather than punished—and killings and disappearances still occur daily, at a rate of more than 100 a month.

In this climate, the generals have declared that elections will be held on October 27, 1985. This may look good to Washington, but what could elections mean to Guatemalans when the army has crippled or destroyed most independent organizations and virtually the entire country is consumed with fear? The average Guatemalan would not presume to criticize or organize openly against the status quo.

Whether or not elections take place, the military is simply not about to relinquish real power. The occupant of the presidential palace may wear a pinstripe suit instead of a uniform, but the army will still remain in charge. The generals will continue to impose the lopsided pattern of landownership and income distribution that has given rise to much of the conflict. All potential civilian candidates recognize this, and none who might favor land reform dare propose it.

Nor does anyone imagine that the military will relinquish the power it has amassed in the countryside through civil patrols and model villages. The army has conscripted 900,000 predominantly Indian men into unpaid patrols and begun to intern 100,000 Indians in 70 model villages. Together, the two policies are forcefully transforming the lives of the indigenous population.

In fact, far from getting ready to give up power, the army is further entrenching itself in realms normally controlled by civilians. A November 1984 law, for example, extends military control over virtually all rural reconstruction and development efforts—precisely the area where much of the proposed United States economic aid would go.

New security assistance could only send a signal that atrocities are acceptable. It would also be sure to further strengthen the military's control. Is there an alternative? Aid should be limited to economic assistance and it should be dependent on three conditions: it should go to local communities and not be managed by the military; those guilty of atrocities must be brought to justice; peasant organizations and grassroots groups must be able to function freely.

The choice is clear: we can bankroll the further entrenchment of the military, or we can support the establishment of a stable and just Guatemalan society.

SUGGESTION FOR FURTHER READING

Manz, Beatriz
    1986   *Refugees of a Hidden War.* Albany: SUNY Press.

CHAPTER 7

ANTHROPOLOGISTS AS SPIES

The Nation, November 20, 2000

DAVID PRICE   In this article, David Price revisits the issue of clandestine anthropological research raised in the earlier
pieces by Boas (Chapter 1) and Berreman (Chapter 4). Using documents obtained through the Freedom of Information Act, Price traces the historical
ties between anthropologists, the CIA, and its precursor (the Office of Strategic Services or OSS) from World War I to the 1991 Gulf War. He also discusses the significance of modifications to the American Anthropological Association's "Principles of Professional Responsibility" (see Chapter 4) that
have diluted the original document's emphasis on nonsecrecy in research and
the primary responsibility of anthropologists to those they study.

  Price concludes with a sobering warning: "Unless the scientific community takes steps to denounce such [espionage] activities using the clearest
possible language and providing sanctions against those who do so, we can
anticipate that such actions will continue with impunity during some future
crisis or war." It remains to be seen whether anthropologists will once again
serve as spies in the "war on terror" declared by George W. Bush.

On December 20, 1919, under the heading "Scientists as Spies," *The
Nation* published a letter by Franz Boas, the father of academic anthropology in America. Boas charged that four American anthropologists, whom he did not name, had abused their professional research
positions by conducting espionage in Central America during the First
World War. Boas strongly condemned their actions, writing that they
had "prostituted science by using it as a cover for their activities as
spies." Anthropologists spying for their country severely betrayed their
science and damaged the credibility of all anthropological research,
Boas wrote; a scientist who uses his research as a cover for political
spying forfeits the right to be classified as a scientist.

The most significant reaction to this letter occurred ten days later at the annual meeting of the American Anthropological Association (AAA), when the association's governing council voted to censure Boas, effectively removing him from the council and pressuring him to resign from the national research council. Three out of four of the accused spies (their names, we now know, were Samuel Lothrop, Sylvanus Morley, and Herbert Spinden) voted for censure; the fourth (John Mason) did not. Later Mason wrote Boas an apologetic letter explaining that he'd spied out of a sense of patriotic duty.

A variety of extraneous factors contributed to Boas's censure (chief among these being institutional rivalries, personal differences, and possibly anti-Semitism). The AAA's governing council was concerned less about the accuracy of his charges than about the possibility that publicizing them might endanger the ability of others to undertake fieldwork. It accused *him* of "abuse" of his professional position for political ends.

In 1919 American anthropology avoided facing the ethical questions Boas raised about anthropologists' using their work as a cover for spying. And it has refused to face them ever since. The AAA's current code of ethics contains no specific prohibitions concerning espionage or secretive research. Some of the same anthropologists who spied during World War I did so in the next war. During the early cold war Ruth Benedict and lesser-known colleagues worked for the RAND Corporation and the Office of Naval Research. In the Vietnam War, anthropologists worked on projects with strategic military applications.

Until recently there was little investigation of either the veracity of Boas's accusation in 1919 or the ethical strength of his complaint. But FBI documents released to me under the Freedom of Information Act shed new light on both of these issues.

The FBI produced 280 pages of documents pertaining to one of the individuals Boas accused—the Harvard archeologist Samuel Lothrop. Lothrop's FBI file establishes that during World War I he indeed spied for Naval Intelligence, performing "highly commendable" work in the Caribbean until "his identity as an Agent of Naval Intelligence became known." What is more, World War II saw him back in harness, serving in the Special Intelligence Service (SIS), which J. Edgar Hoover created within the FBI to undertake and coordinate all intelligence activity in Central and South America. During the war the SIS stationed approximately 350 agents throughout South America, where they collected intelligence, subverted Axis networks, and at times assisted in the interruption of the flow of raw materials from Axis sources. Lothrop was stationed in Lima, Peru, where he monitored imports, exports, and political developments. To maintain his cover he pretended to undertake archeological investigations.

From his arrival in Lima in mid-December 1940, Lothrop was dogged by constant worries that his communications with Washington were being intercepted by British, Peruvian, Japanese, or German intelligence operatives. By August 1941 he became concerned that his lack of significant archeological progress might lead to the discovery of his true work in Peru. Lothrop reported his fears of being detected to FBI headquarters: "As regards the archaeological cover for my work in Peru, it was based on the understanding that I was to be in the country six months or less. It is wearing thin and some day somebody is going to start asking why an archaeologist spends most of his time in towns asking questions. This won't happen as soon as it might because the Rockefeller grant for research in Peru makes me a contact man between the field workers and the government."

Lothrop was referring to the Rockefeller Foundation, which financed twenty archaeologists who were excavating in Peru, Chile, Colombia, Mexico, Venezuela, and Central America. He also used his ties to a variety of academic and research institutions—including Harvard, the Peabody Museum, the Institute of Andean Research, and the Carnegie Institute—as cover in Peru. Archeologist Gordon Willey, who worked on an Institute of Andean Research Project in Peru and had some contact with Lothrop at this time, recalled that "it was sort of widely known on the loose grapevine that Sam was carrying on some kind of espionage work, much of which seemed to be keeping his eye on German patrons of the Hotel Bolivar Bar."

In fact, Lothrop was considered a valuable agent who collected important information on Peruvian politics and leading public figures of a nature usually difficult to secure. An FBI evaluation reported that headquarters "occasionally receive[s] information of sufficient importance from Mr. Lothrop to transmit to the President." Lothrop's principal source was an assistant to the Peruvian minister of government and police. In the spring of 1944 this informant resigned his governmental position and began "working exclusively under the direction of Dr. Lothrop." In May 1944 the U.S. Embassy reported that Lothrop's principal informant was fully aware of Lothrop's connection to the SIS and FBI.

Lothrop's cover was compromised by four Peruvian investigators in the employ of his top informant. His informant had been heard bragging to the Peruvian police that he made more by working for the U.S. Embassy than the police made working for the Peruvian government.

The FBI decided to test the reliability of Lothrop's key informant by assigning him to collect information on nonexistent events and individuals. The informant was given background information about a nonexistent upcoming anti-Jewish rally that he was to attend, including a list of specific individuals who would be present. Though the rally did not occur, the informant provided a full report on it. He also filed detailed reports on a nonexistent commemorative celebration of the bombing of Pearl Harbor held in a distant town, and on a fictitious German spy who supposedly had jumped ship in Peru.

Lothrop was instructed not to tell the informant that his duplicity had been detected; instead, he was to say he was out of funds to pay for informants. Lothrop refused to believe his informant was lying and sent a letter of resignation to J. Edgar Hoover. His resignation was accepted and he returned to the United States to resume his academic duties at Harvard's Peabody Museum and the Carnegie Institute.

What is now known about Lothrop's long career of espionage suggests that the censure of Boas by the AAA in 1919 sent a clear message to him and others that espionage under cover of science in the service of the state is acceptable. In each of the wars and military actions that followed the First World War anthropologists confronted, or more often repressed, the very issues raised by Boas in his 1919 letter to *The Nation.*

While almost every prominent living U.S. anthropologist (including Ruth Benedict, Gregory Bateson, Clyde Kluckhohn, and Margaret Mead) contributed to the World War II war effort, they seldom did so under the false pretext of fieldwork, as Lothrop did. Without endorsing the wide variety of activities to which anthropological skills were applied in the service of the military, a fundamental ethical distinction can be made between those who (as Boas put it) "prostituted science by using it as a cover for their activities as spies" and those who did not. World War II did, however, stimulate frank, though muted, discussions of the propriety of anthropologists' using their knowledge of those they studied in times of war, creating conditions in which, as anthropologist Laura Thompson put it, they became "technicians for hire to the highest bidder." Although the racist tenets of Nazism were an affront to the anthropological view of the inherent equality of humankind, Boas (who died in 1942) would probably have condemned anthropologists who used science as a cover for espionage during World War II. Approximately half of America's anthropologists contributed to the war effort, with dozens of prominent members of the profession working for the Office of Strategic Services (OSS), Army and Navy intelligence, and the Office of War Information.

In the following decades there were numerous private and public interactions between anthropologists and the intelligence community. Some anthropologists applied their skills at the CIA after its inception in 1947 and may still be doing so today. For some of them this was a logical transition from their wartime espionage work with the OSS and other organizations; others regarded the CIA as an agency concerned with gathering information to assist policy makers rather than a secret branch of government that subverted foreign governments and waged clandestine war on the Soviet Union and its allies. Still other anthropologists unwittingly received research funding from CIA fronts like the Human Ecology Fund.

The American Anthropological Association also secretly collaborated with the CIA. In the early 1950s the AAA's executive board negotiated a secret agreement with the CIA under which agency personnel and computers were used to produce a cross-listed directory of AAA members, showing their geographical and linguistic areas of expertise along with summaries of research interests. Under this agreement the CIA kept copies of the database for its own purposes with no questions asked. And none were, if for no other reason than that the executive board had agreed to keep the arrangement a secret. What use the CIA made of this database is not known, but the relationship with the AAA was part of an established agency policy of making use of America's academic brain trust.

Anthropologists' knowledge of the languages and cultures of the people inhabiting the regions of the Third World where the agency was waging its declared and undeclared wars would have been invaluable to the CIA. The extent to which this occurred is the focus of ongoing archival and FOIA research. When the CIA overthrew Jacobo Arbenz in Guatemala in 1954, an anthropologist reported, under a pseudonym, to the State Department's intelligence and research division on the political affiliations of the prisoners taken by the military in the coup.

During the Korean War linguists and ethnographers assisted America's involvement with little vocal conflict of conscience. Norwegian sociologist Johan Galtung's revelations in 1965 of Project Camelot, in which anthropologists were reported to be working on unclassified counterinsurgency programs in Latin America, ignited controversy in the AAA. During America's wars in Southeast Asia the AAA was thrown into a state of upheaval after documents purloined from the private office of UCLA anthropologist Michael Moerman revealed that several anthropologists had secretly used their ethnographic knowledge to assist the war effort.

As a result of inquiries made into these revelations, the 1971 annual meeting of the AAA became the scene of a tumultuous showdown after a fact-finding committee chaired by Margaret Mead maneuvered to create a report finding no wrongdoing on the part of the accused anthropologists. An acrimonious debate resulted in the rejection of the Mead report by the voting members of the association. As historian Eric Wakin noted in his book *Anthropology Goes to War*, this "represented an organized body of younger anthropologists rejecting the values of its elders." But the unresolved ethical issue of anthropologists spying during the First and Second World Wars provided a backdrop to the 1971 showdown. Almost two decades later, during the [1991] Gulf War, proposals by conservatives in the AAA that its members assist allied efforts against Iraq provoked only minor opposition.

Today most anthropologists are still loath to acknowledge, much less study, known connections between anthropology and the intelligence community. As with any controversial topic, it is not thought to be a good "career builder." But more significant, there is a general perception that to rake over anthropology's past links, witting and unwitting, with the intelligence community could reduce opportunities for U.S. anthropologists to conduct fieldwork in foreign nations.

In the course of research in this area I have been told by other anthropologists in no uncertain terms that to raise such questions could endanger the lives of fieldworkers around the globe. This is not a point to be taken lightly, as many anthropologists work in remote settings controlled by hostile governmental or guerrilla forces. Suspicions that one is a U.S. intelligence agent, whether valid or not, could have fatal consequences. As Boas prophetically wrote in his original complaint against Lothrop and his cohorts, "In consequence of their acts every nation will look with distrust upon the visiting foreign investigator who wants to do honest work, suspecting sinister designs. Such action has raised a new barrier against the development of international friendly cooperation." But until U.S. anthropology examines its past and sets rules forbidding both secret research and collaboration with intelligence agencies, these dangers will continue.

Over the past several decades the explicit condemnations of secretive research have been removed from the AAA's code of ethics—the "Principles of Professional Responsibility" (PPR). In 1971 the PPR specifically declared that "no secret research, no secret reports or debriefings of any kind should be agreed to or given" by members of the AAA. By 1990 the attenuation of anthropological ethics had reached a point where anthropologists were merely "under no professional obligation to provide reports or debriefing of any kind to government officials or employees, unless they have individually and explicitly agreed to do so in the terms of employment." These changes were largely accomplished in the 1984 revision of the PPR that Gerald Berreman characterized as reflecting the new "Reaganethics" of the association: In the prevailing climate of deregulation the responsibility for ethical review was shifted from the association to individual judgments.

As anthropologist Laura Nader noted, these Reagan-era changes were primarily "moves to protect academic careers . . . downplaying anthropologists' paramount responsibility to those they study." The current PPR may be interpreted to mean that anthropologists don't have to be spies unless they want to or have agreed to do so in a contract. A 1995 Commission to Review the AAA Statements on Ethics declared that the committee on ethics had neither the authority nor the resources to investigate or arbitrate complaints of ethical violations and would "no longer adjudicate claims of unethical behavior and focus its efforts and resources on an ethics education program."

Members of the current ethics committee believe that even though the AAA explicitly removed language forbidding secretive research or spying, there are clauses in the current code that imply (rather than state) that such conduct should not be allowed—though without sanctions, this stricture is essentially meaningless. Archeologist Joe Watkins, chairman of the ethics committee, believes that if an anthropologist were caught spying today, "the AAA would not do anything to investigate the activity or to reprimand the individual, even if the individual had not been candid [about the true purpose of the research]. I'm not sure that there is anything the association would do as an association, but perhaps public awareness would work to keep such practitioners in line, like the Pueblo clowns' work to control the societal miscreants." Watkins is referring to Pueblo cultures' use of clowns to ridicule miscreants.[1] Although it is debatable whether anthropologist intelligence operatives would fear sanctions imposed by the AAA, it is incongruous to argue that they would fear public ridicule more. Enforcing a ban on covert research would be difficult, but to give up on even the possibility of investigating such wrongdoing sends the wrong message to the world and to the intelligence agencies bent on recruiting anthropologists.

Many factors have contributed to the AAA's retreat from statements condemning espionage and covert research. Key among these are the century-old difficulties inherent in keeping an intrinsically diverse group of scholars aligned under the framework of a single association. A combination of atavistic and market forces has driven apart members of a field once mythically united around the holistic integration of the findings of archeology and physical, cultural and linguistic anthropology. As some "applied anthropologists" move from classroom employment to working in governmental and industrial settings, statements condemning spying have made increasing numbers of practitioners uncomfortable—and this discomfort suggests much about the nature of some applied anthropological work. The activities encompassed under the heading of applied anthropology are extremely diverse, ranging from heartfelt and underpaid activist-based research for NGOs around the world to production of secret ethnographies and time-allocation studies of industrial and blue-collar workplaces for the private consumption of management.

As increasing numbers of anthropologists find employment in corporations, anthropological research becomes not a quest for scientific truth, as in the days of Boas, but a quest for secret or proprietary data for governmental or corporate sponsors. The AAA's current stance of inaction sends the dangerous message to the underdeveloped world that the world's largest anthropological organization will take no action against anthropologists whose fieldwork is a front for espionage. As the training of anthropology graduate students becomes increasingly dependent on programs like the 1991 National Security Education Program—with its required governmental-service payback stipulations—the issue takes on increased (though seldom discussed) importance.

It is unknown whether any members of the AAA are currently engaged in espionage, but unless the scientific community takes steps to denounce such activities using the clearest possible language and providing sanctions against those who do so, we can anticipate that such actions will continue with impunity during some future crisis or war.

Many in the American Anthropological Association are frustrated with its decision neither to explicitly prohibit nor to penalize secretive government research. It is time for U.S. anthropologists to examine the political consequences of their history and take a hard, thoughtful look at Boas's complaint and the implications implicit in the association's refusal to condemn secret research and to reenact sanctions against anthropologists engaging in espionage.

EDITOR'S NOTE

"Miscreants" refers to those who engage in socially deviant behavior. Among the Pueblo and certain other Native American cultures, clowns traditionally mimicked the behavior of deviants in public settings (for example, at ritual celebrations), thereby reproaching the offenders.

SUGGESTIONS FOR FURTHER READING

Price, David
    2002   "Lessons from Second World War Anthropology." *Anthropology Today* 18, no. 3: 14–20.
    2003   *Cold War Witch Hunts: The FBI's Surveillance and Repression of Activist Anthropologists.* Durham, N.C.: Duke University Press.

CHAPTER 8

ABUSE OF POWER BY THE ADVOCATES OF REASON

Acts of Resistance, 1998

PIERRE BOURDIEU, *translated by Richard Nice* — The late Pierre Bourdieu (1930–2001), renowned French sociologist and anthropologist, was a frequent contributor to national debates on culture, economic policy, globalization, and immigration. He once said of his public commentaries: "I would not have engaged in public position-taking if I had not, each time, had the perhaps illusory sense of being forced into it by a kind of legitimate rage, close to something like a sense of duty."[1]

Throughout the 1990s, Bourdieu was particularly concerned about the destructive effects of economic neoliberalism, including the policies of the International Monetary Fund and the World Bank, institutions whose prescriptions have often led to human suffering and political instability in the Third World, according to some economists, for example, Joseph Stiglitz.[2] In the following commentary, originally delivered at a public discussion organized by the International Parliament of Writers at the 1995 Frankfurt Book Fair, Bourdieu describes "terrorist violence" as a revolt against the modern-day "imperialism . . . of international bodies."

From deep inside the Islamic countries there comes a very profound question with regard to the false universalism of the West, or what I call the imperialism of the universal. France has been the supreme incarnation of this imperialism, which in this very country has given rise to a national populism, associated for me with the name of Herder.[3] If it is true that one form of universalism is no more than a nationalism which invokes the universal (human rights, etc.) in order to impose itself, then it becomes less easy to write off all fundamentalist reaction against it as reactionary.

Scientific rationalism—the rationalism of the mathematical models which inspire the policy of the IMF or the World Bank, that of the law firms, great juridical multinationals which impose the traditions of American law on the whole planet, that of rational-action theories, etc.—is both the expression and the justification of a Western arrogance, which leads people to act as if they had the monopoly of reason and could set themselves up as world policemen, in other words, as self-appointed holders of the monopoly of legitimate violence, capable of applying the force of arms in the service of universal justice.

Terrorist violence, through the irrationalism of the despair which is almost always at its root, refers back to the inert violence of the powers which invoke reason. Economic coercion is often dressed up in juridical reasons. Imperialism drapes itself in the legitimacy of international bodies. And, through the very hypocrisy of the rationalizations intended to mask its double standards, it tends to provoke or justify, among the Arab, South American, or African peoples, a very profound revolt against the reason which cannot be separated from the abuses of power which are armed or justified by reason (economic, scientific, or any other). These "irrationalisms" are partly the product of our rationalism, imperialist, invasive, and conquering or mediocre, narrow, defensive, regressive, and repressive, depending on the place and time.

One is still defending reason when one fights those who mask their abuses of power under the appearances of reason or who use the weapons of reason to consolidate or justify an arbitrary empire.

EDITOR'S NOTES

1. Quoted in Pierre Bourdieu, *Acts of Resistance* (New York: New Press, 1998), p. vii.
2. Stiglitz, winner of the 2001 Nobel Prize in Economics, outlines his critique in *Globalization and Its Discontents* (New York: W. W. Norton, 2002).
3. See Pierre Bourdieu, "Deux impérialismes de l'universel," in C. Fauré and T. Bishop, eds., *L'Amérique des Fracais* (Paris: Editions François Bourin, 1992).

SUGGESTION FOR FURTHER READING

Bourdieu, Pierre
    1998   *Acts of Resistance: Against the Tyranny of the Market.* Translated by Richard Nice. New York: New Press.

PART II

PRESCIENT ANTHROPOLOGY
DIAGNOSING CRISES ABROAD

CHAPTER 9

WEST MUST CORRECT ITS MISTAKES IN YUGOSLAVIA

Baltimore Sun, August 16, 1992

ROBERT M.
HAYDEN

In the period following the Cold War, ethnic and religious conflicts flared in numerous parts of the world, in some cases for the first time in many decades. Robert M. Hayden was among the first to document and analyze this phenomenon. As an anthropologist who has conducted field research in Yugoslavia and India, two multiethnic and multireligious states, Hayden has analyzed these cultural dynamics in his work.

Among the first international post–Cold War crises was the disintegration of Yugoslavia and the subsequent civil war between Serbs, Bosnians, and Croatians. In this piece, Hayden analyzes how the diplomatic failures of the United States and European countries led to the escalation and increasing violence of the conflict.

The disgusting brutality of the Serbian campaign in Bosnia makes it easy to view the whole Bosnian tragedy as the fault of the Serbs. Yet the Bosnian war, and Serbian campaign itself, are in large measure the result of diplomatic errors by the Europeans and Americans.

If the war is to be stopped, its causes must be addressed. To do so will require recognition of these errors.

The most fundamental error was to accept the disintegration of Yugoslavia. It was always clear that the country would not fall apart cleanly because of the complex intermingling of nationalities there.

There was a basic error of logic: If Yugoslavia could not exist as a multiethnic state, how could the various republics do so?

At the level of cynical Realpolitik, the answer was simple. In the newly independent republics, state chauvinism would replace state socialism, with the majority in each state permitted to discriminate systematically against the largest scapegoat minority under a pious cover of "democracy." This cynical solution has been applied in Slovenia and Croatia and in the Baltic republics of the former Soviet Union. However, there was a flaw in the reasoning. What if the hated scapegoat minority rose up in arms and rebelled?

With the collapse of Yugoslavia, the most vulnerable minorities in Croatia and Bosnia were the Serbs. In both regions, Serbs were already sensitive because of the ghastly civil war of 1941–45. The then fascist "Independent State of Croatia," which included Bosnia, implemented a policy of genocide against the Serbs. In Bosnia itself, allied Croat and Muslim forces massacred Serbs, who responded by killing Muslims.

Viewed in this historical context, then, Serb fears of oppression and worse were understandable. They were hardly reassured by a Croatian government that today belittles the wartime genocide or by a coalition of Muslims and Croats to separate Bosnia's Serbs from Yugoslavia.

In this context of fear, the European Community and U.S. insistence on the inviolability of borders put the Serbs of Croatia and Bosnia in the unenviable position of the Kurds in Iraq. Their rejection of the borders was to be expected, even as the brutality of their resistance can only be condemned. But this was the first blunder: to ratify the destruction of Yugoslavia without redrawing borders.

The second blunder was the premature recognition of Bosnia before a political solution could be reached. Bosnian Serbs had clearly shown that they rejected such a state unless they could have political autonomy amounting to virtual independence. It was clear to all who knew anything about Yugoslavia that the recognition of an independent Bosnia in these circumstances would ignite a civil war. Lord Carrington, the EC special representative to Yugoslavia, Cyrus Vance, the former U.S. Secretary of State, and Warren Zimmerman, U.S. ambassador to Yugoslavia, had counseled against it. Unfortunately, they were right.

Despite the simplistic war cries of that odd couple, Margaret Thatcher and Bill Clinton, the Bosnian tragedy cannot be solved by military action. While America tries to treat the Bosnian war as an international conflict, it is in fact a civil war. The Serbs fighting the Bosnian government are Bosnian Serbs—albeit supported by Serbia—who have been incorporated into a "sovereign" Bosnia against their own will. They boycotted the referendum on Bosnian independence and did not want to secede from Yugoslavia.

Any attempt to defend the territorial integrity of Bosnia will require a long war of conquest against these Bosnian Serbs. Military action would be as tough as fighting the Viet Cong. Nor would action against Serbia help Bosnia. The United States could destroy Serbia, but to do so would impoverish another 10 million people, most of whom oppose the war. It would also create a few million more refugees. It will not force Bosnia's Serbs to submit to a Muslim-Croat coalition government.

At this stage, any attempt to preserve Bosnia will lead to a longer, bloodier, more horrible war. A better approach would be to accept that the recognition of Bosnia with its existing boundaries was a gross error and to draw new borders, presumably accompanied by transfers of population, a "solution" patterned after the partition of India in 1947.

To save face, the United States and EC may be able to insist on the fiction of a Bosnian "state" which is actually a confederation of autonomous cantons, a temporary solution that would probably soon lead to the secession of the Serbian and Croatian cantons and their attachment to the mother republics.

Patterning the division of Bosnia on the partition of India is hardly a completely satisfactory solution. As that experience shows, such a solution is itself grotesque and will lead only to permanent armed hostility in what used to be Yugoslavia. Yet an unhappy result was foreordained once the EC and the United States gave in to Germany's insistence on the destruction of the Yugoslavia that had been created after the German defeat in World War I and reconstituted after the German defeat in World War II. Having rejected multinational Yugoslavia, the EC and the United States cannot create a multinational Bosnia. To attempt to do so will enlarge the Balkans tragedy.

SUGGESTION FOR FURTHER READING

Hayden, Robert M.
    1999   *Blueprints for a House Divided: The Constitutional Logic of the Yugoslav Conflict.* Ann Arbor: University of Michigan Press.

CHAPTER 10

**NATO FUELS THE
BALKAN FIRE**

Pittsburgh Post-Gazette, March 28, 1999

ROBERT M.
HAYDEN
After the conflicts between Serbs, Bosnians, and Croatians subsided, another dispute exploded in the southern Yugoslavian province of Kosovo. Problems began almost immediately after the breakup of the former Yugoslavia, when Slobodan Milosevic ended a policy (implemented by Tito) which granted autonomy to Kosovo from 1974 to 1989. By the end of this period, the vast majority of those living in Kosovo were ethnic Albanians.

In response to the new policy of direct rule, the Kosovo Liberation Army (KLA) began attacking Serbian police and civilians in 1997. Serb forces responded by killing KLA forces and Albanian civilians, and the conflict quickly escalated, resulting in approximately 2,000 deaths and several hundred thousand refugees.

On March 24, 1999, U.S.-led NATO air forces initiated a bombing campaign against Yugoslav targets, in violation of international law and the U.N. Charter. Although many Clinton administration officials argued that the attacks were necessary to prevent greater bloodshed, U.S. State Department and Pentagon officials indicated that Serbian paramilitary atrocities directed at Kosovar Albanian civilians escalated in the weeks following the bombing.[1] In this article, Hayden issues a sharp critique of the NATO campaign.

On March 24, the United States led NATO into the first campaign of military aggression against a sovereign state in Europe since World War II. It did so against the principles of international law and of the United Nations charter. It also did so against the rulings of the Nuremberg trials, which declared that "to initiate a war of aggression . . . is not only an international crime, it is the supreme international crime."

That NATO is an aggressor is not in doubt. While hardly a "republic" under the dictatorship of Slobodan Milosevic, the Federal Republic of Yugoslavia is clearly a state with internationally recognized borders. NATO is attacking that state militarily, brazenly, although Yugoslavia has not attacked or even threatened any NATO country.

To be sure, Serbian forces have attacked ethnic Albanians in Kosovo, a province that has been part of Serbia since 1913. While Kosovo had a very mixed population in the past, during the years of its "autonomy" under ethnic Albanian rule (1974–1989), it became almost 90 percent Albanian. The Serbian police have been brutal in response to an armed uprising by the Kosovo Liberation Army (KLA), which began to attack Serb police and to murder Serb civilians in 1997.

The resulting conflict has been horrible and tragic. It is hardly unique in the world, however, nor even particularly noteworthy in terms of victims. For example, the Turkish campaigns against the Kurds in Turkey and in Iraq have killed far more people and destroyed far more villages than the Serb campaigns in Kosovo. Yet NATO is not bombing Turkey (which is, of course, a NATO member).

Perhaps the niceties of international law may be forgotten if the cause is right. But what is the cause?

President Clinton has said that we are attacking Yugoslavia to protect the Albanians there from a Serb offensive, to prevent a wider war, to uphold our values, to protect our interests, and to advance the cause of peace. Yet few actions could be less likely to produce these results than the massive assaults now being conducted on Serbia.

Protect the Albanians? It was clear before NATO's aggression that the most likely result of air attacks would be an increase in fighting in Kosovo, and this has happened. The Serbs, committed to holding onto their territory, have increased their attacks on the KLA. The KLA, having gained NATO as its air force, has increased its attacks on the Serbs. Caught in the middle are the people of Kosovo, who are now fleeing the increased fighting. Thus NATO has caused a new wave of refugees.

Prevent a wider war? As the increasing flows of refugees reach Albania and Macedonia, they threaten to disrupt those fragile states. Macedonia is particularly vulnerable, since relations between the Slav Macedonian majority and ethnic Albanian minority there are already uneasy. On the second day of NATO attacks on Serbia, thousands of demonstrators, waving Macedonian flags, attacked the American Embassy, and the Macedonian government stated that anti-NATO sentiment was increasing.

So much for, to use Bill Clinton's words, "defusing the Balkans powder keg." Uphold our values? Which values? Isn't international law one of our values?

Here, the relevant comparison is with Iraq, where the United States conducted the [1991] Gulf war because Saddam Hussein had invaded a neighboring state, thus changing borders by force. In Kosovo, the United States has led NATO into attacking a sovereign state, thus threatening to change borders by force.

Or perhaps the "values" are the need to protect civilians from military attack. In that case, the United States will need to put Turkey on its target list, not to mention Israel, which has attacked civilians in Lebanon (part of which it also occupies) with some frequency for many years now.

Of course, Bill Clinton referred to "genocide" in his speech justifying the attacks on Yugoslavia. Yet in Kosovo, about 2,000 people have died in two years, in the course of the brutal repression of an armed insurrection. This is a condition usually called "civil war." Tragic, yes. Incidents of war crimes, almost certainly. But "genocide," no. This is an insult to the memory of the victims of the Holocaust.

Do our values include terrorizing the innocent populations of Belgrade, Novi Sad, Kragujevac, Nis, and other Serbian cities? Do they include damaging the power and water supplies of these people? Do they include destroying the livelihood of these people? Are our values, in fact, the same as those we condemned during the siege of Sarajevo by the Serbs (and failed to notice during the siege of Mostar by the Croats)?

Advance the cause of peace? Increasing conflict, and radically increasing the risk of even greater war, seems an odd way to achieve this goal. Advance our interests? Perhaps. But what are our interests in this case? Bill Clinton has not said. And when we know what they are, will they justify the violations of international law and the betrayal of our supposed values that are manifested by NATO's massive aggression against Yugoslavia?

In a transparent display of hypocrisy, President Clinton has said that NATO is not waging war against the people of Yugoslavia, but against their government. Can anyone believe that people under attack will hate anyone other than the attackers?

NATO's aggression has betrayed those who oppose Milosevic's dictatorship, thus strengthening the rule of the man whom Bill Clinton accurately described as "a dictator who has done nothing since the cold war ended but start new wars and pour gasoline on the flames of ethnic and religious division."

There is now a new arsonist in the volatile Balkans: NATO.

EDITOR'S NOTE

1. See Noam Chomsky, "Crisis in the Balkans," pp. 34–50 in *Rogue States: The Rule of Force in World Affairs* (Cambridge: South End Press, 2000).

CHAPTER 11

NO EXIT FROM SOMALIA

Washington Post, May 15, 1991

ANNA SIMONS Among the most catastrophic post-Cold War crises was the civil war in Somalia. Like Afghanistan, Somalia was heavily armed by the United States during the 1980s for the alleged purpose of deterring Soviet expansion. The American-backed leadership, however, looted the national treasury and repressed dissent, and many Somalis resented U.S. support of the corrupt regime. By 1991, civil war had exploded.

The following three commentaries by Anna Simons offer an anthropologist's view of the situation over time. They courageously suggest policy options that would be controversial among many anthropologists and government officials, yet reflect intimate knowledge of the region and local cultures.

In the following 1991 article, written at a time when Somalia barely registered in the U.S. media, Simons urges policy makers to take note of the looming crisis there. She also offers a concrete suggestion for helping Somalis escape the bloodshed.

Conditions for many Somalis are as bad as they are for the Kurds and Bangladeshis, yet because there are no journalists in Somalia, news of the catastrophe there barely trickles out.

Since December, Somalia's capital has been unlivable for hundreds of thousands of Somalis, if not more. Beyond the toll of dead and injured, civil war has utterly devastated the social structure, laid waste the infrastructure and destroyed any semblance of civil order throughout the country. Nevertheless, tens of thousands of Somalis are stuck along the borders of a nation which, for all intents and purposes, no longer exists—with no exit.

Many Somalis are perched on the Kenyan border. However, Kenya has long viewed Somalis with suspicion and ambivalence, and to judge from what Somali friends have written, their applications for refugee status are not being processed at all quickly (if at all), nor is Kenya granting Somalis visas to travel in Kenya or through Kenya to anywhere else. Nor must Kenya have much incentive to do so; no country is making it easy for Somalis to enter.

Thus, even the best-educated and most upstanding and middle class of the Somalis—those who worked for the government or ran businesses and owned restaurants—have been left desperate, destitute, and deserted. This is what one Somali on the Kenyan border writes: "Here the condition is something beyond your imagination. Even the water is very scarce. Don't ask about medicine. Never talk about a house to rent. Food is very scarce. Even if you get food you may not get the purchasing power [money]."

Another good friend watched his handicapped sister raped by militia, after bandits stripped his entire family of everything they owned. Now he fears being shot whenever he tries to cross the border into Kenya to mail a letter—to plead for help.

Meanwhile, Kuwait desperately needs hundreds of thousands of pairs of hands for its massive cleanup and repair.

Kuwait has long hosted Somali workers. Indeed, one returned American soldier saw at least one truckload of jubilant Somalis celebrating the liberation of Kuwait City in Kuwait City—some Somalis clearly stuck out the occupation alongside Kuwaitis.

Somalis are Muslims, like Kuwaitis, and Somalia is also a member of the Arab League. Under normal circumstances I am sure Saudi Arabia and the Gulf states would have tried to head off the civil war in Somalia (as they have so often done in the past). However, they can hardly be blamed for having been preoccupied by recent events so much closer to home.

Nevertheless, now there is occasion to pay attention again, and to offer a simple, temporary but life-saving solution to tens—perhaps hundreds—of thousands of Somalis.

Offer those Somalis on the Kenyan border transit to Kuwait, employment in the cleanup effort in Kuwait and refuge in Kuwait until they have the opportunity to return safely to set their own devastated house in order again.

CHAPTER 12

OUR ABYSMAL IGNORANCE ABOUT SOMALIA

Washington Post, December 6, 1992

ANNA SIMONS   Once the fighting in Somalia appeared to be waning in November and December 1992, the outgoing Bush administration decided to move U.S. troops into the country on a massive scale under the auspices of the United Nations. In 1993 Clinton supported the intervention as a humanitarian mission, although critics charged that the famine was ending by the time American soldiers arrived on the scene. In many ways, the operation had the appearance of a public relations mission.

In this article, published as U.S. troops were on the way to Somalia, Simons expresses grave concern that "we Americans literally do not know what we are getting into," and provides readers with basic information about the history and politics of the country. She unambiguously drives her main argument home: the vast majority of so-called Somali experts lack fundamental knowledge about the region.

As the troops and the network anchors head for Somalia, I have this feeling—one that has grown with every passing morning news show, talk show, and evening newscast—that we Americans literally do not know what we are getting into.

The amount of misinformation that has been circulating and recirculating on Somalia is shameful. Perhaps we'll become better informed as U.S. involvement there deepens, but I'm not counting on it. I only hope that we don't learn the truth the hard way.

There are only a handful of non-Somalis in America—a very small handful—who should be regarded as experts on Somalia. Currently, however, the term is being loosely applied to a number of people who may indeed be expert in something—international relations, military strategy, low-intensity conflict, humanitarian assistance, or maybe just

THIS MODERN WORLD by TOM TOMORROW

THE EVENING NEWS PRESENTS SOMALIA AS A SIMPLE MORALITY PLAY...IN WHICH STARVING VICTIMS ARE RESCUED FROM EVIL WARLORDS BY A BENEVOLENT UNITED STATES MILITARY...

THIS INCREDIBLE, SELF-LESS GESTURE OF HUMAN-ITARIANISM *CLEARLY* DEMONSTRATES THE INNATE MORAL SUPER-IORITY OF AMERICA!

GOD BLESS US EVERY ONE!

REALITY IS SOMEWHAT *MURKIER*...THE CRISIS IS LARGELY A LEGACY OF THE COLD WAR, BROUGHT ON BY SUPERPOWER SUPPORT FOR REPREHENSIBLE *DICTATORSHIPS*, MASSIVE *ARMS SHIPMENTS*, AND AGRICULTURAL POLICIES WHICH ENCOURAGED CASH-CROP *EXPORTS* AT THE EXPENSE OF *SELF-SUSTENANCE*...

OH THAT'S ALL MUCH TOO *COMPLICATED*.

I JUST WANT TO WATCH THE SOL-DIERS ON *TEEVEE*.

THE SUBSEQUENT FAMINE IS NOT ONLY *TRAGIC*, IT IS *OBSCENE*...PARTICULARLY WHEN ONE CONSID-ERS THAT ENOUGH GRAIN IS ACTUALLY GROWN EACH YEAR TO *EASILY* FEED EVERY HUMAN ON THE *PLANET*...BUT UNFORTUNATELY, MUCH OF THAT GRAIN IS INSTEAD USED TO FATTEN *LIVESTOCK* SO THAT CITIZENS OF THE DEVEL-OPED WORLD CAN CONTINUE TO ENJOY THEIR *BIG MACS*...

UM...SO WHAT'S YOUR *POINT*?

STILL...EVEN IF NONE OF THESE UNDERLYING FACTORS ARE ADDRESSED, THE FACT REMAINS THAT THIS INTERVENTION *WILL* SAVE SOME LIVES...TO HELP US SORT OUT THIS CONFUSING SITUATION, LET'S SEE WHAT OUR RESIDENT PUNDIT *SPARKY* HAS TO SAY...

WELL...THOSE OF US WHO GET PAID TO HAVE DEFINITIVE OPINIONS ON EVERY SUBJECT AREN'T EVER SUPPOSED TO *ADMIT* THIS... BUT FRANKLY, I JUST DON'T KNOW *WHAT* TO THINK...

GASP!

OH MY GOD!

TOM TOMORROW © 12-29-92

public relations—but don't know much at all about Somalia. Neverthe-less, they're being heard from.

Begin with the military front. To dismiss armed Somalis as an inef-fectual, ragtag lot is to not only underestimate the tenacity of people who might well oppose foreign intervention but also to ignore guerrilla experience that has been built up in Somalia over a long period. Oppo-sition groups have been active for more than 10 years in a region that is, in many ways, far more inhospitable than the wide-open sands where U.S. troops practiced before going to war in Kuwait and Iraq.

Moreover, the military experts are being either overconfident—and thus careless—or are just plain not leveling with the American public in some of their pronouncements. As one military adviser who helped train the Somali army has pointed out, the weapons the Somalis have are the same sort of weapons the North Vietnamese used so effectively against our more massive firepower. Plus, three years ago there were substantive reports of chemical weapons being stockpiled in Somalia. The country received weapons not only from the United States and the Soviet Union, but also from Libya and other Arab nations.

And has anyone mentioned the stockpiles of heavy weapons still buried in the bush? Or the initial effectiveness of the Somalis when they fought the Ethiopians in the Ogaden War?[1]

It is ironic that the same media networks that have previously reported on the skill of Somali poachers in decimating East Africa's wildlife population have not made the connection between such adeptness at outmaneuvering crack police units and the potential ability to outfox some of our own military forces.

At the other end of the expert spectrum are those who claim knowledge of foreign policy and Africa and are spouting things like, "Elders ruled Somalia peacefully for centuries." In fact, Somalia has existed as a sovereign country only since 1960, and even before colonialism drew boundaries, the strength of various clans and subclans was always variable and shifting with regard to who was in control of what areas and what people.

In fact, this is precisely what now appears to have revived in the northern and northeastern sectors of Somalia: zones of influence exist within which there is relative calm. Who is considering the Somalis in those areas and how their balance of power will be altered with the insertion of American or U.N. troops into the south, and the subsequent resurrection by outsiders of some sort of government for all of Somalia?

No Somalis I know who reside in this country are being consulted as to what should or could be done. In part this is because the State Department has rightly viewed Somalis as too partisan; every Somali in this country, whether the holder of a doctorate or the owner of a convenience store, has relatives somewhere in Somalia and thus strong interests and opinions concerning how things should be done there. There is tremendous disagreement within the U.S. Somali community, disagreement that in many ways parallels the discord in Somalia itself.

But this makes it far too easy for Americans at the State Department, in the Pentagon, and elsewhere in government to dismiss the full range of Somali viewpoints. Clearly, it is all part of the broader resolution: If getting food to starving Somalis cannot be handled diplomatically, then maybe it's time to knock heads together. And perhaps it is.

But what is at issue for the long haul is an extremely complicated, extremely different, and extremely foreign situation. We should be heading into it with a good deal more knowledge than has so far been provided us by so-called experts.

EDITOR'S NOTE

1. The Ogaden War (1977–1979) was fought between Somalia and Ethiopia over the disputed Ogaden province. The Soviet-backed Ethiopian army was able to reclaim the territory after a successful invasion by Somali forces in 1977.

CHAPTER 13　THE SOMALIA TRAP

Washington Post, August 15, 1993

ANNA SIMONS　Simons' third commentary urges policy makers in the Clinton administration to act decisively in Somalia, but her recommendations were largely ignored. Less than two months after the publication of Simons' piece, eighteen elite U.S. Army Rangers were killed after their helicopter was shot down in a botched operation in Mogadishu to capture Mohammed Aideed, a local strongman. Within a month, Clinton announced that U.S. troops would begin withdrawing from Somalia.

Before considering withdrawal from Somalia, two key questions must be asked: What was our purpose in embroiling ourselves in Somalia in the first place, and have we achieved our goals?

One reason for choosing withdrawal now may well be that neither question will be any more answerable two years from now than two weeks or two months from now. Our purposes continue to appear as murky today as they did in November and December, while whatever we may have helped achieve for Somalis likely will vanish as soon as we pull out. In other words, we have hoisted ourselves on our own petard such that the real question becomes: At what price can we retreat with honor? And the answer to that question is the simplest by far: We cannot.

The trap we have erected for ourselves is this: Our insertion into Somalia was ill-conceived and impracticable from the outset. Putting the best possible spin on it, it seems to have stemmed from a heartfelt need to get horrific images of starving people off nightly television newscasts. So far, this has been our only success. Somalia remains off the airwaves. It is only when U.S. soldiers have been shot and killed (not even shot and wounded) that broadcasts reluctantly swing from Bosnia back to the Horn of Africa.

Yet this rapidly achieved silence (implying success, but hiding failure) came at the price of not bothering to understand the fundamentals of what was occurring in Somalia. For instance, our assumption that a country with no government would be easy to enter was correct, but our assumptions about restoring order so that we may leave again have been pitifully naive. Even worse, we have never successfully convinced the people we intervened to help that we have had their best interests at heart. Rather, a nagging suspicion for many Somalis (and—not un-coincidentally—many of the soldiers we have sent to Somalia) has been that we seek something more: oil, a military base, a stop to the rise of Islamic fundamentalism, an affirmation of our superpower status, a policeman's trial run at creating order out of lawlessness.

Indeed, such suspicions—that we have ulterior motives and that Somalis themselves are incidental to larger goals—fuel some of what now goes on in Mogadishu. Why should Somalis trust our intentions, particularly when these intentions have yet to be clarified? In this sense, Mohamed Farah Aideed does not deserve all our blame. Or if he does, it is in large measure because he personifies our mistakes in once again treating with and then treating badly someone whose power we initially enhanced but now can't control.

So what should we do?

If we withdraw from Somalia, we must realize we lose more than just face. We potentially lose the ability to intervene easily in countries where other peoples will need us in the future. And we potentially destroy what remains of the Somalia we have been shoring up.

However, if this is the decision that is in the best interests of this country, then for the sake of Somalis all forces should be withdrawn from that country, including all humanitarian assistance organizations. It was the aid agencies that supplied bandits with just enough food and money for ammunition and arms to keep them going and at one another's throats before we intervened. Without their assistance, maybe Somali suffering won't be quite so prolonged, and Somali might will be able to make Somali right much more quickly. Two regions of Somalia (the northeast and the self-declared northern country of Somaliland) already prove this point.

But if it is our might that should make right, then we need to do it with a different attitude. We need to take charge. Critics abroad and in universities here will scream neocolonialism, while many Americans will rightly wonder why we are helping reengineer a remote African country when we have so many dire social problems of our own.

Nevertheless, if our position in the world requires us to help police it, then Somalia is the place to begin because—like it or not—we are already there.

However, should this be our choice, we must recognize that we are already at a disadvantage. Recent history should have taught us to first understand Somalis and Somalia, and sooner rather than later. Still, it might not be too late if we address the hard questions now and answer them honestly.

SUGGESTIONS FOR FURTHER READING

Simons, Anna
    1995   *Networks of Dissolution: Somalia Undone.* Boulder: Westview Press.
    1998   *The Company They Keep: Inside the U.S. Army Special Forces.* New York: Avon Books.

CHAPTER 14

INCREASED U.S. MILITARY AID TO COLOMBIA WON'T CURB DRUG TRAFFICKING

San Francisco Chronicle, August 19, 1999

WINIFRED
TATE

In the 1990s, the official justification for U.S. involvement in many Latin American countries shifted from the Cold War struggle against communism to the "war on drugs." This shift resulted largely in efforts to eradicate sources of narcotic drugs—especially marijuana, coca, and poppy plants.

The "war on drugs," like any conventional war, has relied upon military personnel, equipment, and tactics. In the 1990s, more than fifty thousand U.S. troops passed through nearly every country in the region and approximately fifteen thousand Latin American military and police agents were trained in the United States. Yet evidence indicates that many of the armed forces receiving U.S. assistance have dismal human rights records and that the war on drugs may be a cover for destroying opposition groups and insurgents.

Colombia, which produces much of the cocaine consumed in the United States, is a case in point. For more than thirty-five years the Colombian military and right-wing paramilitary groups have fought a guerrilla war against the Revolutionary Armed Forces of Colombia, or FARC, which have proposed state control over the economy. All sides have used drug money in varying degrees to finance the war, and all have reportedly engaged in human rights abuses, including assaults upon civilians, kidnappings, torture, rape, and extrajudicial executions. According to recent reports, some U.S. contractors have helped plan and support these operations.[1]

The following article, by Winifred Tate of the Washington Office on Latin America, was written as the Clinton administration proposed an escalation of military support for Colombia.

The long-neglected conflict in Colombia is emerging as Latin America's major crisis and pulling the United States ever more deeply into an unwinnable war. Escalating political violence, an entrenched insurgency, increasing illicit drug production, and growing concern from Colombia's neighbors about the conflict spilling over have policy makers in Washington searching for a solution to the problems besetting Colombia.

Many U.S. policy makers and military leaders are calling for increased U.S. aid for the Colombian military. But this will only serve to pull the United States closer to the most abusive military forces in the hemisphere without reducing illicit drug production or contributing to stability and democracy in that beleaguered country.

Though the Colombian army has declared itself "reformed," the nation's military is far from a new institution. Military collusion with paramilitary activity on a local and regional level continues, and paramilitary violence has escalated in the past six months. These groups target alleged guerrilla sympathizers, but their net of terror has been cast wide over a growing number of Colombian peace leaders and members of civil society. More than 400 people have been killed or "disappeared" in the first three months of this year alone, and tens of thousands more have been forced to flee their homes.

Two generals have been cashiered because of evidence of participating in human rights abuses, but the army continues to harbor many officers linked to rights violations, including high-level commanders. General Rafael Hernández López, for example, was named chief of staff of the Colombian Armed Forces, despite a pending investigation for his alleged participation in the 1996 kidnapping and murder of a guerrilla leader's family member. Human rights organizations and Colombian judicial authorities have gathered extensive evidence of his implication in numerous human rights violations, including summary executions, forced disappearances, rape, and torture committed by soldiers under his command. Increased military aid is not likely to improve the military's human rights performance.

In 1990, the United States sent a team of military advisers to Colombia to review that country's military intelligence organizations and recommend changes. Colombia's military intelligence apparatus was reorganized, and clandestine intelligence networks were established that, in at least one case, functioned as paramilitary death squads. One such group, Naval Intelligence Network No. 7, was responsible for the murder of more than 50 civilians. Five military officials, including Lt. Col. Rodrigo Quiñónez, were found guilty last year of creating and financing this paramilitary group in order to murder local opposition leaders and union organizers. Quiñónez remains on active duty, with only a letter of reprimand in his file.

Now, drug czar Barry McCaffrey has requested $40 million in aid for "regional intelligence programs," part of a nearly $600 million emergency aid package for Colombia. This despite concerns substantiated by a General Accounting Office report revealing that U.S. intelligence shared with the Colombian military lacks mechanisms "to ensure that it is not being used for other than counternarcotics purposes."

Support for the Colombian military is pulling the United States into the quagmire of a protracted and dirty counterinsurgency struggle, with no clear policy objective. There is no evidence that focusing counternarcotics efforts on battling the country's largest guerrilla group, the Revolutionary Armed Forces of Colombia or FARC, will reduce coca production. In fact, right-wing paramilitary groups, linked to the Colombian security forces, are more deeply involved in drug trafficking. Aerial fumigation has pushed a desperate peasant population further into the jungle—or into the arms of the insurgency.

While only Colombians can resolve their crisis, the international community—and particularly the United States—can and should do much to support an eventual negotiated settlement. We should begin by correcting the overwhelming imbalance in U.S. aid: more than $230 million in predominantly military assistance for counternarcotics operations, less than $10 million for development, judicial and law enforcement, and human rights.

On March 10, President Clinton apologized for the U.S. role in Guatemala's long internal conflict, saying that "support for military forces or intelligence units which engaged in violent and widespread repression . . . was wrong, and the United States must not repeat that mistake." Now, a matter of months after the president's historic apology, we risk repeating that mistake by intervening in a counterinsurgency war that the United States cannot win.

Clear support for human rights and civilian democracy will prevent the need for future apologies to Colombians who have suffered enough in the name of misguided counternarcotics policies.

EDITOR'S NOTE

1. See T. Christian Miller, "Colombia: Videotape Shows Americans' Role in Village Bombing," *Los Angeles Times*, March 16, 2003, p. A4.

CHAPTER 15

COLOMBIA: RULES OF THE GAME

Foreign Policy in Focus, February 16, 2001
www.foreignpolicy-infocus.org

WINIFRED
TATE

In July 2000 the U.S. Congress passed the Clinton administration's "Plan Colombia," a $1.3 billion three-year program to ratchet up U.S. military aid and training to Colombia. Colombia is now the third-largest recipient of U.S. military assistance. In this article, Winifred Tate cautions against the possible consequences of increasing such aid, given the miserable human rights record of the Colombian military.

When the U.S. and Colombia meet on the soccer field in Miami this Saturday, the rules are clear, the time is fixed, the game is officiated, and one team will win. In contrast, the U.S. is playing a far different game in Colombia: there are no rules, no referee, a maze of different "teams," and no clear end. The playing field is a battlefield. No one wins; everyone loses.

I have just returned from a five-day fact-finding trip to Colombia's southern state of Putumayo, where U.S.-trained army battalions have been deployed since December and where thousands of acres are being sprayed with herbicides.

The results are not good. Indigenous and peasant farmers have had their food supply destroyed by U.S.-funded aerial spraying. A grade school garden and a government-sponsored alternative agriculture project designed to teach peasants to grow cash crops other than coca were destroyed by fumigation. Paramilitary gunmen have gone on killing sprees whose total toll will never be known.

There are some very unhappy conclusions to be drawn:

First, the U.S. is teamed up with the most abusive military force in the hemisphere. And Colombia's military, in turn, frequently works hand in glove with brutal paramilitary forces that are estimated to be responsible for three-quarters of the politically motivated civilian murders. Members of the Colombian military help the paramilitaries with intelligence, logistics, and transportation, and by blocking official investigations into their activities. This directly violates the human rights conditions set by Congress as a prerequisite for U.S. military assistance. During the first 18 days of January alone, paramilitary groups committed 26 massacres; in one incident paramilitary thugs beat more than 20 people to death with sledgehammers and stones. Yet U.S. aid continues to flow.

Second, there's no clear end. The $1.3 billion extraordinary aid package passed by Congress last July was sold as a one-time emergency appropriation, a part of "Plan Colombia" that would end the civil war and bring peace and economic growth. Now the U.S. military is asking Congress for an additional $1 billion a year, continuing into the foreseeable future.

Third, the strategy is unclear. While Plan Colombia was sold to the American public as a counter-drug plan, U.S. funds were earmarked primarily for military aid to train, equip, and transport three new Colombian army battalions, blurring the lines between counterinsurgency and counternarcotics missions. U.S. policy makers are desperate to appear hard on drugs; but for Colombians this is not a war on drugs, it is the fifth decade of a counterinsurgency struggle.

Fourth, there aren't two sides: there's a maze of intertwined, overlapping, and heavily armed competitors. The drug cartels, under the protection of paramilitary forces, have diversified their operations, finding new production and trafficking routes. Colombian guerrillas, primarily the Revolutionary Armed Forces (FARC), have financed their expansion through profits from the drug trade, but their objective is territorial control and pursuing a war against the state. After more than 40 years, this war will not be won on the battlefield, but at the negotiating table.

Fifth, there are no winners. Ordinary Colombians lose. Human rights lose. Peace loses. The region loses. There have already been clashes between guerrillas and paramilitaries in surrounding countries. And the United Nations High Commissioner for Refugees has begun preparing camps along the border for thousands of displaced persons. The U.S. war on drugs is pushing drug cultivation and trafficking into floundering Ecuador, Peru, and the fragile Amazon ecosystems.

The U.S. loses. Our most important interests and objectives in the region—including strengthening democracy, promoting human rights and the rule of law, and fostering trade and investment—are being severely undermined. Treatment programs for addicts go underfunded at home, and, despite spending some $19 billion a year on the war on drugs, illegal narcotics remain cheap and plentiful within America.

It's time for a new U.S. game plan in Colombia. First, we must send an unequivocal message to the Colombian military that it must cut its ties with paramilitary forces. Second, we must put our money into proven programs of supporting human rights, rule of law, and economic development. Finally, we must solve our drug problem at home with effective medical treatment and educational solutions to this largely public health problem.

If the U.S. team played soccer the way we're engaging Colombia, we'd score minus 50 goals, the team would be billions of dollars in the red, and 10 percent of the spectators would wind up dead. Maybe it's time for a new game plan.

CHAPTER 16

UNVEILING U.S. POLICY IN COLOMBIA

Foreign Policy in Focus, April 19, 2002
www.foreignpolicy-infocus.org

LESLEY GILL   Lamentably, the Bush administration has not only maintained the levels of military support established under Plan Colombia but expanded funding to other South American countries. Under the Andean Regional Initiative, military funding has been expanded to six neighboring countries.

By February 2002, when peace talks between the Colombian government and FARC leaders collapsed, it was clear that U.S. involvement in Colombia was likely to expand beyond the realm of counternarcotics efforts, especially in the post–September 11 climate. In this article, Lesley Gill describes the potential pitfalls of labeling the FARC a terrorist group while ignoring the violence perpetrated by right-wing paramilitaries. Her commentary is a sharp condemnation of U.S. aerial fumigation policies that destroy the livelihood of peasant farmers in the name of counterterrorism.

As the drumbeat in the "war against terror" becomes louder in Washington, the Bush administration is prepared to involve the U.S. more directly in Colombia's 40-year civil war. President Bush now advocates the use of U.S. advisers and equipment in a campaign against guerrillas who want to overthrow the Colombian government. Although the U.S. has already been tacitly supporting counterinsurgency operations in Colombia, Bush's initiative would up the policy ante by openly committing the U.S. to the defeat of the guerrillas and eliminating the distinction between counternarcotics and counterinsurgency operations.

The September 11 tragedy provides the administration with the rationale to directly target guerrilla insurgents, whom it labels "terrorists" and blames for the recent collapse of peace talks. As I discovered on a recent fact-finding trip to the coca-growing region of southern Colombia, however, the aims of U.S. policy have been evident to peasants there for some time. It is here that indiscriminate aerial spraying of coca fields serves less to promote alternative development than to displace peasants from an area controlled by the FARC, Colombia's oldest and largest guerrilla organization.

In the department of Putumayo, over half of the 350,000 inhabitants depend on coca for a livelihood. It is the only crop that can be marketed in a region where stable roads do not exist, and it provides some families with a modest living that would be unobtainable by other means. But coca—the basis of cocaine—also exposes them to intense levels of violence, as profits from its cultivation are sustained by the illegal drug traffic. Families are therefore eager to adopt viable alternatives.

Yet alternative development has always been subordinate to a repressive military and fumigation strategy. The U.S. seems less interested in assisting peasants to find substitutes for coca than in reducing the area under cultivation by almost any means necessary. The U.S. government now states that it will no longer promote alternative crops to peasants whose coca fields are eradicated in U.S.-financed fumigation operations. Only $145 million of Plan Colombia—a $1.3 billion, mostly military aid package approved in mid-2000 by President Clinton—is dedicated to crop substitution programs, and a coercive system of social pacts, designed to channel aid to peasants who agree to manually eradicate coca, has little credibility with local people.

In the southern department of Putumayo, where most of Colombian coca is produced, some 37,000 growers consented in 2000 to destroy their coca within six months after the arrival of financial assistance or face the fumigation of their fields with herbicide. Peasants soon discovered that financial assistance was either slow to arrive or never came, and by the end of 2001, the U.S. Agency for International Development had spent only 10 percent of what it had allocated for alternative development. To make matters worse, adhering to the terms of the government's pacts turned out to be no guarantee against fumigation.

The first round of aerial fumigation took place between December 24, 2000, and January 7, 2001, and, according to the U.S. embassy, it destroyed 30,000 hectares in the municipalities of Orito, San Miguel, and Valle de Guamuez. The Catholic Church, however, stated that coca represented only 15,000 hectares; the rest of the area was planted in food crops. In November 2001, spraying began again in San Miguel and Valle de Guamuez, even though little or no U.S. government aid had reached pact signers who remained in compliance with the eradication agreements.

The experience of one peasant whom I met in Putumayo reflected those of many others. This individual signed a pact along with 70 members of his community, but, because he never received the promised development aid, the man borrowed $12,000 to plant black pepper and offset the imminent loss of his coca. Then he stuck a white flag in the field to signal that the black pepper crop was legal. When the spray planes returned on November 24, 2001, they destroyed the entire pepper field as well as fruit trees, coffee bushes, cassava, corn, and pasture. All of this raises disturbing questions both about Washington's commitment to alternative development and about the real aims of its fumigation program in guerrilla strongholds.

A U.S. embassy official who requested anonymity told me that reducing the total area under coca cultivation—not alternative development—is the cornerstone of U.S. policy in Colombia. "It may be best that people simply abandon the area or make their own decisions about how to survive," he said. "People need to understand that the [U.S.] government absolutely will not tolerate coca cultivation." Yet since the fumigation operations began, coca cultivation has increased rather than decreased. In addition, a U.S.-trained counternarcotics force has been unable to dislodge the FARC from rural areas of Putumayo.

When confronted with evidence of food crop destruction, embassy officials explain that, although aerial spraying is supposed to be done from 30 feet up, the presence of guerrillas in Putumayo forces planes to 90 feet, which causes the herbicide to drift onto neighboring fields. But though drift may explain some of the damage, it does not account completely for the level of destruction in Putumayo. Independent Colombian and U.S. observers have reported the devastation of food crops that are far from coca fields. In these cases, one Colombian expert on alternative development notes, "the only explanation is that [fumigation] was intentional," calculated to destroy peasant morale in areas under FARC control and displace them to other areas of the country. In fact, analysts and peasants alike conclude that displacement has long been a strategy, not an effect, of Colombia's civil war. The fumigation campaign has unfolded in a context in which the Colombian government cannot defeat the guerrillas militarily and peace talks have collapsed.

Guerrillas control nearly half of the national territory, and last year alone, they repeatedly attacked an oil pipeline operated by Occidental Petroleum. For the U.S., protecting the supply of Colombian oil is especially important as conflicts in the Middle East worsen, and President Bush recently requested $98 million to train and equip Colombian counterinsurgency battalions who guard the pipeline. In addition, the administration's $882 million "Andean Regional Initiative," which was approved last December, earmarked 63 percent of the Colombia funding for military uses.

The portrayal of the FARC as international terrorist "evil doers" is simply the latest in a series of Washington's label shifts. During the cold war, Washington defined the FARC as "communist subversives," but this label became obsolete with the collapse of the Soviet Union and the expansion of the drug war in the 1990s, when U.S. propagandists deployed the more politically expedient term "narcoguerrilla" to delegitimize the rebels. Although today both the FARC and the other main guerrilla group, the National Liberation Army (ELN), benefit from coca production and processing, they do not control the major national and international drug trafficking networks.

Moreover, the narcoguerrilla concept blurs the social and political differences that distinguish the two guerrilla groups from the drug traffickers and from each other. It also obscures the involvement of the paramilitaries, sectors of the military, and members of the political establishment in the drug traffic. Since September 11, new portrayals of the FARC as an international terrorist organization have not been supported by evidence. Although guerrilla tactics against Colombian citizens and select foreigners working in Colombia expose the insurgents to charges of terrorism, the FARC's military operations beyond Colombian borders are restricted to occasional forays into the sparsely populated border regions of neighboring countries.

Equating the FARC with international terrorism creates a double standard with respect to other armed actors in the Colombian conflict. Washington policy makers say relatively little about the Autodefensas Unidas de Colombia (AUC), a federated organization of local paramilitary groups allied with the U.S-backed Colombian security forces. Although the State Department lists the AUC, along with the FARC and ELN, as a terrorist organization and agrees with human rights groups who blame paramilitaries for 70 percent of Colombia's human rights violations, U.S. policies largely ignore the AUC's links to the Colombian military, which uses the organization as an ally in the battle against leftists. The AUC is therefore relatively free to expand its power and to murder ordinary Colombians, as Bush's war on terror targets the FARC.

The U.S. should stop using the threat of terrorism to justify its involvement in counterinsurgency operations in Colombia. Colombia is in the middle of a complex civil war, and the Bush administration needs to recognize the differences between this 40-year-old domestic conflict and global terrorism.

CHAPTER 17

THE PRICE OF FREE TRADE: FAMINE

Los Angeles Times, March 22, 2002

MARC
EDELMAN

This article focuses on another part of Latin America undergoing rapid upheaval—Central America. Marc Edelman examines the negative impact of "free" trade agreements on the livelihood of farmers struggling to survive in an era of economic deregulation. International coffee prices are at forty-year lows, due largely to the World Bank's promotion of coffee cultivation in Vietnam and Indonesia. This has led to a global glut that undermines the ability of millions of Latin American farmers to provide their families with an adequate cash income. At the same time, local markets have been flooded with U.S.-produced corn (which is heavily subsidized by taxpayers), making it unprofitable to cultivate the region's most important subsistence crop.

The appearance of this article in March 2002 was especially timely, since the Bush administration was promoting the idea of a "Free Trade Area of the Americas," designed to further lower tariff barriers in the region.

Increasingly, Central Americans face two choices: migrate or starve. Edelman's piece may be read as a diagnosis of a steadily deteriorating situation in the United States' own backyard.

Central America is in the grip of famine, and if President Bush mentions it when he visits El Salvador on Sunday, he will likely suggest that free trade is the solution.

Yet Bush's proposed Central American Free Trade Agreement is hardly going to remedy the worsening disaster in rural Guatemala, El Salvador, Honduras, and Nicaragua. Unregulated markets are a large part of the reason why 700,000 Central Americans face starvation and nearly one million more suffer serious food shortages.

Hardest hit are coffee plantation workers and maize farmers. Coffee prices have spiraled downward since the 1989 collapse of the International Coffee Agreement, which assigned countries production quotas. In the past few years, prices plummeted further with a surge in exports from Vietnam and Indonesia, where the World Bank encouraged expansion of coffee acreage.

With the market glutted, many coffee farmers did not bother to harvest this year. The result has been evictions from plantation housing, increased migration to teeming slums, and severe hunger among unemployed coffee workers.

Maize farmers too have been feeling the free-market squeeze. Since 1992, Central America has had intra-regional free trade in grains and almost no tariff protection against low-cost imports. Forced to compete with highly subsidized U.S. farmers, many Central American farmers have abandoned food production, gone bankrupt, and lost their land.

Some of Central America's most conservative figures—Guatemalan President Alfonso Portillo and Nicaraguan Cardinal Miguel Obando y Bravo—acknowledge that the intensity and suddenness of the food emergency make it a famine, worse than the hunger characteristic of the region.

Famine is always rooted in economic policies and political decisions, as Amartya Sen, the 1998 Nobel Prize winner in economics, has long maintained. Sen also points out that famines do not occur in democracies, where contested elections and vigorous journalistic oversight force policy makers to try to prevent occurrences that might threaten constituents or allow opponents to make political hay.

U.S. policy makers should ask, then, what the widening famine says about Central American democracy, for which Washington spent billions of dollars and waged three proxy wars during the 1980s.

Apparently, the gap between rulers and ruled in the four affected countries is so large that policy makers feel little pressure to address the crisis. No wonder polls show that a mere 35 percent of Hondurans, 24 percent of Nicaraguans, 21 percent of Salvadorans, and 16 percent of Guatemalans say they are "satisfied" with how democracy functions in their countries.

Right now, tens of thousands of Central Americans are heading north. In contrast to the 1980s and early 1990s, most are not escaping war and repression. Many are abandoning farms that failed because of globalized trade and the dumping of U.S. grain. Others are fleeing liberalized interest rates so high that they have no hope of ever starting a small business. Still others are trying to escape life in the free trade zones, where factory owners enjoy huge public subsidies and workers face immense obstacles in organizing for a living wage.

Central American land could produce decent living standards for small farmers if they could obtain small-scale irrigation systems, better access to land, secure title to property, low-cost credit, and shelter from unfair competition and the ravages of global market forces.

These measures would give even the poorest of the poor a stake in their societies, but they would require elites to take popular needs seriously. Public sectors eviscerated by privatization and budget cuts can't address the inequalities that globalization generates.

Rural Central Americans are already reeling after a decade or more of free-market reforms. President Bush's trade proposals could be the knockout blow.

SUGGESTIONS FOR FURTHER READING

Edelman, Marc
    1992   *The Logic of the Latifundio.* Stanford: Stanford University Press.
    1999   *Peasants against Globalization: Rural Social Movements in Costa Rica.* Stanford: Stanford University Press.

CHAPTER 18

HOW TWO TRUTHS MAKE ONE TRAGEDY

The Independent, October 22, 2000

ALI QLEIBO   On September 27, 2000, Ariel Sharon, then leader the of the Israeli opposition Likud party, entered the Haram al-Sharif in East Jerusalem, the site of the gold Dome of the Rock that is among the holiest Islamic shrines. The esplanade is also revered by Jews, who call it the Temple Mount after a temple destroyed there in A.D. 70. When Sharon, who was protected by hundreds of Israeli riot police, descended nearly an hour later, he was met by Palestinians who heaved chairs, trash cans, and stones at the Israeli forces. The latter retaliated by firing tear gas and rubber bullets. Predominantly Arab East Jerusalem has been under illegal Israeli occupation since 1967.

Sharon's unannounced visit provoked outrage on the part of Palestinians because of his leading role in the 1982 Sabra and Shatila massacres in the Palestinian refugee camps of Beirut, in which Lebanese militiamen—allied with and armed by the Israeli Defense Forces—killed more than 1,000 men, women, and children. At the time, Sharon was defense minister. Not surprisingly, his visit to the Haram al-Sharif sparked a spontaneous popular uprising that has now become known as the Second Intifada.

The following article, written by Palestinian anthropologist Ali Qleibo weeks after the beginning of the Second Intifada, examines the dilemma faced by Palestinians in the wake of escalating violence. His words speak of the extreme forms of everyday violence suffered by the people of the region, of hopelessness, despair, and courage.

As the violence continued last week, Palestinians could be divided into two groups—those who feel that if they don't fight they will be overlooked, and those who feel that to resort to violence is to undermine their human dignity.

But what is the same for all Palestinians is that they have sustained a major blow. Any sense of security they could have entertained has faded. *"El-hamdillah ala Salamtak"* ("Welcome back to safety") has replaced the more traditional greeting *"Salaam aleik'um"* ("Peace be upon you").

As people adjusted to the upheavals of the past three weeks they started to leave their houses. In a state of shock they wandered around, searching for familiar faces, reassuring themselves that life still went on, that our city was still there and that others had survived the disaster.

I remember the night, three weeks ago, after Ariel Sharon, the Israeli opposition leader, had visited the Muslim shrine, the Haram al-Sharif. Violence had broken out. I went into the old city to visit my neighbors. All my friends had survived the ordeal unscathed.

"Did you go and defend the Haram al-Sharif [Temple Mount]?" I asked. Ghassan, a friend and once an activist, said: "If Arafat needs martyrs, the politicians ought to send their own sons. I am happy my son is in medical school in Cairo. Before, I would gladly offer my children as martyrs. I would still offer them provided the leaders stand with their children next to us."

Everyone I knew faced things with disengaged interest. The "stone throwing" was seen as a political contrivance to prod the stalling peace talks. The news leaked out that the Israelis were planning to take over a part of the mosque as a synagogue. Danger threatened our Haram al-Sharif. The Palestinians split into two groups. As I waited in line to buy bread, I overheard a middle-aged man lecture a youth. "If we do not protect the Dome of the Rock," he said, "who would?" The young man answered: "A good Muslim is one who does his Muslim duties and stays alive." The older man explained: "This is not a question of nationalism, it is a matter of faith." The young man retorted. "The Noble Sanctuary has a God to protect it." Before the Oslo peace talks everyone would have rushed to the Noble Sanctuary. Most people I ran into had turned skeptical, suspicious of dubious politics, and apathetic.

At this critical point the picture of Mohammed el-Durrah came into the foreground. This was the boy whose father, trying to avoid the fighting at Natzarim, led him home from school through a short cut, only to get caught in the crossfire. The sight of the boy being shot dead hit a deep chord.

The Oslo agreement has actually made it worse for Palestinians, because it appeared to the outside world that we were enjoying peace. All that has happened is that Israeli occupation has become the status quo. Palestinians continue to suffer—they are harassed, their travel is restricted, their land confiscated, unemployment is high, salaries are low.

It was after the burial of one of the Palestinian martyrs that "the lynching" took place. Two Israeli soldiers were caught and it was immediately assumed that they were "Arabists"—Israelis who disguise themselves as Arabs and infiltrate the protesters, planting bombs, shooting, and killing. The soldiers were escorted to the police station past the funeral parade.

My friend Khalil was horrified. "It is not Muslim, it is not Arab, it has nothing to do with our culture," he said. Victims to the mob, victims to corrupt leadership, victims to military occupation; blind hate triumphed momentarily.

Remorse followed. In Ramallah vigils have been held for the past two nights. Candlelit "peace parades" have taken place in which people walk mournfully past el-Manarah square. A voice mumbled: "But no one cares about our hundred martyrs. Settlers attack helpless farmers. Last week they stoned one to death." Another voice answered: "It is our dignity as human beings that we must struggle for."

Israeli occupation puts the Palestinian in a dilemma: if he is quiet he is overlooked; once he expresses resistance he is condemned.

SUGGESTION FOR FURTHER READING

Qleibo, Ali H.
    1992   *Before the Mountains Disappear: An Ethnographic Chronicle of the Modern Palestinians.* Cairo: Kloreus Books.

CHAPTER 19

THE MATRIX OF CONTROL

Media Monitors Network, 2001
www.mediamonitors.net

JEFF HALPER   The following piece was written in the months following the second Palestinian intifada, which began
in September 2000 in response to the provocative visit of Ariel Sharon to the
Islamic shrine of Haram al-Sharif, in East Jerusalem (see Chapter 18). At the
time, Sharon was leader of the Israeli right-wing opposition party.

In this piece, Jeff Halper describes the Israeli strategy of maintaining control over the West Bank and Gaza by means of a matrix of roads, checkpoints,
settlements, waterways, and other barriers that segment the Palestinian territories. This matrix, he argues, is crucial to understanding why Palestinians
are unwilling to accept Israel's offer to give back 94 percent of the Palestinians' pre-1967 borders—the 6 percent would effectively slice the West Bank
and Gaza into a series of isolated islands, not contiguous territories.

Such an arrangement violates U.N. Security Council Resolution 242,
which calls for an end to Israeli occupation of the West Bank and Gaza and
the reestablishment of the pre-1967 borders between Israel and the Palestinian territories. Although Israel has not complied with this resolution, the
United States currently provides the country with more than $3 billion an-
nually in aid, most of which is used for military purposes.

The Japanese and East Asians have a game called Go. Unlike the Western game of chess, where two opponents try to defeat each other by
taking off pieces, the aim of Go is completely different. You win not
by defeating but by immobilizing your opponent by controlling key
points on the matrix. This strategy was used effectively in Vietnam,
where small forces of Viet Cong were able to pin down and virtually
paralyze some half-million American soldiers possessing overwhelming firepower.

In effect, Israel has done the same thing to the Palestinians on the

West Bank and Gaza and in East Jerusalem. Since 1967 it has put into place a matrix, similar to that of the Go board, that has virtually paralyzed the Palestinian population. The matrix is composed of several overlapping layers.

First is the actual physical control of key links and nodes that create the matrix of control—settlements and their extended "master plans"; a massive system of highways and bypass roads (including wide "sanitary" margins); army bases and industrial parks at key locations; closed military areas; "nature preserves;" control of aquifers and other natural resources; internal checkpoints and control of all border crossings; areas A, B, C, D, H-1, H-2, and much more. These define the matrix of constricted Palestinian enclaves and effectively divide them from one another. They also give Israel control of key nodes.

The second layer of the matrix is bureaucratic and legal—all the planning, permits, and policies that entangle the Palestinian population in a tight web of restrictions. These include political zoning of land as agricultural in order to freeze the natural development of towns and villages; a politically motivated system of building permits, enforced by house demolitions, designed to confine the population to its constricted enclaves; land expropriation for (solely Israeli) "public purposes"; restrictions of planting and the wholesale destruction of Palestinian crops; licensing and inspection of Palestinian businesses; closure; restrictions on movement and travel; and more. Although Israel is careful to present its policies as "legal," in fact they are not. The failure to guarantee Palestinians the basic human rights provided by the Geneva Convention and other international covenants—upon which Israel has signed—is patently illegal. The extensive use of the Israeli court system, which invariably rules against Palestinians, as a means of controlling the local population makes a mockery of the link between law and justice. All these confine Palestinians to isolated cantons, control their movement, and maintain Israeli hegemony.

The third layer of the matrix involves the use of violence to maintain control over the matrix—the military occupation itself, including massive imprisonment and torture; the extensive use of collaborators to control the local population; pressures exerted on families to sell their lands; the undemocratic, arbitrary, and violent rule of the Military Commander of the West Bank and the Civil Administration. What Israelis know of this system they justify in terms of "security."

The average Israeli has no concept of this matrix, and so for most Israelis "peace" means simply giving up the minimum territory that would "satisfy" the Palestinians and ending "terrorism." Average Palestinians are highly attuned to the presence of the matrix, since they hit up against it every time they move. But it is crucial to the achievement of a just and viable peace that the nature of the matrix as an integrated system of control be fully comprehended. The Palestinians can wrest 95 percent of the Occupied Territories from Israel, can oversee the dismantling of almost all the settlements, and can establish a recognized state, but unless they effectively dismantle the matrix of control a viable Palestinian state will elude them. It is not control of territory alone that is important; it is identifying and neutralizing the key nodes of the matrix.

The structure and workings of the matrix—and especially its controlling nodes—are subtle and require careful analysis. Some of its control points are obvious. The E-1 area of 13,000 dunums[1] between Jerusalem and Ma'aleh Adumim that was recently annexed effectively cuts the West Bank in two and is antithetical to any notion of a viable Palestinian state. Still, Barak apparently promised the National Religious Party that the order would not be rescinded, and not much protest to that has been voiced. Other nodes are less obvious. The Israeli-conceived road system of Jerusalem and the West Bank, for example, converges in the area of Ma'aleh Adumim. Even if the Palestinians gain control of the surrounding region but leave that one settlement, Israel simply has to declare Ma'aleh Adumim a "closed military area" in order to paralyze movement within any Palestinian entity. Even more subtle nodes of control exist elsewhere. Only a several-meter-wide strip between Ramallah and Bir Zeit, just enough for one Israeli military jeep, is sufficient for controlling movement in that area. A narrow Israeli strip between Bethlehem and Beit Sahour, as well as similar slivers all over the West Bank, contribute to the matrix of control.

Settlements are crucial to preserving the matrix, not so much because of the land they occupy, but because of the control mechanisms that necessarily surround them. Thus, while the settlements take up only about 1.5 percent of the West Bank, their master plans cover more than 6 percent. Add to that the supporting infrastructure of roads (bypass roads, conceived in Oslo as being only minor roads connecting settlements, have become a major mechanism of control), of industrial areas, of military installations and other "security" arrangements, of checkpoints and so on, and it becomes obvious that leaving a tiny yet strategically located settlement in place effectively nullifies the gaining of territory around it.

The only meaningful way to dismantle the matrix is to eliminate it completely. That means removing all the settlements from Palestinian territory, replacing closure and checkpoints by normal (and minimal) border arrangements agreed upon by both sides, and removing Israeli military presence to agreed-upon security points on the external borders, only for a limited period of time. But if this turns out not to be possible and an Israeli presence remains, it is imperative that it not constitute a matrix of control.

Understanding the matrix and its workings is critical for Palestinian success in the negotiations. The very gap between Israel and Palestinian map-making abilities and uses is worrying. As an Israeli who seeks a just and viable peace between our peoples, I hope the Palestinian negotiating team utilizes all the expertise at its disposal to avoid concessions that will in the end leave Palestine little more than a Bantustan.

EDITOR'S NOTE

1. Equivalent to 13 square km.

SUGGESTIONS FOR FURTHER READING

Carey, Roane, Jonathan Shainin, and Tom Segev, eds.
   2002   *The Other Israel: Voices of Refusal and Dissent.* New York: The New Press.
Halper, Jeff
   1990   *Between Redemption and Revival: The Jewish Yishuv of Jerusalem in the Nineteenth Century.* Boulder: Westview Press.
Said, Edward W. and Christopher Hitchens, eds.
   1988   *Blaming the Victims: Spurious Scholarship and the Palestine Question.* London and New York: Verso.

CHAPTER 20

AFTER THE INVASION: NOW WHAT?

CounterPunch, April 12, 2002

JEFF HALPER   As this book is going to press, it is clear that Halper's words have accurately predicted the escalation of the conflict. The Israeli Defense Forces mounted bloody invasions of the West Bank and Gaza beginning in March 2002. Dozens of Palestinian suicide bombers retaliated with brutal attacks upon densely populated civilian and military areas. This article was written after U.S.-made Apache helicopters attacked Palestinian refugee camps in the towns of Jenin and Nablus, in March and April 2002. More than 50 Palestinians were killed in Jenin alone.[1] In July 2002, 15 people—nearly all women and children—were killed in a nighttime F-16 missile attack on a crowded Gaza apartment building.[2]

Two years after the beginning of the Second Intifada, approximately 2,000 Palestinians and 300 Israelis have been killed. There is no immediate end in sight to the Middle East crisis.

The fall of the Jenin refugee camp and the crushing of resistance in the casbah of Nablus, April 9—the twelfth day of the Israelis' final push to defeat the Palestinians—marks the end of yet another stage of the Palestinians' struggle for self-determination. On April 10, when Powell meets the Spanish president of the European Union, it will become clear whether the "political process" that must now emerge will lead to a viable and truly sovereign Palestinian state or to the dependent ministate Israel has had in mind since the start of the Oslo process in 1993.

This is an either-or situation; nothing can bridge the fundamental interests separating the two sides. The Palestinians, who have already agreed on a demilitarized and semisovereign state on only 22 percent of mandatory Palestine, must receive a state that is territorially coherent, economically viable, and in control of its borders and natural resources, with full access to Jerusalem and a meaningful degree of sover-eignty. Israel, which needs a Palestinian ministate to "relieve" it of the 3 million Palestinian residents of the Occupied Territories who pose a threat to the "Jewish character" of the state, will not agree to relin-quish control or to fully dismantle its infrastructure of settlements and bypass roads. It is determined to maintain its occupation in one form or another. Only one of these two options is possible: either a viable Palestinian state or a dependent Bantustan.

With the breaking of Palestinian resistance on April 9, Sharon would appear to have reasons to rejoice. The multipronged strategy of his "na-tional unity" government to force the Palestinians to accept a Bantu-stan seems to have achieved its major goals:

1. A campaign of attrition has steadily eroded the Palestinians' ability to resist the occupation. The demolition of hundreds of Palestinian homes, massive expropriation of fertile farmland, a permanent eco-nomic "closure" that has imprisoned and impoverished the population, curfews and sieges lasting months, induced emigration of thousands of middle-class families, and the widespread use of collaborators to under-mine Palestinian society have all taken their toll.

2. Massive military actions against the fragile Palestinian infrastruc-ture and population centers using the most sophisticated and power-ful of U.S. conventional weapons—F-16s, Apache helicopters equipped with laser-guided missiles, tanks and artillery—culminating in the cur-rent all-out invasion of Palestinian areas—are intended to beat the Pal-estinians into submissiveness. Although seemingly in response to Pal-estinian terrorist attacks and carefully cast as part of America's War against Terrorism, these military actions are proactive, exploiting ter-rorist attacks to achieve political goals of continued domination.

3. Delegitimizing Arafat, whom Sharon has called "our bin Laden," "irrelevant," and head of a "terror-sponsoring entity" (the Palestinian Authority), is essential if Israel is to install (with American help) a more "compliant" Palestinian leader who will agree to a ministate. Just as South Africa had to find African "leaders" that would lend legitimacy to their Bantustans, so must Israel find a Palestinian figure willing to be president of a ministate, thereby agreeing to and legitimizing Israel's control over most of the West Bank, Greater Jerusalem, and perhaps parts of Gaza.

4. Creating irreversible "facts" on the ground. While deflecting at-tention to its role as a peace-seeking "victim" of Palestinian aggres-siveness, Israel never paused for a moment in expanding settlements

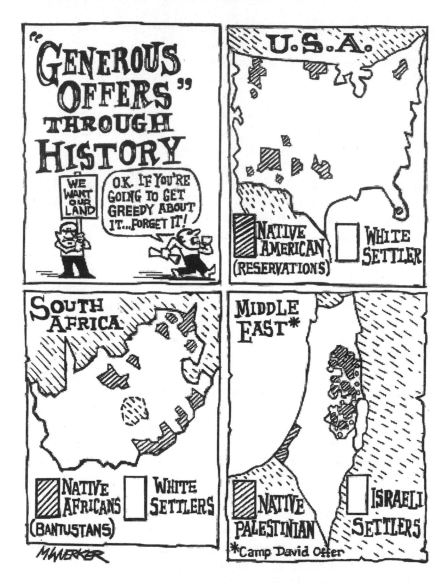

and constructing its own infrastructure that would ensure its control over the Occupied Territories, even if a Palestinian ministate were to come into being. The vaunted Mitchell Commission's recommendations of freezing Israel's settlements have already been rendered irrelevant. Israel has all the land, settlements, and settlers it needs. Once it completes the construction its 480 kilometers of highways and bypass roads linking the settlements while creating massive barriers to Palestinian movement—a $3 billion project entirely funded by the United States—its hold on the Occupied Territories may be irreversible.

5. Reliance on the American Congress to protect Israel from those forces—European, Arab, international (member states of the U.N.)—who would pressure it to dismantle its occupation completely in the interests of a viable Palestinian state. The uncritical support of Congress is Israel's trump card; it provides it with an impenetrable shelter from outside pressures. The U.S. administration may (only may) press for a meaningful political process following Israel's suppression of Palestinian "violence," but Congress will ensure that it be an open-ended process of negotiations lasting years. At best, Israel strives for interim agreements rather than a final status settlement, for these will preserve its de facto control over the Occupied Territories.

Will Israel succeed? Sharon thinks so. He believes that Europe, critical as it might be, has no independent foreign policy apart from the U.S. The Arab countries have some limited clout—the U.S. will press Israel to make concessions so that the Arabs will submit to an attack on Iraq—but those concessions will stop far from a complete end to the occupation. Both Israel and the Arab world know Congress's "red lines" on Israel, and they fall much closer to a Palestinian ministate than to a viable and truly sovereign one.

Still, it is up to us, the international civil society of NGOs, faith-based organizations, political groups, human rights advocates, and just plain world citizens, to monitor the fateful period we are now entering. April 10 begins our test. Having shed the naïveté of Oslo, we must follow the upcoming political process with eyes wide open and critical. Our goal must be to see a viable, sovereign state emerge in all the Occupied Territories (giving the Palestinians the right to negotiate border adjustments and other compromises they see fit). Unlike Oslo, the political process must have a just peace—a viable Palestinian state and a just resolution of the refugee issue, as well as Israel's security concerns—as its explicit goal. And it must have a binding timetable.

In the Oslo process and during the past year and a half of Israeli repression, the international community let the Palestinians down. It did not insist on negotiations that would lead to Palestinian self-determination (after seven years of negotiations, the Palestinians ended up confined to tiny, impoverished islands while Israel doubled its settler population). And it did not provide the protection and support available to the Palestinians through international law, according to which the occupation was illegal, unjust, and immoral in every respect. One cannot criticize an oppressed people's resort to armed resistance—even terrorism—when it finds itself abandoned by the international community that offers its only source of redress. We must not again allow occupation, repression, and violence to overwhelm the progress towards a just peace as we have over the past decade. It is truly time to end the occupation.

EDITOR'S NOTES

1. See Justin Huggler, "Jenin: The Camp That Became a Slaughterhouse," *The Independent*, April 14, 2002.

2. See John Kifner, "Gaza Mourns Bombing Victims," *New York Times*, July 24, 2002.

CHAPTER 21

IF U.S. DUMPS TEST BAN TREATY, CHINA WILL REJOICE

Los Angeles Times, July 29, 2001

HUGH
GUSTERSON

The Comprehensive Test Ban Treaty (CTBT), negoti-ated in the mid-1990s, completely prohibited the test-ing of all nuclear weapons. Bill Clinton signed the treaty in September 1996 and although the Senate refused to ratify it, the United States has abided by its terms.

Under the presidency of George W. Bush, the future U.S. commitment to the terms of this treaty is uncertain. During the 2000 presidential campaign, Bush repeatedly voiced his opposition to CTBT, and in the months following his inauguration he continued to express criticism of the treaty.

In this commentary, Hugh Gusterson argues that if the United States buries the CTBT, China, Russia, India, and Pakistan are likely to use this as a pretext to accelerate the development and testing of their own nuclear stockpiles. Gusterson, who was an antinuclear activist in the 1980s, did field research in the town of Livermore, California, the site of a nuclear weapons development facility.

The prescience of the piece is extraordinary in light of recent events. In 2001, the Bush administration commissioned a study to determine how quickly mothballed Nevada nuclear test sites could be made operational. Then, in March 2002, the *Los Angeles Times* reported that a "Nuclear Pos-ture Review" had been prepared by administration officials, which among other things advocated the development of new, low-yield "bunker-busting bombs" with nuclear warheads.

At approximately the same time, the conflict between India and Pakistan over the Kashmir region led many to speculate that a nuclear war might be within the realm of possibility in South Asia. Although the tension eased somewhat in the summer of 2002, critics argue that a nuclear confrontation still threatens the region.

According to recent news reports, President Bush is looking for ways to bury the Comprehensive Nuclear Test Ban Treaty (CTBT) and has directed the nuclear complex to move into a higher state of readiness for a nuclear test. Chinese President Jiang Zemin and hardliners in his government must be getting ready to break out the champagne, since no country stands to gain as much from a resumption of testing as China — except perhaps Russia, India, and Pakistan. The country with the most to lose is the United States.

When the CTBT was being negotiated in the mid-1990s, some Pentagon officials and scientists within the U.S. nuclear-weapons complex pushed for a treaty that would allow small nuclear tests of a few hundred tons. The Russian and Chinese delegations to the test-ban talks also wanted a treaty that permitted some testing: China wanted to exempt "peaceful" nuclear explosions (for canal and dam construction); the Russians wanted a treaty that allowed tests of a few hundred tons, thinking that this would make it easier to ensure that their aging nuclear weapons still worked and to maintain expertise at their nuclear-weapons laboratories.

After an extensive interagency debate, the U.S. government decided to hold out for a complete test ban. The U.S. concluded that it was much easier to verify such a ban than a treaty that permitted, say, 200-ton but not 300-ton tests. U.S. defense officials also decided that, with 1,030 nuclear tests under its belt (versus 715 by the former Soviet Union and 45 by China), the U.S. had a well-tested and reliable nuclear stockpile that could not be greatly improved. The U.S. feared that further nuclear testing might enable other countries to catch up and hoped that a global ban on nuclear testing would be a daunting obstacle to countries seeking to develop anything but the most primitive and unreliable nuclear weapons. This decision, endorsed by the Joint Chiefs of Staff, was made not by starry-eyed antinuclear idealists but by hard-headed realists in the defense bureaucracy, who saw a test ban as in the vital interest of the U.S. Retired Gen. John Shalikashvili, former head of the Joint Chiefs of Staff, was commissioned by the White House last year to reevaluate that decision. He concluded that "an objective and thorough net assessment shows convincingly that U.S. interests, as well as those of friends and allies, will be served by the treaty's entry into force."

Conservative critics of the test ban treaty say that it prevents us from knowing if our weapons still work. While it is true that detonating a weapon provides the most literal assurance that a weapon works (or did until it was destroyed by the test), such tests were infrequent even in the heyday of nuclear testing, when they were mainly used to validate improvements to the arsenal. However, as part of a bargain within the defense bureaucracy, the Clinton administration replaced nuclear explosive testing with a handsomely funded program for simulated testing and nondestructive surveillance of the stockpile. This Stockpile Stewardship and Maintenance Program currently receives about $5 billion a year. No other country's nuclear-weapons establishment comes close to this.

When the CTBT was negotiated, the Russians and the Chinese grumbled that it put the U.S. at an unfair advantage because its nuclear test experience and top-of-the-line simulation technology would enable it to care for its nuclear stockpile while theirs crumbled.

If the U.S. kills the CTBT, Russia and China will be able to test again. This will make it easier for the Russians, who cannot match the U.S. weapons stewardship program, to ensure that their poorly maintained weapons work and to train a new generation of weapons scientists. It will also make it easier for the Chinese, who currently have only single-warhead missiles, to perfect new missiles with multiple warheads. These will, of course, be a valuable asset against the Bush administration's cherished ballistic missile defense system.

Meanwhile, India, which tried to block the CTBT in the United Nations in 1996, would also welcome a resumption of testing. India's 1998 tests revealed design flaws in its hydrogen bombs, and Indian scientists are eager to test again to find out whether they have succeeded in correcting these flaws. If India tests, Pakistan will follow.

If the U.S. resumes nuclear testing, it will also run the risk of being perceived as what it likes to call a rogue state. When France broke its self-imposed testing moratorium in the early 1990s, it was surprised to find itself the target of protests and boycotts all over the world. President Francois Mitterand hurriedly cut short the series of tests. One of the reasons the five official nuclear powers agreed to surrender nuclear testing in the mid-1990s is that the Non-Proliferation Treaty of 1970 — one of the few arms control treaties the Bush administration has not attacked — committed them to "pursue negotiations in good faith on effective measures relating to cessation of the arms race at an early date."

By 1995 the nonnuclear powers, running out of patience, were threatening not to extend the Non-Proliferation Treaty indefinitely without a test ban. In exchange for their extension of the treaty, the nuclear powers made a commitment to end nuclear testing. It would be no small thing to renege on this commitment.

Finally, a resumption of nuclear testing could well reawaken a sleeping giant at home—the domestic antinuclear movement. The Reagan administration's intensification of the arms race in the 1980s brought hundreds of thousands of people into the streets of New York City for a protest in 1982—the largest street demonstration in American history. On a single day the same year, 1,300 people were arrested for civil disobedience at one of the three nuclear weapons laboratories in the U.S. Does the Bush administration want to return us to those days?

If the Bush administration buries the CTBT, it will enable the Russians, the Chinese, the Indians, and the Pakistanis to narrow the gap between their nuclear stockpiles and ours, it will exacerbate international perceptions that the U.S. government lectures others on their behavior while doing as it pleases, and it threatens to unleash social unrest at home. This is a high price to pay for being a little more certain that the greatest nuclear arsenal on earth is still reliable.

SUGGESTION FOR FURTHER READING

Gusterson, Hugh
    1996   *Nuclear Rites: A Weapons Laboratory at the End of the Cold War.*
           Berkeley and Los Angeles: University of California Press.

PART III

PRELUDE TO SEPTEMBER 11

CHAPTER 22

CUT OFF THE ARMS FLOW AND LET AFGHANS UNITE

Los Angeles Times, February 15, 1989

ASHRAF
GHANI

In January 1989, the Soviet army retreated from Afghanistan following a bitter ten-year war to defend the country's communist government against Afghan resistance groups. Many of them were armed by the U.S.-backed Pakistani intelligence agency. Also supported by the Pakistani and Saudi governments were the mujahedeen or "holy warriors," radical Muslim fighters who had come from dozens of countries to drive out the Soviets. Among them was Osama bin Laden, who would spend much of his time in Afghanistan seeking to spread Wahhabism.[1] In 1986, CIA director William Casey personally went to Afghanistan to review the mujahedeen groups who had been supplied with American-made Stinger antiaircraft missiles and trained by U.S. advisers.[2] This war—essentially a Cold War conflict between the Soviets and U.S. mercenary armies—left the country in shambles, with millions of Afghans in dire need of humanitarian aid.

In this commentary Ashraf Ghani, a native of Afghanistan who studied and taught anthropology in the United States before his appointment as Afghan finance minister in 2002, implored the Bush administration to discontinue arms shipments to the region, which was rapidly slipping into political chaos. He also strongly recommended that the United States and United Nations initiate a process of political and economic reconstruction—advice which was effectively ignored.

Ultimately, Ghani's warnings proved to be prophetic. Warring factions terrorized the country for the next five years. Then, at the end of 1994, a radical Islamic organization emerged—the Taliban. Their triumph was due in part to continued military support from U.S.-backed Pakistani intelligence. By 1996 they gained control of the major Afghan cities and ruled the country for the next five years.

The Soviets have left Afghanistan, making the collapse of the besieged puppet regime in Kabul just a matter of time. President Bush has a unique opportunity to define a positive agenda for the future of that country, yet for now he has chosen to merely affirm that the United States will continue to supply the Afghan resistance with military assistance.

Rather than additional means of destruction, the Afghan people are most in need of constructive measures. The Bush Administration could insist that the Afghan people be given the right to self-determination and take the initiative by channeling future economic assistance only to a government so freely chosen. By doing so, it could help thwart blatant Pakistani and Iranian attempts at determining the future of Afghanistan and at fanning the flames of civil war.

The Afghan people have no desire that the United States micromanage their politics. Rather, they wish that the United States would stop colluding with the Pakistani generals in choosing the cast of political actors and writing the script for the future of their country.

Over the years Washington has been entrusting Pakistani military intelligence with the distribution of more than $2 billion in military and financial aid and with the allocation of Stinger missiles to the Afghan resistance.

As long as the Soviet army was occupying their country, Afghan refugees had no choice but to accept the price exacted by Pakistan. Pakistani generals not only insisted on picking seven individuals acceptable to them to act as leaders of the resistance based in Pakistan; they also considered it their privilege to decide how and when to favor any of these groups. Local leaders inside Afghanistan, in need of arms and money, had no choice but to declare affiliation with one of these parties. The departure of the Soviet forces, however, frees the resistance inside Afghanistan from this dependence. Should a legitimate interim government emerge, one reflecting the aspirations of the Afghan people and committed to the reconstruction of the country, the commanders are likely to support its authority.

But the situation as it stands now finds Islamabad frantically trying to give its seven-party alliance the mantle of legitimacy by convening a consultative council, or *shoora*.

Simultaneously, Tehran is adding a sectarian dimension to the already intricate balancing act by demanding a significant role for eight Shiite parties that are based in Iran. Reports filtering out from inside Afghanistan also tell of Pakistani generals who have been urging resistance commanders to attack the cities, regardless of the bloodbath and the chaos that are sure to ensue. Only the restraint shown by commanders of the resistance has thus far prevented the execution of these plans.

In the absence of an interim government truly representative of the Afghan people, there is no incentive for the peaceful surrender of Kabul and other cities still in the hands of the Soviet-backed regime. Nearly three million civilians, locked in besieged Kabul and already on the brink of starvation, are sure to suffer tremendous losses should the encircling resistance groups attack the capital.

Surely the slaughtering of civilians of Kabul is not what the Bush administration wants its "kinder, gentler America" to contribute to.

There is still time for Bush to act decisively by delaying any shipment of arms and clearly supporting a political solution. The President can call for a referendum under the auspices of the United Nations—a logical choice following the Geneva Accords of last April that made the withdrawal of the Soviet forces possible. The referendum would be held simultaneously in Pakistan, Iran, and the parts of Afghanistan that are free of the Soviet-backed regime.

Such a referendum would ascertain the relative weight of each of the 15 pro-Pakistani or pro-Iranian parties, as well as that of independent groups or leaders. It would allow the emergence of a responsible and accountable leadership that the Afghan people could call their own.

After all, let us not forget that, aside from the nine years of Soviet occupation, Afghanistan can boast of nearly 300 years of recorded history of self-rule. And, as one resistance commander has been quoted by Western correspondents, there can be no compromise on "liberty, dignity and honor." If Washington ceases to view Afghans as mercenaries in its anti-Soviet crusade, it might be able to understand their longings for independence, peace, and prosperity.

EDITOR'S NOTES

1. Wahhabism is a strict and austere form of Islam within the Sunni tradition. It was begun by Abdul Wahab (1703–1792) as a movement to curb the influence of Sufism among the Arab Bedouin, but beginning in the 1970s its spread became an important part of Saudi foreign policy.

2. See Ahmed Rashid, *Taliban: Militant Islam, Oil, and Fundamentalism in Central Asia* (New Haven: Yale University Press, 2000), p. 127.

SUGGESTIONS FOR FURTHER READING

Ghani, Ashraf
    1987   "The Afghan State and Its Adaptation to the Environment of Central and Southwest Asia." In *Soviet-American Relations with Pakistan, Iran, and Afghanistan,* edited by Hafeez Malik, pp. 310–33. New York: St. Martin's Press.
    1993   "Gulab: An Afghan Schoolteacher." In *Struggle and Survival in the Modern Middle East,* edited by Edmund Burke III, pp. 336–351. Berkeley and Los Angeles: University of California Press.
Rashid, Ahmed
    2000   *Taliban: Militant Islam, Oil, and Fundamentalism in Central Asia.* New Haven: Yale University Press.

CHAPTER 23

U.S. CAN STRENGTHEN AFRICAN TIES IN WAKE OF TERRORISM WITH AID, CLEAR POLICIES

Harrisburg Patriot-News, August 24, 1998

JAMES
MERRYMAN

On August 7, 1998, two car bombs exploded outside of U.S. embassies in Kenya and Tanzania. Nearly three hundred people died (nearly all of them Africans) and approximately five thousand were injured in the two blasts. Several months later, investigators concluded that operatives linked to Osama bin Laden had probably orchestrated the attacks.

In this piece, anthropology professor James Merryman (who was in Kenya at the time of the bombings) argues that the "Africans are the major victims, not the cause," of the attacks. He suggests that U.S. officials provide emergency assistance and continue to promote Africa's economic development as a way of preventing further instability.

In spite of Merryman's advice, the Clinton administration responded to the embassy attacks by sending U.S. warplanes on bombing raids in August 1998 to destroy a factory in Sudan and terrorist training camps in Afghanistan. It was alleged that bin Laden operatives were producing chemical weapons at the factory site. The buildings were, in fact, an important pharmaceutical complex that produced medicine for the Sudanese people. Later it was revealed that the United States had no conclusive evidence that chemical weapons had been produced there.[1]

The United States has an obligation to assist Kenya and Tanzania to repair the physical damage to their respective capitals following the insidious terrorist attacks on the U.S. embassies in those East African countries. The U.S. also needs to continue short-term economic and medical aid to the residents impacted by the terrorists' violence.

Following President Clinton's historic visit to Africa, the United States has a unique opportunity to make good on its promises of support. Failure to do so will undermine U.S. credibility and subvert our attempts to work closely with African governments elsewhere to increase U.S. embassy security and ensure the welfare of Americans living abroad in Africa.

The U.S. can have a more secure diplomatic presence and create a productive business climate only by cultivating the best possible relations with each host country in Africa.

Although the Cold War with its ideological struggle for Third World minds has ended, the global community will not allow the U.S. to comfortably slip back into isolation. The mantle of singular superpower means that Africa's problems are not easy for us to avoid, be it the debacle of intervention in Somalia or suffering condemnation by world opinion for refusing early intervention in the genocidal bloodbath of Rwanda.

Economically, Africa holds vast resources including the world's largest reserves of gold and diamonds and a wide array of exotic metals vital to aerospace and information technology. Africa has more than a half-billion potential consumers of American products at a time when our Asian export markets are weakening.

There are major opportunities for U.S. investment in Africa, along with an increasingly well trained workforce. These potentials, however, can only be realized in the context of political and economic stability. U.S. interests are served by a secure Africa.

Both Tanzania and Kenya have maintained uninterrupted civilian rule since gaining their independence and stand in stark contrast to the model of anarchic civilian rule and the jack-booted oppression of military regimes played out across the continent. Although the U.S. has maintained largely positive relations with Kenya and Tanzania, the political ambience of U.S. foreign policy with the two countries has been mixed over the past 35 years.

U.S.-Kenya relations have been strained in recent years in response to America's persistent insistence on Western-style multiparty elections and linking that position to levels in U.S. economic aid to Kenya. There is growing political unrest, coupled with a runaway population growth rate that has not kept pace with economic growth.

Tourism, based on Kenya's abundant wildlife and majestic scenery, has long been the country's main foreign exchange earner. However, Kenya's position as Africa's premier safari center has eroded due to a somewhat deserved reputation for "iffy" political stability and increasing personal security problems due to regionally unchecked highway banditry and growing bands of urban thieves and hooligans.

Unfortunately, the bombings will undoubtedly have an additional negative impact on tourism, at least in the short run.

In all fairness to Kenya and Tanzania, the U.S. must make its message clear. Africans are the major victims, not the cause, of these atrocities. The terrorists, having inflicted their damage, are unlikely to strike again in these two locations.

The U.S. has a major role to play in promoting Africa's development. Supplying appropriate interim aid to sustain stability in Kenya and Tanzania is a vital piece of this development.

As Americans we owe this much to the 200–plus Africans killed and 5,000 injured for merely being there as innocent bystanders on the battlefield of America's global war with terrorism.

EDITOR'S NOTE

1. See Seymour Hersh, "The Missiles of August," *New Yorker*, October 12, 1998, pp. 34–41. See also Tim Weiner and James Risen, "Decision to Strike Factory in Sudan Based on Surmise," *New York Times*, September 21, 1998.

CHAPTER 24

**EGYPTIANS DON'T LIKE
SADDAM, BUT . . .**

Austin American-Statesman, January 14, 1991

ROBERT
FERNEA

On August 2, 1990, Iraq's armed forces invaded and occupied Kuwait, a small country rich in oil reserves. Although the U.S. government had maintained exceptionally friendly relations with Iraqi president Saddam Hussein throughout the 1980s—even after he ordered Iraqi troops to use poison gas against Kurdish people in his own country in 1988—the invasion of Kuwait dramatically changed the relationship.

In the tense months that followed, the U.N. Security Council passed resolutions giving Iraq until January 15, 1991, to withdraw from Kuwait. Otherwise, "all necessary means" would be used to ensure compliance. Hussein ignored the resolutions. In the meantime, the Bush administration assembled a coalition of thirty-three countries for military operations, including Saudi Arabia, which allowed the United States to construct military bases on its soil for the first time. (This outraged many Muslims, since Mecca and Medina—both in Saudi Arabia—are Islam's two holiest sites.) On January 17, the U.S.-led coalition attacked Iraq and the first Gulf War had begun.

The following commentary was written by Robert Fernea shortly after a failed January 9, 1991, meeting in Geneva between U.S. Secretary of State James Baker and Iraqi Foreign Minister Tariq Aziz. Fernea, with more than forty years of experience working in the Middle East, gives insight into why many people in the countries of the region feel enmity toward the United States. In particular, he draws attention to the fact that U.S. support for Israel's invasion and occupation of the Palestinian territories—actions which violate U.N. Security Council resolutions—contrasts sharply with the condemnation of Iraq's invasion and occupation of Kuwait.

The collapse of peace talks in Geneva has left my friends here in Egypt convinced that there will be a war between Iraq and, principally, the

United States. However, their attitudes toward this vary, just as they have varied toward the gulf crisis since its outset.

Especially among younger Egyptians, a feeling of wanting to get on with a change of the status quo outweighs the more cautious outlook typical of the older generation, who fear the unforeseeable consequences of an armed conflict in this region. Among Egyptians of all ages, the more optimistic see a war ending quickly; the less optimistic are not so sure.

Perhaps these feelings are shared by many Americans.

It may be more difficult for Americans to appreciate how successful Saddam Hussein's repeated attempts to link the gulf crisis with the Palestinian-Israeli conflict have been in this part of the world.

Over and over again, editorial writers and Egyptians of all ages and walks of life point out that while the United States has rushed to the aid of Kuwait, an undemocratic state with an elitist government, we have refused to pressure Israel to follow the many United Nations resolutions unfavorable to Israel's perceived interests. The Gaza Strip and the West Bank, plus the more recently acquired Israeli security zone in southern Lebanon, are all seen by Arabs to be illegal occupations, basically no different from the Iraqi occupation of Kuwait.

Iraq is not popular in Egypt. Many thousands of expatriated Egyptians suffered directly from the Iraqi invasion of Kuwait.

Nevertheless, enmities between Egypt and Iraq are between fellow Arabs, who feel they have a common reason for complaint about Western policies toward the long-standing Arab-Israeli conflict. The old Middle Eastern saying, "My brothers against my cousins, but my brothers and cousins against the world," should be borne in mind in this regard.

As the likelihood of war increases by the hour, one also thinks of the story about Pandora's box; what miseries will be released upon the world if the lid is removed from armed conflict by our failure to find a peaceful solution to the present crisis? Will America and the West find itself standing against the whole Arab world? Will Christians and Jews end up pitted against Muslims—everywhere?

So here in Cairo, many hope that President Bush might be flexible about agreeing to discuss all the territorial disputes in the Middle East in return for Saddam's departure from Kuwait.

The Arab-Israeli conflict has gone on nearly a half-century. Thousands of lives have been lost and the normal course of human lives interrupted. Surely the United States could be responsive to the desire for peace in the Middle East without making a hero of Saddam and without going to war.

SUGGESTIONS FOR FURTHER READING

Fernea, Elizabeth Warnock
    1969   *Guests of the Sheik: Ethnography of an Iraqi Village.* New York: Doubleday.
Fernea, Elizabeth Warnock, and Robert Fernea
    1985   *The Arab World: Personal Encounters.* Garden City, N.J.: Anchor Press/Doubleday.
Fernea, Robert
    1970   *Shaykh and Effendi: Changing Patterns of Authority among the El Shabana of Southern Iraq.* Cambridge: Harvard University Press.

CHAPTER 25

GRAVESITES— ENVIRONMENTAL RUIN IN IRAQ

Depleted Uranium Education Project, ed.,
Metal of Dishonor, 1997

BARBARA
NIMRI AZIZ

The first Gulf War ended with a full Iraqi retreat from Kuwait followed by a cease-fire that went into effect on February 28, 1991. In this 1997 commentary, anthropologist and radio journalist Barbara Nimri Aziz focuses on the environmental and human costs of the war. Depleted uranium munitions fired by U.S. tanks and warplanes have irradiated cities and the countryside, and seem to have triggered a chain of diseases including leukemia, cancers, and birth defects. The release of toxic chemicals has also contributed to these problems. And the destruction of Iraq's infrastructure (including sources of fresh water and hospitals) has also made it more difficult for Iraqis to stay healthy.

Strict economic sanctions imposed by the United Nations in August 1990 soon took a devastating toll on the country. More than one million Iraqis died as the result of the sanctions, which blocked the importation of vital medicines such as chemotherapy drugs and agricultural inputs.

As this book goes to press, Iraq is gripped with the devastation of a second Gulf War, which has left thousands of civilians dead and many others in dire need of humanitarian aid. In addition, U.S. and British forces used depleted uranium shells in March and April 2003, according to reports.[1]

The chain of death created by the [1991] Gulf War is a scary thing. I'm not talking about black skies over the blazing oil wells of Kuwait, or charred remains of soldiers on the sand, or the incinerated families who had sought protection in a bomb shelter. Those are familiar images of death, recognizable, and however painful, they are finite. With the end of hostilities, they disappear.

The really scary part comes later—now—when we find that things which looked alive are really dead or doomed.

I refer to a chain of deadly pollution, the kind that creeps up on us, first with vague complaints, then with the persistence of strange illnesses, then with more testimonials of similar symptoms. We slowly recognize that disparate efforts which first appear unrelated are, in fact, connected.

We have the sickening sense of something spreading, without limits, of something embedded so deep within the system that it's unreachable. Our inquiries are met with denials. So, to begin, all we seek to do is confront it. We just want to stand on the gravesite as if it were a known, finite place.

This is our feeling, I think, as we hear more and more documentation regarding Gulf War syndrome and its link to the use, by the Pentagon, of depleted uranium weaponry during the 1991 war.

Evidence is mounting, and those soldiers who find themselves stricken are growing in number, networking and uniting in a swelling movement of people who refuse to accept government disclaimers that these soldiers might be the victims of some new dangerous materials the Pentagon used. A public movement to ban depleted uranium is growing and attracting more media attention in the U.S.

Many Iraqis were killed outright by the weapons that blew apart their vehicles and their bunkers. Those who survived the onslaught and fled must have ingested and carried with them the fumes and toxic dust created by the bombardments. There is also the uranium waste—three hundred tons of it, according to reports—left on the battlefield.

Today the entire population of Iraq is besieged by diseases. We know that waterborne parasites and bacteria and malnutrition in Iraq are responsible for many recognizable diseases, and for wasting and death. But what about reports of a sharp rise in spontaneous abortions, cancers, and other "new diseases"? The Iraqi Ministry of Health is systematically documenting some of these health problems. Dr. Siegwart Guenther of the Austrian Yellow Cross International is also studying evidence of possible Gulf War syndrome inside Iraq and the high incidence across the country of abnormal births.[2]

Iraqi Scientists Most Concerned about Radiation

Those most concerned about radiation and other kinds of pollution are Iraqis. Their entire population is probably afflicted. And essential empirical evidence of strange illnesses in the Iraqi population is being gathered by their own scientists. Iraq still has a highly trained community of biologists, environmentalists, energy specialists, cancer researchers, etc., most of whom earned advanced degrees in the U.S. or Great Britain. With access to the entire country, they are capable of conducting the needed research.

Until the embargo and war, these scholars were in the international scientific community; they published widely and they took part in international scientific gatherings.

Because of the embargo, however, their careful on-site work and their disturbing findings are not as widely known as they should be, partly because these men and women are now denied professional contact with their peers overseas and are therefore unable to offer comparative statistics and work together with concerned scientists worldwide to find solutions and recommend treatments.

This is happening when health and environmental conditions inside Iraq are deteriorating, and bad conditions generated by the war are spreading, creating a catastrophe of accelerating proportions and unknown ramifications.

The Pentagon, which has been trying so hard to suppress information about the extent, occurrence, and possible source of Gulf War syndrome among its own personnel, would doubtless want to keep any Iraqi source silent on this matter as well. Even a scientist researching the hazardous effects of the war finds herself or himself effectively blocked from reporting important relevant findings.

Dr. Huda Ammash is one of those Iraqi scientists who should be speaking to her international colleagues. She is presently an environmental biologist and professor at Baghdad University, having undertaken graduate studies in the U.S. where she obtained her Ph.D. from the University of Missouri.

Working with governmental departments of agriculture, health, and environment, Ammash is now undertaking research in Iraq. When I met her in 1995, she kindly shared her report with me. She is most concerned with the enormous energy emission and light energy from the massive bombing in the forty days of war in 1991 and the resulting ionization.[3]

"We know that ionization causes radiation," she said. "It is now diffused throughout the entire airspace of Iraq and has likely spread to our neighbors as well, possibly as far north as the southern border of Russia."

Dr. Ammash calculates that "the prolonged effect of this ionization is, over a period of more than ten years, equal to one hundred Chernobyls."

Dr. Ammash and others note that "an outbreak of meningitis in children concentrated in one Baghdad locality is highly unusual and may be a manifestation of high ionization levels. It has never been seen in Iraq before and, under the circumstances of the embargo, Iraq can provide no immunization against it." She notes the alarm among doctors she interviewed who report that "99 percent of the victims of this disease are children." Ammash accumulated reports that show cancer increasing at rapid and abnormal rates; child leukemia is especially rampant, with some areas of south Iraq showing a fourfold rise in these few years. Breast cancer in young women (age thirty and under) is also many times higher than in 1990 in certain parts of Iraq.

In addition, the Iraqi environment is subject to a mass of other chemical and microbial pollutants released into the atmosphere because of indirect results of the war. Ammash points out, for example, how "damage to bombed and crippled industrial plants resulted in the leakage of millions of liters of chemical pollutants—black oil, fuel oil, liquid sulfur, concentrated sulfuric acid, ammonia, and insecticides—into the atmosphere. Fumes created by the bombardment of more than 380 oil wells produced toxic gases and acid rain."

Bombardment of chemical factories damaged their gas purification units and thus created tremendous air pollution as well. If these filters can't function, dangerous gases are allowed to escape from cement factories. Up to the present, the imposition of sanctions prevents the repair of these industrial filters. Untreated heavy waters from industrial centers are the media for growth of microbes, mainly typhoid, malta fever, and other pathogenic bacteria.

Ammash also reports fourteen crop diseases—including covered smut, sazamia moth, yellow crust, spickulated drought disease, gladosporium disease, and epical bent—which were never before recorded in Iraq's history. These are now infecting date trees and citrus trees.

When I arrived back in Baghdad, I followed up my research in Mosul with discussions with agriculture officials and with visits to small, local farms engaged in mixed agriculture. I spoke with experts at the Food and Agriculture Organization (FAO), a U.N. agency in Baghdad since before the [1991] Gulf War. Their mandate is to assist any nation to increase its food production, and they are trying to help Iraq in this area. Now, more than ever, with food unobtainable from abroad, Iraq is obliged to reverse its rather neglected agricultural policy with active food production schemes. Since the imposition of the embargo, Iraq has been trying to do so, bringing more land under grain production and improving irrigation.

Iraq Could Be Self-Sufficient

FAO officials were unequivocal about prospects. "Iraq could be self-sufficient in grain," said director Amir Khalil. "It has the water; it has the land; it has the expertise." Yet, despite efforts and the growing food crisis, production was declining. Why?

For agriculture experts and farmers alike, the explanation is simple: "No herbicides, no pesticides, no fertilizer, no improved seed." The animal husbandry and poultry situation is as severe as the grain crisis. Without vaccines and other medicines, all of which Iraq cannot furnish itself, animals—like people and plants—cannot survive.

According to a 1995 FAO report, dairy herds had gone down 40 percent since 1990. Before the war, dairy cows numbered just over 1.5 million; by 1995, their number fell to only 1 million. Water buffaloes suffered an even worse fate, and goat herds have declined from 1.3 million to fewer than a quarter of a million. Iraq's poultry system with 106 million hatching hens was virtually wiped out overnight by the bombing when electrically run poultry sheds across the country—8,400 units—shut down. Without vaccines and specialized, treated food, moreover, hens cannot survive long.

Why this devastation? Largely because agricultural imports, all essential in food production in any modern state today, are unavailable.

If we are to believe FAO's own reports, it seems that another weapon in this cowardly secret war is the denial of agricultural essentials—a kind of sabotage—to ensure Iraq cannot become food self-sufficient.

It is ominous that it was also during my field research in a farming community that I found the first shocking evidence of a little discussed plague in the human population.

In the course of extended conversations with local farmers after my inspection of the fields, we spoke about social life. One farmer remarked that marriages were fewer now. "Why?" I asked. The answer was straightforward. "Young people fear the birth of malformed fetuses and stillbirths." How was this?

"We look around our village," they said. "Everyone knows couples in the village who had deformed babies in the last four years."

With the help of these farmers and the local schoolteacher, I took an ad hoc survey. They had 160 houses here, and among these they counted 20 households where malformed babies had been born. My hosts noted that most of the fathers of these stillborn and abnormal births in their village are men who served in the army during the [1991] Gulf War. They noted many spontaneous abortions, but we did not include these. I had heard in Baghdad that more spontaneous abortions are reported across the country now than were before 1990.

The Iraqi Ministry of Health could not provide me with any statistics about this development at that time. But my inquiries at five hospitals (in Mosul, Baghdad, and Kerbala) revealed that the number of abnormal births recorded in hospitals had dramatically increased. Recalling their personal experience, all doctors with whom I spoke estimated they see ten times more such births today than five years ago. One doctor in Mosul said she saw two cases a year before 1991; she now sees four or five cases a month. The symptoms?

"Babies born without ears, without eyes, without limbs or with foreshortened limbs, without formed genitalia, with cleft palate, clubfoot, enlarged heads." One doctor reported her first knowledge of a case of congenital leukemia.

"How Can I Have Any Plans?"

A professor of poultry science had accompanied us to the fields in Mosul. From seeing how he walked and stood, I already suspected he himself was unwell. Nevertheless, I inquired about his plans for further research. I still remember the bewildered look on his face when I asked him this.

"Plans? Madam," he said softly, "I am trying to feed my family; I am looking for medicine for my ill father. How can I have plans?"

I asked Dr. Ammash the same question. "It is difficult for anyone to have a plan," she quietly explained. "You have a plan when you have a settled situation—known circumstances. We don't have that anywhere in Iraq. My immediate plan is to provide tomorrow's means for life for my children, to help my students into another successful day. After that, I don't know."

EDITOR'S NOTE

1. See Neil Mackay, "U.S. Forces' Use of Depleted Uranium Weapons Is 'Illegal,'" *Sunday Herald* (Scotland).

2. For information on depleted uranium and its effects, see Siegwart Horst-Guenther, "How DU Shell Residues Poison Iraq, Kuwait, and Saudi Arabia," in Depleted Uranium Education Project, ed., *Metal of Dishonor*, 2d ed. (New York: International Action Center, 1997). See also Akira Tashiro, *Discounted Casualties: The Human Cost of Depleted Uranium* (Hiroshima: Chugoku Shimbun Press, 2001).

See also *La Guerre Radioactive Secrete* [*Invisible War: Depleted Uranium and the Politics of Radiation*], February 2000; Martin Meissonier, director; Paul Moreira, executive producer. A film produced by Canal+ and available at <www.canalplus.fr/emissions/90mn/contact.asp>. U.S. distributor: Damacio López, 1322 Lopezville, Socorro, NM 84801; tel.: 505-838-0263; e-mail: idust@sdc.org.

3. See Huda Ammash, "Toxic Pollution, the Gulf War, and Sanctions," in Anthony Arnove, ed., *Iraq under Siege* (Boston: South End Press, 2000), pp. 205–215, and Barbara Nimri Aziz, "Targets, Not Victims," in Anthony Arnove, ed., *Iraq under Siege* (Boston: South End Press, 2000), pp. 161–170.

CHAPTER 26

U.N. SHOULD ACT TO PROTECT MUSLIM WOMEN

Newsday, April 13, 1998

FADWA
EL GUINDI

The civil war that has gripped Algeria for more than a decade has claimed more than a hundred thousand lives, mostly civilians. Since its independence from France in 1962, the country has been ruled by a single party, the National Liberation Front (FLN). By the mid-1980s an opposition group, the Islamic Salvation Front (FIS), had appealed to Algerians unhappy with the incompetence and religious repression imposed under FLN rule. By the early 1990s, the FIS had gathered a wide base of popular support.

The FIS's popularity pressured the country's leadership to reform the political process, and in 1993 Algeria's first democratic multiparty elections were held. When it was apparent that the FIS would win parliamentary elections, military and secular elites ousted the president, annulled the elections, banned the FIS, and declared a state of emergency. Then the country descended into a spiral of violence from which it has yet to emerge.

Although the Algerian government claimed that operatives from the FIS and the radical Armed Islamic Group (GIA) were responsible for terrorist attacks, massacres, and atrocities, it consistently refused to allow U.N. observers entry into the country to investigate these claims until mid-1998. Human rights groups report that Algerian security forces are responsible for much, if not most, of the violence.

In the following article Fadwa El Guindi appeals for the United Nations and United States to act quickly to improve the Algerian situation. She focuses on the atrocities committed against Muslim women.

Lamentably, the situation has not improved appreciably since the time this commentary appeared. According to a recent Amnesty International report, "A human rights crisis continues to blight Algeria. The number of people killed each month by the security forces, state-armed militias and armed groups in the context of the armed conflict remains shockingly high. Reports of torture and ill-treatment by the security forces—including of women and children as young as 15—continue to be . . . widespread, even though the climate of fear in the country means that reported cases may represent only the tip of the iceberg."[1]

By 1993, the Islamic Salvation Front had galvanized a wide and popular Algerian base of support and was expected to win elections. The Arab street, a popular and growing force of public opinion and nonmilitant resistance, had expressed desire for political change.

Had the will of the people been allowed to take its course democratically, the world would have seen a different political landscape in Algeria.

Instead, more than 60,000 people have reportedly died in the civil war between the government and the Islamic opposition since the voided 1993 election. In more recent developments, many innocent Algerian civilians in villages—mostly women and children—have been killed in brutal attacks blamed on Islamic groups. There is a clear need for human rights groups and the United Nations to take active roles in seeking to halt such atrocities. The United States has a responsibility to ease regional tensions that contribute strongly to the local instabilities by, for example, putting pressure on Israel to comply with peace agreements and U.N. resolutions. It must also end sanctions against Iraq, which have caused human suffering and bitterness in the region.

For members of Islamic groups to engage in senseless brutalities contradicts patterns of resistance consistent throughout the Arab world among similar organizations. It is also contrary to common sense. After all, the victims in Algeria's case are the attackers' own mothers, sisters, wives, and daughters. Why should Islamic groups challenging local undemocratic regimes and simultaneously destabilizing postcolonial forces unleash their anger on their own families? In the past six years, more than 3,700 women were killed in Algerian attacks, including massacres of villagers. Many women, kidnapped and raped, have subsequently been found dead with their throats cut. These brutalities confused observers and analysts of Arab politics.

Rape is an ultimate violation designed to break Muslims by dishonoring their families and humiliating Muslim men. This was the case in the Serbian attacks on Bosnians. But these rapists were considered "enemies from outside the Islamic fold." It makes no sense for groups whose identity de guerre is Islamic to rape their own Muslim women, whatever the nature of the conflict. And, in the case of Algeria, Muslims around the world dissociated themselves from these un-Islamic brutalities and violations of sanctity.

The questions remain, however: Who is doing this? And why? Recent reports by the U.S. State Department, Amnesty International, and Human Rights Watch implicated Algerian security forces in systematic torture, arbitrary arrests, and summary executions.

The Algerian government has consistently refused to allow an international committee of inquiry access to the country to investigate human rights abuses by both sides in the civil war. The reason is likely that such an investigation will prove embarrassing to the Algerian government.

The gravity of the violations can be explained in cultural terms. In traditional Arab culture, the family is the center around which the sociomoral universe exists. Women are the center of the family's sacred identity and the guardians of the Arab family's honor and reputation. Motherhood is considered sacred. Nationhood is expressed in "motherland" terms. The Arabic words for women, household, and sacred sanctity are close derivatives of the same root.

To undermine or attack the Muslim woman destabilizes the core of the sociomoral system. The Arab-Islamic judicial system long recognized rape as a serious crime that received capital punishment—at a time when rape in America was considered sex, not crime. That is precisely why those at war with Muslims and trying to break them choose the path of raping and killing Muslim women. A cultural strength, Islam's placing women at the heart of sacredness is turned into a grave human rights violation in times of conflict and crisis. These are not random acts. They are systematic, racist, and sexist, and they violate international human rights.

Whether these brutalities are by insiders or outsiders, the world organizations entrusted with protecting human rights and lives must intervene. Just as in Bosnia, the world cannot remain a spectator. The raping of Muslim women must be entered as a crime tried in international tribunals. Western feminist groups, which on short notice become activated over issues of whether Muslim women have the right to drive cars, unveil, or join the workforce, must now demonstrate compassion for the more serious issue of brutal raping and butchering of Muslim women.

This is particularly significant since the strong destabilizing factor underlying such crises comes from a poorly conceived U.S. foreign policy that consistently underestimates the role of the Arab street and is too static to adjust flexibly to the emergent political (Islamic) landscape in the region.

EDITOR'S NOTE

1. See Amnesty International Document MDE 28/009/2002 (April 19, 2002). Online version at <http://web.amnesty.org/ai.nsf/Index/MDE280092002? OpenDocument&of=COUNTRIES/ALGERIA>.

SUGGESTION FOR FURTHER READING

El Guindi, Fadwa
    1999   *Veil: Modesty, Privacy, and Resistance.* Oxford and New York: Berg
        Publishers.

CHAPTER 27   WOMEN UNDER THE TALIBAN

Dateline (Australia) March 14, 2001

ZIEBA
SHORISH-
SHAMLEY,
interviewed by
Jana Wendt

In March 2001 the Taliban provoked widespread outrage when they sent fighter planes to destroy two colossal statues of Buddha in Afghanistan's Bamiyan province, approximately one hundred miles northwest of Kabul. One of the statues, thought to have been constructed in the seventh century A.D. (during Central Asia's pre-Islamic era), measured more than fifty meters high.

In the following interview, Zieba Shorish-Shamley, anthropologist and executive director of the Washington, D.C.–based organization Women's Alliance for Peace and Human Rights in Afghanistan, notes that the destruction of the statues was a loss to humanity, but so too are the Taliban's human rights violations against women and ethnic minorities. Women in particular have become "ghosts" in their own country.

In the late 1990s, Shorish-Shamley persuaded the Feminist Majority to organize a petition drive to garner support for Afghan women living under the Taliban regime. Her efforts eventually helped to pressure the Clinton administration to take a tougher stance against the Taliban, who were once unconditionally accepted by most U.S. policy makers.

The destruction of two stone Buddhas in Afghanistan this week has cast new light on the Taliban regime which now claims control of 90 percent of the country. While thousands of people have been killed in more than 20 years of war in Afghanistan, it seems that no single act has so outraged the world community. Even fellow Muslims have condemned the destruction of the Bamiyan Buddhas as not sanctioned by the Koran. Ironically, it has taken this very public and defiant act of cultural vandalism to draw new attention to the plight of the Afghans themselves.

JANA WENDT: Zieba Shorish-Shamley, there has been an international outcry over the Taliban's destruction of the Bamiyan statues. As someone who's been working for women living under the Taliban, what did you make of all this attention?

ZIEBA SHORISH-SHAMLEY: I think the attention is great in the sense that as an anthropologist, obviously I care a great deal for our national heritage and historical artifacts.

However, I think the world and the international community should have had an outcry such as this when a lot of ethnic people were massacred by the Taliban about two or three times, as well as thousands of Afghan women that have died, and are dying under the Taliban rule because they're not allowed to work, they're not allowed to have equal access to the health care system, and they're virtual prisoners in their own society under the Taliban rule.

I think the genocide and the culture of genocide and human rights violations and war crimes, crimes against humanity—all of this goes together, and the word "outcry" should include all of those atrocities as well.

JW: You've been working for women's rights for a long time. Why do you think that these statues have suddenly captured the imagination and harnessed the outrage of the world?

ZSS: The outcry is because these Buddhas, or the statues, did not belong just to the Afghan people. They belonged to humanity. Afghanistan has been the crossroad of Asia, and during the time of the Silk Route many cultures went through there, so destroying them and denying humanity and future generations such beautiful, irreplaceable works of art is a crime against mankind, humankind.

JW: I wonder if you can give me a brief picture of the life of a woman today under the Taliban.

ZSS: A woman, an Afghan woman, today under the Taliban rule is voiceless, an invisible nonbeing, and does not have the most basic rights that are necessary for human existence. The Afghan women have become ghosts, shadows, and cannot participate in the public sphere of their society. And although they are the majority of the Afghan population, they have no voice.

So they are prisoners, they are virtual prisoners, and most of them are dying—hundreds of times we have appealed to the world, and it seems that the world doesn't hear their cries and their voices. So Afghan women's condition is the most horrible that you can think of or can imagine. That is the [plight of the] Afghan woman.

JW: Is there any way that the world attention to the Bamiyan statues may help you to press the point of women's human rights inside Afghanistan?

ZSS: . . . My organization, Women's Alliance for Peace and Human Rights in Afghanistan, has called for a tribunal. We want an international tribunal to be formed by the U.N. and to bring the Taliban and other criminals that commit war crimes, crimes against humanity, genocide—cultural genocide—to justice.

However, the issue has to be pushed, and that is why we are appealing to all the people of the world to write to their governments, to urge their governments to put pressure on the U.N. to form this tribunal, an international tribunal, and to find a solution and end the misery of Afghan people. They have been going through this for 23 years of war, and instead of it getting better, it is getting worse and worse, and now under the Taliban rule . . . it is the darkest moment in the Afghan people's life and history.

JW: Zieba Shorish-Shamley, I appreciate your time this evening.

ZSS: Thank you so much for giving me the opportunity to bring the voices of my suffering people to the people of Australia.

CHAPTER 28

FOLLOW THE OIL TRAIL— MESS IN AFGHANISTAN PARTLY OUR GOVERNMENT'S FAULT

Pacific News Service, August 24, 1998
www.pacificnews.org

WILLIAM O.
BEEMAN

In this commentary, anthropologist and Pacific News Service contributor William O. Beeman eloquently traces the complex connections between the 1998 terrorist bombings of U.S. embassies in Kenya and Tanzania (see Chapter 20), the rise of the Taliban regime in Afghanistan (see Chapters 19 and 24), Osama bin Laden, and the economics of oil. He analyzes how pipeline politics in the Caspian Sea—one of the world's richest oil regions—is driving U.S. foreign policy in Central Asia. Beeman's piece is both a critique of American Realpolitik and an appeal for U.S. policy makers to seriously consider the roles played by religion and ideology in the world of politics.

We must face the fact that if President Clinton is right about who bombed our embassies in Tanzania and Kenya, the action came in part as the result of the muddled actions of our own government.

The story is worthy of a Tom Clancy novel.

It is no secret, especially in the region, that the United States, Pakistan, and Saudi Arabia have been supporting the fundamentalist Taliban in their war for control of Afghanistan for some time. The U.S. has never openly acknowledged this connection, but it has been confirmed by both intelligence sources and charitable institutions in Pakistan.

Given U.S. rhetoric regarding the Middle East, the Taliban would seem to be strange partners. They are a brutal fundamentalist group that has conducted a cultural scorched-earth policy for Afghanistan. They have committed atrocities against their enemies and their own citizens—according to extensive documentation. So why would the United States support them?

Middle Easterners understand. As the ancient saying goes, "The enemy of my enemy is my friend." In Afghanistan the dominant ethnic

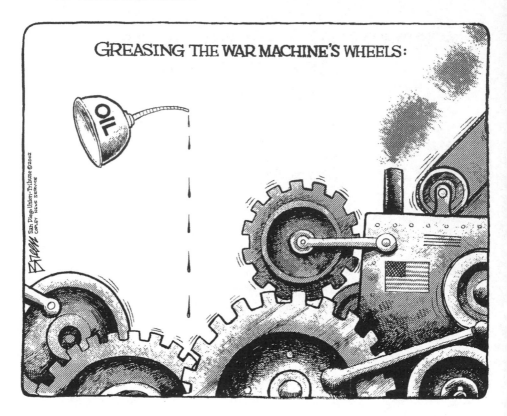

groups are the Pushtuns, who spill over the border into Pakistan, and the Tajiks, whose language is a form of Persian. The Pushtun Taliban have virtually eliminated their Tajik opposition, which had been heavily supported by Iran. And so, according to this line of reasoning, the United States—as an enemy of Iran—must be a friend of the Taliban.

But this does not fully explain why the United States would support such a group—or for that matter why Pakistan, itself a fundamentalist Islamic state, would risk the wrath of Tehran's religious government. The answer to this part of the question has nothing to do with religion or ethnicity—but only with the economics of oil.

To the north of Afghanistan is one of the world's wealthiest oil fields, on the eastern shore of the Caspian Sea in republics formed since the breakup of the Soviet Union. Here, U.S. oil companies are involved in a boom larger than any in the last 40 years in this region. Untold wealth is at stake—but it depends on getting the oil out of the landlocked region through a warm-water port.

The simplest and cheapest route is through Iran. This route is favored by all oil companies, because it involves building a short pipeline and then transshipping the oil through the existing Iranian network.

The U.S. government has such antipathy to Iran that it is willing to do anything to prevent this. An alternate route would go through Afghanistan and Pakistan—but this would require securing the agreement of the powers-that-be in Afghanistan.

From the U.S. standpoint, the way to deny Iran everything is for the anti-Iranian Taliban to win in Afghanistan and agree to the pipeline through their territory. The Pakistanis would also benefit from this arrangement—which is why they are willing to defy the Iranians.

Enter Osama bin Laden, a sworn enemy of the United States living in Afghanistan. His forces could see that the Taliban would eventually end up in the American camp. Thus his bombing of U.S. embassies in East Africa (there are none in Afghanistan) was accompanied by a message calling for Americans to get out of "Islamic countries." By this he meant specifically Afghanistan.

The U.S. response was to bomb bin Laden's outposts while carefully noting that his forces were "not supported by any state." This statement is an attempt to rescue the Taliban relationship, while sending Taliban leaders the message that they must ditch bin Laden. American missiles also took out a factory in the Sudan, but that was only a smokescreen.

Now matters are really in a mess. Iran has actually issued a statement supporting the U.S. actions. The Taliban are angry, and American citizens across the globe are now the targets of the most fanatical of Islamic militants. The U.S. may even lose control of the pipeline.

Every time the United States attempts one of these slick back-door deals, U.S. citizens get burned. Our foreign policy community never seems to learn that religion and ideology are as strong a force in this region as money or guns.

We underestimate these factors every time, and this gets us in trouble every time.

PART IV

ANTHROPOLOGICAL INTERPRETATIONS OF SEPTEMBER 11

CHAPTER 29

OUR LEGACY OF WAR

Chronicle of Higher Education,
September 28, 2001

CATHERINE   In the 1990s Catherine Lutz conducted anthropologi-
LUTZ   cal research in Fayetteville, North Carolina, near Fort
                   Bragg, one of the largest military bases in the United
States. Her work has focused on the effects of militarism at home, and in
the book *Homefront* she notes that the United States has been in a permanent state of war for most of the last century—although rarely has this been
visible to most Americans since World War II.

Now, as she argues in this response to the attacks of September 11, the
war has finally come home.

Although I was deeply saddened and angered by the horrific events
of September 11, I was not shocked, because in the decade I have spent
studying American society and its military, I have learned that we have
already been in a permanent state of war since the late 1930s. Mainly
outsourced to the global south since 1945, this war has now come home
to roost.

While this long war has sometimes drawn on elevated ideals like
antifascism, more often it has been carried on in the name of stability
for any regime that would don an anticommunist mantle and allow
American business access, hiding a rotten core of systematic terrorism
against its own people, often with our weapons and training. Those terrorists were labeled realists, and the long reign of nuclear terror by the
Soviet Union and the United States—who together took aim at millions
of people in skyscrapers and hovels—was called defense, or even peace.
Its architects were called men of honor.

This new war that President Bush has declared can draw on the
decades-long public-relations campaigns intended to convince us that

THE "BAD GUYS WHO ONCE WERE **OUR** BAD GUYS" HALL OF FAME GETS A NEW INDUCTEE...

JVALIER   PINOCHET   SUHARTO   NORIEGA   BIN LADE

REX BABIN THE SACRAMENTO BEE

the larger the American arsenal, the safer we are, and on the idea that war elevates moral character in its supporters.

But my research has shown me that many American soldiers and veterans are not nearly so sure. Some have been among war's most ardent critics, and some remain soul-wounded and attached to each other in fellowships of affliction. Their experiences will never match the rhetoric and safety of the elites now planning a conflagration.

As Bush talks about hunting the terrorists from their holes, and begins to elide terrorists and whole populations, I am reminded of the racial hatred that has preceded, stoked, and been inflamed by nearly every one of the twentieth century's wars. But over the past several days, hope has overtaken my pessimism as I've talked with students. So far, they have refused the simplicities and the vengefulness of the voices on television, whose framing devices overwhelmingly ask when and where the United States will strike, not how that could possibly accomplish a safe future.

Instead, students are questioning and seeking meaning in these events. The instructor of one class I attended as a guest speaker described how angry she was at the perpetrators and asked people to say if they were, too. Many hands went up along with mine, but when asked why, their reasons were many and nuanced. One was angry that the New York and Washington victims had not been protected (despite a

$300 billion military budget), another that human beings continue to stoop to violence, another that her world had lost its security. While the administration has reduced all this into a single feeling, with one swift sword attached, those students' thoughtful, passionate varieties of anger are openings to reflection, learning, and a response more ethical than indiscriminate force.

The parallel of this day of infamy is not Pearl Harbor—in 1941, a colonial outpost in a once-sovereign Hawaiian nation. It is 1947, when a new kind of war was also declared, via executive orders and the National Security Act—a war, it was said, in which the enemy would no longer fight in the open, a war requiring the sacrifice of some freedom and principle. It gave birth to McCarthyism, to slaughters in places like Vietnam and Guatemala; and it took the fruits of our labor and our children.

The perpetrators of this latest terror should be identified in an open process and imprisoned. If one is Osama bin Laden, send the international police for him, and pick up Henry Kissinger and Augusto Pinochet on the way home. The weeping, surviving families of New York, Washington, Chile, Haiti, South Africa, the Somme, Ukraine, Cambodia, and Vietnam call us to bring their murderers to account, not to send legions more to join them in their grief.

SUGGESTIONS FOR FURTHER READING

Lutz, Catherine
    1984   *Micronesia as a Strategic Colony: The Impact of U.S. Policy on Micronesian Health and Culture.* Cambridge: Cultural Survival.
    2001   *Homefront: A Military City and the American Twentieth Century.* Boston: Beacon Press.

CHAPTER 30

LOCAL HORROR/
GLOBAL RESPONSE

Chronicle of Higher Education: Colloquy,
September 2001
www.chronicle.com

DAVID
HARVEY,
TALAL ASAD,
CINDI KATZ,
NEIL SMITH,
AND IDA
SUSSER

This article, written days after the September 11 attacks, reflects the horror and outrage felt by many Americans in the aftermath of the tragic events of that day. But the authors—most of whom are affiliated with the anthropology program at City University of New York—are also critical of the "erroneous policies and practices" of the United States around the globe.

This is a difficult time for those of us who are deeply critical of U.S. military, financial, and commercial policies and practices around the globe. There is, we categorically insist, nothing, absolutely nothing, in those policies and practices that would even remotely justify the insane horror unleashed in the United States on September 11. We share the sense of shock, outrage, sadness, and anger felt in New York and Washington, around the country, and across the globe.

By the same token, there is nothing in these horrendous events to justify the continuation, let alone the intensification, of erroneous policies and practices. The catalog of flaws that have for so long distressed us still stands. The callous disregard shown by U.S. financial and commercial interests for global poverty and suffering; the militarism that backs authoritarian regimes wherever convenient to U.S. interests; the broad indifference (widespread throughout the U.S.) to the death and suffering inflicted on repressed, marginalized, or minority populations around the globe; the insensitivity of U.S.-led globalization practices to local cultures, interests, and traditions; the failure to act to prevent genocidal practices (in Rwanda, for example); the disregard for environmental degradation and resource depletion; irresponsibly self-interested behavior with respect to a wide range of international issues such as missile defenses, global warming, AIDS, and labor rights; the use of international institutions such as the IMF and the World Bank for partisan U.S. political purposes; and the shallow and often hypocritical stances with respect to human rights—none of these can be justified by last week's events.

We wish to reaffirm our critical postures with respect to all such issues no matter how difficult it may be to articulate them freely in these times.

The sheer horror and insanity of what happened last week is a crushing burden on rational thought and reasoned action. Signs of distinctively American brands of zealotry and fanaticism, of ethnic scapegoating, of authoritarianism to the detriment of basic freedoms and civil liberties, abound. Such trends must be resisted. It is also our fervent hope that the righteous wrath and indignation felt around the country (understandable sentiments which we share) might mature into serious reflection on how to make the world a decent habitation for all, how to make real democracy work everywhere, how to make freedom mean something more than freedom of the market, and how to create a more egalitarian and caring world characterized by justice, tolerance, diversity, and love.

This, far more than any amount of saber rattling and military action, is, surely, a far more constructive way to secure a safer and juster world for our children.

SUGGESTIONS FOR FURTHER READING

Asad, Talal, ed.
    1973   *Anthropology and the Colonial Encounter.* London: Tavistock.
Harvey, David
    2000   *Spaces of Hope.* Berkeley and Los Angeles: University of California
           Press.
    2001   *Spaces of Capital: Towards a Critical Geography.* London: Routledge.
Owen, Roger, and Talal Asad, eds.
    1983   *The Middle East.* New York: Monthly Review Press.

CHAPTER 31

A WAR OUR GREAT-
GRANDCHILDREN
WILL BE FIGHTING—
UNDERSTANDING
OSAMA BIN LADEN

Pacific News Service, September 14, 2001
www.pacificnews.org

WILLIAM O.
BEEMAN

This piece by William O. Beeman was among the first anthropological commentaries that appeared nationally in the wake of the September 11 attacks. Based upon his research on the Middle East, terrorism, and U.S. foreign policy, he succinctly outlines why bin Laden and his associates might have been involved in orchestrating the attacks, and describes the structure of their organization. He suggests that the brutality of the acts of September 11 is an indication of the level of anger and frustration generated abroad by U.S. actions that restrict movements for self-determination in other parts of the world. By drawing examples from Saudi Arabia, Israel, and the Palestinian territories, as well as other countries, Beeman outlines some of the possible motives for the attacks.

The United States risks a severe miscalculation in dealing with the destruction of the World Trade Center and the attack on the Pentagon on Tuesday.

This event is not an isolated instance of violence. This is not an act of war. It is one symptom of a cancer that threatens to metastasize. The root cause is not terrorist activity, as has been widely stated. It is the relationship between the United States and the Islamic world. Until this central cancerous problem is treated, Americans will never be free from fear.

Merely locating and hunting down a single guilty party in this case will not stop future violence: Such an action will not destroy the organization of terrorist cells already established throughout the world. Of greater importance, it will do nothing to alleviate the residual enmity against America that will remain at large in the world, continuing to motivate violence.

The perpetrators of the first attack on the World Trade Center, in 1993, were caught and convicted. This did not stop the attack on Tuesday.

The chief suspect is the Saudi Arabian Osama bin Laden or his surrogates. He has been mischaracterized as an anti-American terrorist. He should rather be thought of as someone who would do anything to protect Islam.

Bin Laden began his career fighting the Soviet occupation of Afghanistan in 1979, when he was 22 years old. He has not only resisted the Soviets but also the Serbians in Yugoslavia. His anger was directed against the United States primarily because of the U.S. presence in the Gulf region, more particularly in Saudi Arabia, the site of the most sacred Islamic religious sites.

According to bin Laden, during the [1991] Gulf War, America co-opted the rulers of Saudi Arabia to establish a military presence in order to kill Muslims in Iraq. In a religious decree issued in 1998, he gave religious legitimacy to attacks on Americans in order to stop the United States from occupying the lands of Islam in the holiest of places. His decree also extends to Jerusalem, home of the second-most sacred Muslim site, the al-Aqsa Mosque.[1]

The depth of his historical vision is clear when, in his decree, he characterizes Americans as crusaders, harking back to the Medieval Crusades, in which the Holy Lands, then occupied by Muslims, were captured by European Christians.

He will not cease his opposition until the United States leaves the region. Paradoxically, his strategy for persuading the United States to do so seems drawn from the American foreign-policy playbook. When the United States disapproves of the behavior of another nation, it turns up the heat on that nation through embargoes, economic sanctions, or withdrawal of diplomatic representation.

In the case of Iraq following the Gulf War, America employed military action, resulting in the loss of civilian life. The State Department has theorized that if the people of a rogue nation experience enough suffering, they will overthrow their rulers or compel them to adopt more sensible behavior. The terrorist actions in New York and Washington are a clear and ironic implementation of this strategy against the United States.

Bin Laden takes no credit for actions emanating from his training camps in Afghanistan. He has no desire for self-aggrandizement. A true ideologue, he believes that his mission is sacred, and he wants only to see clear results. For this reason, the structure of his organization is essentially tribal-cellular, in modern political terms. His followers are as fervent and intense in their belief as he is. They carry out their actions because they believe in the rightness of their cause, not because of bin Laden's orders or approval.

Groups are trained in Afghanistan, and then establish their own centers in places as far-flung as Canada, Africa, and Europe. Each cell is technologically sophisticated, and may have a different set of motivations for attacking the United States.

Palestinian members of his group see Americans as supporters of Israel in the current conflict between the two nations. In the Palestinian view, Ariel Sharon's ascendancy to leadership of Israel has triggered a new era, with U.S. government officials failing to pressure the Israeli government to end violence against Palestinians.

Palestinian cell members will not cease their opposition until the United States changes its relationship with the Israeli state. The mujahedeen fighters in Lebanon also direct their hostility against Israel and the United States. They also operate against the Maronite Christian community in their own country, who were supported by the French from World War I until the end of World War II. They will not cease their operations until the region is firmly in Islamic hands.

Above all, Americans need to remember that the rest of the world has an absolute right to self-determination that is as defensible as our own. Despicable acts of mayhem such as those committed in New York and Washington are a measure of the revulsion that others feel at our actions that seemingly limit those rights. If we perpetuate a cycle of hate and revenge, this conflict will escalate into a war that our great-grandchildren will be fighting.

EDITOR'S NOTE

1. Also known as Haram al-Sharif (see Chapters 18–20).

CHAPTER 32

WHAT HAVE THE 9/11 INVESTIGATORS OVERLOOKED?

Christian Science Monitor, July 11, 2002

JANET
MCINTOSH

In May 2002, reports surfaced indicating that the FBI, the CIA, and members of the Bush administration failed to "connect the dots" regarding specific clues and warnings which might have prevented the September 11 attacks. In this commentary, Janet McIntosh argues that the administration also suffers from a "lapsed ability to see the global political landscape from any perspective" outside its own—that is, ethnocentrism. Based on her research and experience in a predominantly Muslim area of Kenya, she suggests that each act of hypocrisy, false denial, or fabrication made by U.S. officials can potentially fan the flames of terrorism.

McIntosh's article implies that the ongoing international "war on terror," focused on disrupting terrorist plots, is a short-term palliative likely to exacerbate anti-U.S. sentiment over the long run.

Last month, we heard quite a furor about how the FBI and CIA failed us in the months leading up to September 11. How, like children wielding a dull crayon, they failed to "connect the dots." Congress is probing; the media is probing; even Egypt and Britain claim that they warned the U.S. about terrorist attacks. And now the government is gearing up for a new federal information clearinghouse: the freshly empowered and consolidated Department of Homeland Security.

While pundits consider the nuts and bolts of such a proposal, we seem to have forgotten that the administration was ill informed, not only about the means of terrorism, but about one of the deepest motives behind it.

The USA is widely loathed, but our leaders never fully grasped that before last September. Shortly after the attacks, President Bush claimed to be "amazed" that anyone hates America, because "I know how good we are." This naïveté is a failure of "intelligence"—not the kind the FBI and CIA specialize in, but a lapsed ability to see the global political landscape from any perspective outside one's own.

My own exposure to such alternative perspectives was painfully enhanced during my fieldwork as an anthropologist in East Africa. I happened to be living in a Muslim area of coastal Kenya in 1998 when the U.S. embassies were bombed in Nairobi and Dar-es-Salaam. The FBI swarmed to the Muslimized areas of the coast, eventually arresting a man (Mohammed Sadiq Odeh) who had circulated through the same towns, even the same apartment buildings, where I did my research.

The vast majority of my Muslim Swahili friends and acquaintances would never dream of committing such vicious acts and were sorry for the loss of life. At the same time, however, a conspiracy theory began to billow through the community: the United States, through a CIA operation, had willfully obliterated its own embassies in order to have an excuse for open season on Muslims. President Clinton's subsequent bombings of a pharmaceutical company in Sudan and an Al Qaeda training site in Afghanistan (back when Al Qaeda was not so infamous) merely confirmed my friends' impression that Muslims worldwide were victims of a capricious American bully.

Conspiracy theories, it turns out, were hardly new to them; several Swahili men bolstered their case by showing me a photocopied letter ostensibly written by then British prime minister John Major to his Foreign Office minister, Douglas Hogg, in 1993. In the letter, Major describes colluding with the United States and other Western nations to ensure that the Muslim population are "totally displaced" from Bosnia-Herzegovina to prevent the emergence of a "possible Islamic state in Europe." These harsh prescriptions, he writes, emerge from a "real-politic [sic]" based on a broader European "Christian-Civilization and ethic [sic]."

At first, I was maddened by what I saw as the paranoid slant of these narratives, and I argued vigorously against them. I pointed out the wild exaggerations and near-hilarious grammatical solecisms in the "John Major" letter that clearly indicate it wasn't penned by an elite Englishman. I argued that while the CIA is hardly a compassionate body, it would never cost the U.S. so much financial damage and inconvenience only to justify Clinton's haphazard retaliatory gestures. My friends were unmoved. Why?

Conspiracy theories say a lot about their perpetrators. They are weapons of the weak, usually circulated by subordinate groups who feel oppressed. They don't require evidence to make the rounds; what they need is perceived plausibility. My Swahili friends pointed to the scores of children who have died in Iraq because of U.S. sanctions. They pointed to Western media bias that favors Israel over Palestine and even to the sixteenth-century Portuguese destruction of Muslim towns on the East African coast, a historical moment that stands, to them, as a synecdoche for Western/Christian hostility.

They are knowledgeable about world history (even if such knowledge is marred by bias and fear), well connected to Muslim communities in other nations, and, as a result, highly suspicious of the United States government. The conspiracy theory surrounding the embassy bombings seemed like one way of saying: We may not have direct evidence for our claim, but judging from your track record, you might well have done it.

President Bush might be baffled by such accusations, but they are a potent symptom of the low regard in which our country is held. I wonder, furthermore, if our future attackers are aggrieved, not only by U.S. political actions, but also by the failure of our country to validate their feelings of oppression. Dare I say, in fact, that the despicable final videotape of Daniel Pearl contains a vital clue about terrorism that has been overlooked.

Pearl's murderers force him to say that he had come to a new understanding of their point of view, and to compare his anguish in captivity to that of the prisoners in Guantanamo Bay. The video-makers interspersed Pearl's scripted words with images of dead and weeping Middle Easterners, presumably victims of U.S. political and military actions. In crafting this pastiche, it is as if they were splicing together a fantasy world in which Americans finally understood, in the depths of their hearts, the suffering and resentment of some Muslim peoples.

Our government should know that fathoming the point of view of potential terrorists is not the same as approving of their acts, but it became "un-American" right around the time Lynn Cheney's ACTA task force spit-roasted a list of academics for pointing out why the U.S. is so reviled. Yet to refuse to grasp terrorists' perspective is to encourage a shortsightedness that will cost everyone dearly.

So what solution could possibly remedy this problem? I don't aspire to fix a global mess, but my experiences in Kenya provided a sharp reminder of the fact that a vast number of Muslims across the world (most of them peaceful, humane people, and a few of them not) are weighing our country's actions. Every U.S. hypocrisy, fib, or denial is registered;

every U.S. policy is picked over for the way it affects Muslims on political, economic, and humanitarian grounds. A just foreign policy then, especially on issues like sanctions against Iraq and the U.S. support for Israeli prime minister Ariel Sharon, is the avenue to peace.

Social justice and fairness have not yet motivated the United States government to overhaul such policies, but perhaps, once it realizes this is the only long-term solution to terror at home, it will be willing to do so on grounds of self-defense.

CHAPTER 33

WE NEED A GLOBAL DECLARATION OF INTERDEPENDENCE

International Herald Tribune, July 6, 2002

WADE DAVIS   In this article, Canadian anthropologist Wade Davis reflects upon the events of September 11 to explore a potential source of further conflict—the deepening rift between the world's rich and poor. Western development models have often led to "disparity, dislocation, and dispossession" in the Third World, which may well be among the most profound dangers to world peace in the coming years. Davis informs readers that "anthropology suggests that when peoples and cultures are squeezed, extreme ideologies sometimes emerge."

When President George W. Bush asked, after September 11, "Why do they hate us?" this was not a rhetorical question. Americans really wanted to know, and still do, for their innocence had been shattered.

The president suggested that the reason was the very greatness of America, as if the liberal institutions of government had somehow provoked homicidal rage in fanatics incapable of embracing freedom.

Other, dissenting voices claimed that, to the contrary, the problem lay in the tendency of the United States to support, notably in the Middle East, repressive regimes whose values are antithetical to the ideals of American democracy.

Both sides were partially right, but both overlooked the deeper issue, in part because they persisted in examining the world through American eyes.

America, of course, has always looked inward. A nation born in isolation cannot be expected to be troubled by the election of a president who has rarely been abroad, or a Congress in which 25 percent of members do not hold passports. Wealth too can be blinding. The United States with less than 5 percent of the world's population produces 21 percent of the global economic output.

M. WUERKER

Such a country does not easily grasp the reality of a world in which 1.3 billion people get by on less than $1 a day. A land wired for the Internet readily forgets that the majority of the world's population has never had a phone call, let alone sent an e-mail.

A culture that celebrates the individual at the expense of family and community has difficulty understanding that in most of the world the community still prevails, for the destiny of the individual remains inextricably linked to the fate of the collective.

Even as the United States came to dominate the geopolitical scene, as it has since 1945, the American people resisted engagement with the world. Such cultural myopia was rendered obsolete in an instant on September 11. In the immediate wake of the tragedy, I was often asked, as an anthropologist, for explanations.

Condemning the attacks in the strongest terms, I nevertheless encouraged people to consider the forces that gave rise to Osama bin Laden's movement. While it would be reassuring to view Al Qaeda as an isolated phenomenon, I feared that the organization was a manifestation of a deeper and broader conflict between those who have and those who have nothing.

I also encouraged my American friends to turn the anthropological lens upon their own culture, if only to catch a glimpse of how Americans might appear to people born in other lands. When the rest of the world looks to the West, and to America in particular, they see many wondrous things. But they also see a culture that reveres marriage yet allows half of its marriages to end in divorce; that admires its elderly yet permits grandparents to live with grandchildren in only 6 percent of its households; that loves its children yet embraces a slogan—"24/7"—that implies total devotion to the workplace at the expense of family.

Technological wizardry is balanced by a model of production and consumption that compromises the life supports of the planet. Extreme would be one word for a culture that does little to curtail industrial processes that threaten to transform the biochemistry of the atmosphere. The American way of life, brilliant and inspired in so many ways, is nevertheless not the paragon of humanity's potential.

For much of the Middle East in particular, the West is synonymous, not only with questionable values and a flood of commercial products, but also with failure. Gamal Abdel Nasser's notion of a pan-Arabic state was based on a thoroughly Western and secular model of socialist development, a dream that collapsed in corruption and despotism. The Shah of Iran provoked the Iranian revolution by thrusting not the Koran but modernity as he saw it down the throats of his people.

The Western model of development has failed in the Middle East and elsewhere because it has been based on the false promise that people who follow its prescriptive dictates will in time achieve the material prosperity enjoyed by a handful of nations of the West. Even were this possible, it is not at all clear that it would be desirable.

To raise consumption of energy and materials throughout the world to Western levels, given current population projections, would require the resources of four planet Earths by the year 2100. To do so with the one world we have would imply so severely compromising the biosphere that the Earth would be unrecognizable.

Given the values that drive most decisions in the international community, this is not about to happen. In reality, development for the vast majority of the peoples of the world has been a process in which the individual is torn from his past, propelled into an uncertain future, only to secure a place on the bottom rung of an economic ladder that goes nowhere.

Anthropology suggests that when peoples and cultures are squeezed, extreme ideologies sometimes emerge, inspired by strange and unexpected beliefs. However unique the circumstances that forged its abominable impulses, Al Qaeda is nevertheless reminiscent of these revitalization movements. We must strive to understand its roots, for the chaotic conditions of disintegration and disenfranchisement that led to Al Qaeda are found among disaffected populations throughout the world.

We live in an age of disintegration. At the beginning of this century there were 60 nation states. Today there are 190, most of them poor and highly unstable. The real story lies in the cities. Throughout the world urbanization, with all of its fickle and forlorn promises, has drawn people by the millions into squalor.

The nation-state, as Harvard sociologist Daniel Bell wrote, has become too small for the big problems of the world and too big for the little problems of the world. Outside of the major industrial nations, globalization has not brought integration and harmony, but rather a firestorm of change that has swept away languages and cultures, ancient skills and visionary wisdom. This is the hidden backdrop of our era.

In the immediate aftermath of September 11, I was asked at a lecture in Los Angeles to name the seminal event of the twentieth century. Without hesitation I suggested the assassination of Archduke Ferdinand in 1914.

The question then turned to September 11, and it struck me that a hundred years from now that fateful date may well loom as the defining moment of this new century, the day when two worlds, long kept apart by geography and circumstance, came together in violent conflict. If there is one lesson to be learned from September 11, it is that power does not translate into security.

The voices of the poor, who deal each moment with the consequences of environmental degradation, political corruption, overpopulation, the gross distortion in the distribution of wealth and the consumption of resources, who share few of the material benefits of modernity, will no longer be silent.

True peace and security for the twenty-first century will only come about when we find a way to address the underlying issues of disparity, dislocation, and dispossession that have provoked the madness of our age. We desperately need a global acknowledgment of the fact that no people and no nation can truly prosper unless the bounty of our collective ingenuity and opportunities are available and accessible to all.

We must aspire to create a new international spirit of pluralism, a true global democracy in which unique cultures, large and small, are allowed the right to exist, even as we learn and live together, enriched by the deepest reaches of our imaginings. We need a global declaration of interdependence. In the wake of September 11 this is not idle or naive rhetoric, but rather a matter of survival.

SUGGESTION FOR FURTHER READING

Davis, Wade
  2002   *Light at the Edge of the World.* Washington: National Geographic
          Society.

PART V

ON AFGHANISTAN, CENTRAL ASIA, AND THE MIDDLE EAST

CHAPTER 34

NATION IS HOME TO AFGHANS, MUJAHEDEEN, TALIBAN, AFGHAN-ARABS, TO NAME A FEW

St. Louis Post-Dispatch, September 23, 2001

ROBERT
CANFIELD

Immediately following September 11, U.S. media attention zeroed in on Afghanistan, whose Taliban government hosted Osama bin Laden and members of the Al Qaeda network, prime suspects in the World Trade Center and Pentagon attacks.

In this piece, anthropology professor Robert Canfield provides a wealth of background information for understanding the linguistic, ethnic, religious, and political complexity of Afghanistan. In describing the rise of the mujahedeen (holy warrior) groups in the 1980s, he reminds readers that these organizations were officially supported by Pakistan and the CIA in an effort to repel the Soviet army and defeat Afghanistan's communist government. When the United States withdrew support without any plan for helping to reconstruct the country, rival factions began fighting for control. Out of this chaos emerged the Taliban.

Two weeks after the publication of this commentary, U.S. forces initiated a massive bombing campaign that killed thousands of Taliban troops, Al Qaeda fighters, and Afghan civilians.

No Afghans participated in the bombings of September 11 and only one kind of "Afghan," the Taliban, has any connection with Osama bin Laden (the presumed mastermind). The Taliban are not typical "Afghans" anyway.

Afghanistan, which may be a crucial target of U.S. forces, is notoriously diverse. Almost two dozen language groups exist in that country, which is divided religiously among Sunni, Shia and Ismaili Muslims, along with a few historically accepted Hindus (and now a tiny group of Christian converts from Islam, most of them fearful and secretive).

Indeed, the Muslims are subdivided in their orientations toward Islam and even Islamic radicalism comes in several varieties.

Scarcely any Muslim in Afghanistan would have approved of the bombings of September 11. Most Afghans' commitment to Islam has never been particularly shrill, perhaps because Afghanistan was never under sustained colonial domination.

The places where radical Islamic ideologies developed, notably Egypt and India, were long subject to European control. The radical Islam that exists in Afghanistan was imported during the anti-Soviet struggle of the 1980s. And the Islam of the notorious Taliban is something else, a creation of special circumstances after the Soviet-Afghan war.

The term "Afghan" originally referred to a particular ethnic type, who are otherwise known as "Pushtun" or (in Pakistan) "Pathan." These "true Afghans" speak Pushtu (Pashto) and are organized tribally, at least in many rural areas. The elite of the country have typically been of Afghan extraction.

Some of the peoples in the country have resented and resisted Pushtun domination and call themselves by their ethnic and linguistic identities—"Hazara," "Uzbek," "Tajik," etc.—to distinguish themselves from the Pushtun. They nevertheless identify themselves as "Afghan" to people (like most Americans) who know little about internal Afghanistan affairs.

Mujahedeen means "holy warriors" and was claimed, especially after 1980, by those people who opposed the Afghan communist government and its Soviet sponsors. Seven of the many mujahedeen organizations were supported officially by Pakistan and the CIA, which tried (with only moderate success) to orchestrate the resistance activities against the communist regimes.

The mujahedeen were able to force the Soviets out of Afghanistan in 1989 and eventually to bring down the Afghan communist government in 1992. Between 1992 and 1996 they fought fiercely among themselves over control of Kabul. Elsewhere in the country they carved the landscape into their own respective fiefdoms, effecting a widespread collapse of social order.

The Taliban arose in the context of that disorder. They are the products of the Islamic schools that were set up among the Afghan refugees during the war. Most of the schools were small and taught by local mullahs, but they were a useful escape from the refugee camps, as they provided food and lodging for the boys that their own families could scarcely muster.

The Taliban are mostly Pushtun and generally they have little understanding of the other groups in the country. In truth, they know nothing about the history of Afghanistan, even of the recent Soviet-Afghan conflict.

Centered on the religious schools and their dormitories, the Taliban ("students") had a different understanding of the world from their families in the refugee camps. Journalist and author Ahmad Rashid calls them "orphans" of the war whose essential anchorage was the "puritan Islam" they were taught. Most of the Taliban speak only Pushtu and Urdu—an indication that in fact they are (at least culturally) Pakistanis, not Afghans.

Arab-Afghans, including Osama bin Laden, joined the resistance against the Soviets. They were accepted among the Pushtun parties, especially those favored by the Pakistanis and Saudis, but were rebuffed by the Persian-speaking parties of the north. Many of them were trained during the war and dispersed into other parts of the Arab world after the war, where they became active in radical movements.

In recent years, however, as the Taliban have been fighting what is left of the mujahedeen, now known as the Northern Alliance, many Arab-Afghans have become allied with the Taliban. These Arab-Afghans are the only elements in the country that have any affinity with or commitment to the destruction of Western society and culture.

It remains to be seen which, if any, of them were involved in the bombing on September 11.

SUGGESTIONS FOR FURTHER READING

Canfield, Robert, ed.
1991   *Turko-Persia in Historical Perspective.* Cambridge: Cambridge University Press.
Hauner, Milan, and Robert Canfield, eds.
1989   *Afghanistan and the Soviet Union: Collision and Transformation.* Boulder: Westview Press.
Shahrani, M. Nazif, and Robert Canfield, eds.
1984   *Revolutions and Rebellions in Afghanistan.* Berkeley: Institute for International Studies.

CHAPTER 35

THE FOLLY OF QUICK ACTION IN AFGHANISTAN

Financial Times, September 27, 2001

ASHRAF
GHANI

In this article, published days before the U.S. military initiated bombing raids over Afghanistan in an effort to destroy the Taliban and Al Qaeda, Ashraf Ghani warns of the possible consequences of a hastily planned war. He notes that the rise of the Taliban can be linked to ill-devised U.S. policies in the region in the 1990s, and that only a credible U.N. plan for reconstruction will succeed in gaining the trust of the population.

By November 2001, the Taliban had abandoned Kabul and Kandahar, their last remaining strongholds. After Hamid Karzai was elected president at a meeting of elders in May 2002, he appointed Ashraf Ghani as finance minister.

As this book goes to press, much of the international support recommended by Ghani has not been forthcoming. Only a fraction of the $2 billion pledged by donor countries for reconstruction has arrived, and this may represent one of the greatest challenges facing the new administration.[1] Although international peacekeepers have achieved relative tranquility in the capital city of Kabul, other regions remain unstable as local bosses struggle for power.

The battle of Afghanistan is the Bush administration's to lose. The Afghan population is ready for change. The networks of support from Pakistan that have been the mainstay of the Taliban regime are disrupted. Afghanistan's neighboring countries and the Arab and Islamic regimes would all be pleased to see a change of regime.

Afghans are poor but have sophisticated notions of legitimacy. Compared with the average American, the average Afghan is keenly interested in world events that affect them and do not miss a single broadcast of the BBC.

Most are disenchanted with the Taliban for its failures to address the well-being of the people, its subordination of the internal needs of the country to external adventurism, and for bringing confrontation with the U.S.

Having witnessed massive use of force by the Red army and the destruction wrought by a long civil war, Afghans are fearful of anarchy and a new phase of warlordism supported by the U.S. Should use of force lead to large-scale civilian casualties, disruption of the lives of people, and a new exodus of the Afghan population to neighboring countries that do not want them, the disenchantment with the Taliban could easily be turned into sympathy and then support for a new militant movement in the region.

The U.S. administration has two options. It can either deal with the symptoms and the visible symbols of the extremist movement or it can address the underlying causes of terrorism and support forces that would be willing to disrupt and destroy the networks that have turned Afghanistan into a launching pad for isolationist and extremist movements.

Dealing with the symptoms would involve military assaults within days or weeks, funneling large amounts of money and matériel to warlords opposed to the Taliban and the creation of alliances with neighboring regimes that could use the opportunity to deny the aspirations of their own people for democratic change. Such an approach would enmesh the U.S. in a series of very complicated relationships in the region. These relationships could in turn spawn networks that could be turned against the West in the longer term.

A more methodical approach would begin from the premise that the fundamental issue in Afghanistan is the creation of a state that would have legitimacy at home, in the region, and internationally. Only a nationalist state would have the capacity and commitment to break and destroy the networks of terror.

There is a significant asset and a central constraint in addressing this issue. In spite of nine years of civil war, no group in the country has asked for the dismemberment of the country. Afghan nationalism is strong and a potential basis for the creation of a stable and legitimate government that would offer a formula for accommodating the aspirations of various linguistic and regional groups. Yet no group or individual commands sufficient legitimacy or has articulated a vision and concrete program of action to convince the population that their aspirations for peace and prosperity can be addressed.

Forging a methodical approach would require acting on lessons from past U.S. engagement in Afghanistan. First, dealing with Afghanistan cannot be outsourced to one of the governments in the region. The U.S. outsourced the management of the resistance to the Soviet occupation of Afghanistan to Pakistan, and the current situation is a tragic consequence of that decision.

Second, the U.S. cannot funnel large amounts of money and arms to discredited warlords who are now lining up to offer their services. This approach has been tried and resulted in the destruction of the capital city and the emergence of the Taliban.

Third, an interim Afghan government cannot be cobbled together in a couple of weeks. That was tried and led to the civil war among armed factions that had little unity of purpose or sense of accountability.

Fourth, funneling resources to political parties or nongovernmental organizations that are not willing to be accountable to the people for the use of those resources can onl lead to alienation of the population. Adoption of that strategy during the Soviet occupation brought little benefit.

Fifth, the United Nations cannot play a constructive role if it does not receive the full backing of the U.S. In recent years, there have been several very capable special envoys whose efforts have not succeeded because of the lukewarm support of the U.S. and the opposition of regional governments.

Establishing a legitimate government in Afghanistan requires a multipronged approach. To gain the trust of the population, a credible program for reconstruction of the country has to be offered. This would require assembling the younger group of Afghan technocrats who have gained success in industrialized countries, as well as many agencies that have had the commitment to stay through the course of the events in Afghanistan.

Critical to the success of this effort would be to design mechanisms for accountability and transparency of management of resources to be provided for reconstruction. Pakistan and the neighboring states should be persuaded to accept and support the creation of a broad-based Afghan nationalist government. The role of the U.N. special envoy could be enhanced to help establish a transitional government composed of a cross-section of Afghans. This process would only be credible if officials in the U.S. government avoided the temptation of imposing lists drawn on the basis of their personal contacts or insistence on giving Afghanistan's octogenarian former king a decisive role in the process.

Establishment of the transitional government would also require the establishment of an army and a police force. Once these arrangements are in place, the use of military force against Osama bin Laden and the hard core of his Taliban allies could be followed by an orderly process of transfer of power.

The administration has an option. It can act quickly, or wisely. The world prays that wisdom may guide policy.

EDITOR'S NOTE

1. See Ian Fisher, "Ready to Rebuild, Afghans Await Promised Aid," *New York Times*, August 25, 2002.

CHAPTER 36

AFGHANISTAN CAN LEARN FROM ITS PAST

New York Times, October 14, 2001

NAZIF
SHAHRANI

Even before U.S. war planes began bombing Taliban positions in October 2001, concerned observers asked: Who will rule Afghanistan once the Taliban is gone?

In this article, Professor Nazif Shahrani argues that the country will enjoy a democratic government only if a decentralized political system is established. He warns that "the painful lesson of Afghanistan's history has been that strong centralized government in any form leads to abuses of power" because the country is marked by ethnic divisions.

The context of Shahrani's editorial is important. There was great concern at this time that the U.S. government would seek to reestablish the octogenarian former monarch, Muhammad Zahir Shah, who had been living in exile in Italy for twenty years.

The people of Afghanistan, after a century of misrule, are in desperate need of a way to govern themselves that will offer some defense against the abuses of power that have marked Afghan history. Now that President Bush has acknowledged the need to help build a stable government in Afghanistan, perhaps under leadership of the United Nations, many are asking: Who should rule? Once the Taliban are defeated, several parties want to rule: the ex-king, Muhammad Zahir Shah; the Pashtun ethnic group; the opposition Northern Alliance; and of course the Taliban. But the better question is: How should Afghanistan govern itself?

The mechanism most often being mentioned is centralized government controlled by an alliance of some combination of ethnic groups. Yet the painful lesson of Afghanistan's history has been that strong centralized government in any form leads to abuses of power. The

United Nations special envoy, Lakhdar Brahimi, is probably in the best position to sort out the complex inner conflicts and alliances inside Afghanistan. But everyone concerned should realize that democratic governance cannot be achieved by handing power over to a party, tribe, or group, or a combination of these, no matter how broad-based.

Instead, what Afghanistan needs is a loosening of centralized power and help in envisioning and creating a decentralized government with a strong national constitution. Providing this help could be the longest-lasting accomplishment the antiterror coalition could make, not only for Afghanistan, but in the service of its own wider goals.

Modern Afghanistan was cobbled together as a buffer state in the late nineteenth century by British India and czarist Russia, with its first modern ruler, Amir Abdur Rahman Khan, picked from among the princelings of a warring Pashtun clan. In return for giving up control of the country's foreign affairs to Britain, he received arms and money to conquer various ethnic and linguistic groups: other Pashtuns, Tajik, Farsiwan, Uzbek, Turkmen, Baluch, Hazara, Aimaq, and others. Infamous for his cruelty and dubbed the Iron Amir by his colonial masters, he established a firm foundation for an oppressive, corrupt centralized system. A brief experiment with constitutional monarchy from 1965 to 1973, under Zahir Shah, was aborted by a palace coup, followed in 1978 by the Soviet-inspired communist regime that plunged the country into an abyss of continual proxy wars culminating in the rise of the Taliban.

The aims of the Taliban under Mullah Muhammad Omar are similar to those of the British-installed Iron Amir: the military conquest and subjugation of all the self-governing non-Pashtun territories. And like him, they use an extremist form of Islam as a justification for terrorizing those they assume to be enemies into submission. What is novel in the Taliban's effort is their alliance with international terrorism.

The old monarchy and Taliban regimes also share the common myth, first fabricated by British India, that the Pashtun have the exclusive right to rule in Afghanistan. This myth, echoed approvingly today by Pakistani generals and politicians, has brought Afghanistan to disaster.

The international community should encourage the creation of a government that recognizes the crucial role of the local and regional communities in self-governance, as existed in earlier eras in Afghanistan. Indeed, these kinds of local governing structures reemerged in the period of anti-Soviet and anticommunist jihad during the 1980s and early 1990s. Areas then controlled by mujahedeen groups established rudimentary governments that ran schools, police units, and courts; these local groups evolved into five major regional coalitions of communities, consisting of several provinces each. The new government of Afghanistan should embrace the principles of community self-governance at village, district, and provincial levels.

Local autonomy and the political integrity of every ethnic and sectarian segment of Afghan society should be guaranteed by a national constitution and a decentralized federal governance structure.

Giving Afghanistan a functional and stable governing system will require patience and an honest transitional government. It will also require the supervision of a United Nations–mandated international peacekeeping force in Afghanistan. While the ex-king should be allowed to play a role in such a transitional government, every effort must be made to keep his old corrupt cronies from infiltrating the new government. Care must also be taken to keep Pakistan from dictating the shape of the new government and to keep the corrupt elements of the mujahedeen groups and the previous communist regime from any positions of power.

The task is daunting, but the rewards are liberation from terror for the people of Afghanistan and a new precedent for combating the conditions that give rise to terrorism elsewhere.

SUGGESTIONS FOR FURTHER READING

Shahrani, M. Nazif
   1979   *The Kirghiz and Wakhi of Afghanistan: Adaptation to Closed Frontiers.* Seattle: University of Washington Press.
Shahrani, M. Nazif, and Robert Canfield, eds.
   1984   *Revolutions and Rebellions in Afghanistan.* Berkeley: Institute for International Studies.

CHAPTER 37

WOMEN IN THE
NEW AFGHANISTAN

Democracy Now! (Pacifica Radio), December 4,
2001

ZIEBA
SHORISH-
SHAMLEY,
interviewed by
Amy Goodman

By mid-November 2001, U.S. and British forces had ousted the Taliban from power. In the final days of that month, the United Nations convened a series of meetings in Bonn, Germany, between Afghan factions to create a political plan for the future. Despite protests from many organizations, all but a handful of the participants in the conference were male.

On December 4, anthropologist and activist Zieba Shorish-Shamley of the Women's Alliance for Peace and Human Rights in Afghanistan was interviewed from Brussels, Belgium, by Amy Goodman. There, approximately fifty representatives participated in an Afghan women's conference to discuss unified demands on women's issues in post-Taliban Afghanistan. Shorish-Shamley emphasizes the need for women to participate in all phases of the reconstruction process.

AMY GOODMAN: The four Afghan factions holding talks in Bonn, Germany, have reached agreement on a U.N. blueprint for rebuilding the country's political system. The deal came early yesterday morning after the Northern Alliance, the largest delegation, finally submitted a list of its candidates for a 29-member interim administration to rule Afghanistan. The next step, expected to begin immediately, will be to choose which factions get which jobs. The interim administration will rule for six months, until a commission is formed to convene a *loya jirga*, a traditional grand assembly. The assembly would then elect a transitional government to rule for about two years, until a constitution is drawn up and elections are held. Under intense international pressure, the interim administration is expected to include at least one woman as one of the five deputy prime ministers and several other women as ministers. While talks continue in Bonn, talks of another sort are under way in Brussels, Belgium, where the first Afghan women's summit is being held. Fifty Afghan women representing a wide range of ethnic and religious groups and political views have gathered, supported by women's rights groups from around the world. They are working to forge unified demands on the need for women's equality and for their full participation in conflict resolution efforts and in the formation of a future Afghan government. We go now to Brussels, to Zieba Shorish-Shamley, with the Women's Alliance for Peace and Human Rights in Afghanistan. Thanks for stepping outside the meeting. Can you tell us what the situation is there?

ZIEBA SHORISH-SHAMLEY: The gathering at Brussels is for Afghan women to come up with a blueprint of their own as to what they want and their involvement in the peace process, as well as reconstruction of the future government of Afghanistan. In other words, whoever the Afghan government may be in the future, our message is that there has to be a proportionate representation of women in every aspect of the Afghan future—not only [in] the reconstruction [but in] the government [as well], because the women were not really represented proportionately at the Bonn process. So at this [meeting] the women are talking about what they want, and hopefully by the end of this summit we will have come up with a declaration of what their requests are and what their demands are.

AG: But this summit isn't binding in any way?

ZSS: No, it is not binding, but we will try to push what comes out of this summit at the U.N. (international level), as well as [with] the key government players, Six plus Two,[1] . . . who are involved in Afghanistan. Afghan women's rights have been violated for too long; they have been kept out of the reconstruction and actually . . . everything has been stripped from them, all the basic human rights that are required for human existence. So, therefore, without the Afghan women I do not think that Afghanistan will be adequately reconstructed, because 55 to 60 percent of the population of Afghanistan are women. And there won't be any peace without justice and the Afghan women demand to be involved in every aspect of their society.

AG: Zieba Shorish-Shamley, what do you think of the formulas they came up with in Bonn? The interim administration of Afghanistan is expected to include at least one woman as one of the five deputy prime ministers, and several other women as ministers.

ZSS: Well that tells you right there, it doesn't represent Afghan women. Afghan women are up to 55 percent or 60 percent of the population of the country. I do not understand, as an Afghan woman, why the U.N. and other countries always tell us Afghan women . . . [have] to please the warring factions and the political parties who have been in power who were the cause of the op-pression of Afghan women. Somebody has to listen to the Afghan women because they . . . [are] not going to be satisfied with one woman represented in the interim government. They would not be represented proportionately; by that I mean there should be more women than the men in the loya jirga. So again I say there will not be peace without justice and we will demand and we will deliver our message to the future so-called government of Afghani-stan, whoever it may be . . . Another message—I am talking about Women for Peace and Human Rights in Afghanistan—if they do not include proportional representation of Afghan women in the government in the reconstruction and future of Afghanistan . . . we will resist them, we will mobilize the world as we did against the Taliban, and we will mobilize it against them as well. So we are determined on this, and we will not compromise these rights, because the rights are not only given to us by Islam, they are also given to us by the United [Nations] charter. So we want these rights, and we want full participation, and we want the restoration of Afghan women's rights, and that is our demand, and we will not budge.

AG: Is the U.N. participating in your talks?

ZSS: Yes, the [OXFAM] executive director, Ms. Heizer, is here, as well as Ms. Angela King, who is representing the Secretary-General, Kofi Annan. So they are here as well as people from the European Parliament or Union. So there are many important women here and as I said, we don't have any problem with the women [who are] important people, we have a problem with the men in the U.N., as well as in Afghanistan, as well as in governments, because they seem to be selling us out to please the warring factions who have abused our rights and who have caused the severe oppression of the Afghan women. So they should negotiate with us, with the Afghan women, as well as with the people of Afghanistan. And an-other demand that we have is that the local autonomy of Afghanistan—the local populations' autonomy—must be respected. No one can impose a government from outside onto Afghan people.

AG: To what extent are you, the Women's Alliance for Peace and Human Rights in Afghanistan, communicating with or possibly negotiating with the Afghan military, the Northern Alliance—those that are going to be in power now?

ZSS: They haven't contacted us. I don't think they care for us because we ask for something that is ours, we ask for justice. Neither have the other political parties who are involved in the Bonn process. They know that we would not compromise the rights of Afghan women for anything . . . We haven't been contacted, and that doesn't bother us. We want the rights of the women to be restored, so we go to the international community and we go to the people of Afghanistan . . . If this government or future government is elected, [if] it's democratic, representing all women, all different ethnic groups of Afghanistan as well as women, and women are included in reconstruction and every other aspect of the public domain, [then] we don't have any problem with that government, we will support it 100 percent. But if they're going to play the game again, and just hang on to the power and do not share the power with more than half of the society, that's not going to work out—that's going to fail. And the reason the U.N. peace negotiations so far have failed in Afghanistan is because the U.N. has always negotiated with the warring factions, the people in power, or countries surrounding Afghanistan who supported the warring factions and caused all the misery . . . So what we want is for the U.N. and U.S., which is a key player, and the other Six plus Two [countries] who are involved in Afghanistan to . . . stop negotiating with them. They should negotiate with the people of Afghanistan—the people . . . have the right to self-determination. And I don't think the people of Afghanistan in any way are against women's involvement in the reconstruction and other building of our country, or in the government of Afghan society.

AG: Zieba Shorish-Shamley of the Women's Alliance for Peace and Human Rights, when the Northern Alliance took Kabul, the women, a group of about 100 women led by Suralia Perlika attempted to march to the United Nations demanding their rights and lifting up their burqas.[2] They were stopped, not by the Taliban, but by the Northern Alliance. What do you know of the group in Kabul right now?

ZSS: Well there are some elements within the Northern Alliance that are not bad, but there are elements in the Northern Alliance [who], according to . . . Women's Alliance for Peace and Human Rights in Afghanistan, are war criminals. We have . . . called on the U.N. to investigate and bring to justice the war criminals of the Soviet era, war criminals during the mujahedeen, and war criminals during the Taliban . . . Well, that tells you by itself [what happens] when the women are stopped from demonstrating and from expressing themselves, which is their right. Not only the U.N. rights which came fifty years ago . . . these rights were [also] given to the Moslems, to the Afghan women in sixth century A.D. When the Northern Alliance does that, not only does it violate the international law, it violates the Islamic law . . . We have to get women involved and we have to struggle for full restoration of Afghan women, it doesn't matter who the government is.

AG: Finally, how do you see women on the ground in Afghanistan building up civil society right now?

ZSS: Well they are trying in this meeting that we have. There are women already in the refugee camps, and some inside Afghanistan, that are trying to put their lives together, trying to educate children, to help on many, many issues that are too vast to talk about. What is happening in Afghanistan to Afghan women right now [is that] Afghan women and children need food, shelter, and medical care. Many women are dying, and the latest report . . . by the World Health Organization last week [reported that] because of wearing the burqa, the rate of tuberculosis has risen very high among Afghan women, because they were denied sunshine under the Taliban rule. As well . . . there are 300,000 to 400,000 pregnant women inside Afghanistan without any prenatal, delivery or postnatal care . . . So that tells you how dire the need is for medical attention in Afghanistan. At the same time, what we want is for the U.N. to move and demilitarize the city of Kabul. The peace-keeping forces of the U.N. — or as they decided, of some Moslem countries that have offered [to participate] — should move into the city of Kabul. There has to be security, and security for women. For the women of Afghanistan, there is no security . . . there is no sense of peace. So they should be protected, but the first thing that I urge the international community [to do] is to get food to them as soon as possible . . .

AG: Zieba Shorish-Shamley, thank you for taking time — coming out of the meeting where you are in Brussels—to speak with our listeners and viewers around the country on the "War and Peace Report." Thank you.

EDITOR'S NOTES

1. "Six plus Two" countries are the six countries bordering Afghanistan (Iran, Turkmenistan, Uzbekistan, Tajikistan, China, and Pakistan), plus the two Cold War superpowers (United States and Russia).

2. The burqa is a garment for women that covers the entire body, including the face. Under the Taliban's rule, Afghan women were required to wear burqas, which became a symbol of the government's repression of females.

CHAPTER 38

ENLISTING AFGHAN AID

People's Geography Project, September 2001
www.peoplesgeography.com

DAVID B.
EDWARDS
AND SHAH-
MAHMOOD
MIAKHEL

In this article, which appeared in late September 2001, anthropologist David B. Edwards and Afghan journalist Shahmahmood Miakhel argue that U.S. leaders may be stepping into a trap if they attack Afghanistan. Rather than see Afghans as enemies, the Bush administration should see them as potential allies against the Taliban regime. They conclude by emphasizing the need to create a secure future for Afghanistan as a strategy to avoid future terrorist infiltration there.

Osama bin Laden is waiting for George Bush to attack Afghanistan. It is the response he expects, and he can't wait. For him, this is a holy war, a clash of civilizations, and he has no compunction about using Afghans as kindling to start a conflagration that would involve the entire Muslim world. One hopes the policy makers in Washington realize where bin Laden's strategy leads and will think carefully about how to avoid his trap.

To develop a strategy that confounds bin Laden's plans, we must begin by thinking of Afghans not as enemies but as potential allies. It is no coincidence that none of the names so far identified in the list of hijackers are Afghans. Bin Laden and his Arab followers live in restricted enclaves, and few Afghans outside the Taliban regime itself harbor any sympathies for his cause. Afghanistan now, no less than during the decade of Soviet control, is an occupied nation, and we must enlist in our struggle the many Afghans inside the country and out who would welcome the opportunity to unseat the Taliban and get rid of the Arab interlopers in their country. Two steps must be taken to draw these people into the international community in its attack on bin Laden and his supporters.

First, the international community must assemble experienced Afghan leaders to provide the nucleus of an interim government. This group should include exiled moderates who were forced out of the political picture first by the extremist resistance parties in Peshawar back in the 1980s and then by the Taliban. They must be joined by the handful of moderate commanders forced into exile by the Taliban that Afghans still trust. The number of recognized Afghan leaders who have managed to both survive and maintain their reputation in the polarized politics of the last two decades is small, but they exist and must be persuaded to put aside their partisan disputes and participate in a transitional coalition to govern Afghanistan until democratic elections can be held. As this group is brought together, Afghans generally must be convinced that these leaders will not be puppets of the United States or any other foreign power. Similarly, Afghanistan's neighbors must understand that the interim government will avoid foreign entanglements and dedicate itself to the immediate goals of reestablishing the foundations of government, helping the Afghan people become economically self-sufficient, and preparing the ground for general elections.

The second step is an international commitment made up front to provide a massive influx of development assistance to reconstruct the economic and social infrastructure of Afghan society. After 23 years of foreign occupation and civil war, the country's roads, irrigation systems, and electrical grid are in a state of ruin, and Afghanistan now is in the grip of a drought that has turned much of the region into a desert. Afghans remember well that the international community largely forgot about them after the Soviets withdrew from their country, and they must be assured that this will not happen again and that we will work with them to rebuild the vibrant and modernizing society that existed prior to the Marxist revolution of 1978. Without such commitments, Afghans will find little reason to take the risks that opposing bin Laden and the Taliban will entail. On the other hand, the promise of sustained international support for Afghanistan will send a message not only to Afghans, but to Muslims generally that the West is committed to their welfare rather than their destruction.

No group has suffered more in the last quarter century than the Afghans, but they are a resilient people and will be a formidable foe again if they believe themselves to be under invasion from a foreign enemy.

We must frame our response to the terrorist outrage not as an assault but as a liberation—from oppressive rulers, unwanted guests, and the economic calamity that is their everyday reality. Respected Afghan leaders must be at the forefront of our efforts, and it must be clear that our intentions are to help rebuild rather than to destroy. Those of us who have enjoyed the prosperity of the last two decades must recognize that terrorism is born of political and economic despair. If we fail to take into account Afghanistan's future, as well as its past and present, Afghanistan will remain a place where terrorists can find safe haven, and all the military might in the world won't make us safe again.

SUGGESTIONS FOR FURTHER READING

Edwards, David B.
    1996   *Heroes of the Age: Moral Fault Lines on the Afghan Frontier.* Berkeley and Los Angeles: University of California Press.
    2002   *Before Taliban: Genealogies of the Afghan Jihad.* Berkeley and Los Angeles: University of California Press.

CHAPTER 39

PAKISTAN'S DILEMMA

Middle East Report Online, September 19, 2001
www.merip.org

KAMRAN
ASDAR ALI

Throughout the late 1980s and into the 1990s, Afghan resistance fighters and mujahedeen groups received funding and support channeled through the Pakistani intelligence agency from CIA sources (see Chapter 28). The Pakistani government provided the Taliban with support after their rise to power in the mid-1990s, and was one of only two countries to grant the Taliban government formal recognition (the other was Saudi Arabia). The Bush and Clinton administrations, seeking to undercut Iran's role in Afghan politics, largely ignored the Taliban's repressive policies and Pakistan's responsibility in supporting them.

This article by Kamran Asdar Ali describes the dilemma faced by Pakistani officials in the critical days following September 11, when the Bush administration began shifting its focus away from the alleged suicide hijackers (nearly all of whom were Saudi nationals legally in the United States) to toppling the Taliban regime, hosts of Osama bin Laden. U.S. officials sought Pakistani support for the impending Afghan war, and placed that country's leaders in the position of alienating orthodox Muslims outraged by the possibility of aerial attacks that would eventually inflict thousands of civilian casualties.

As this book goes to press, political instability continues to plague Pakistan. U.S. special forces began operating within the country's borders in February 2002, allegedly in search of Al Qaeda members, to the dismay of many Pakistanis. Hardly a week goes by without news of attacks on civilian targets by Muslim extremists. President Pervez Musharraf has responded with increasingly repressive policies that may further undermine the country's stability.

Pakistani media reports indicate that on the evening of September 14 the president, General Pervez Musharraf, met with his cabinet and national security team in a marathon session lasting until the early hours of the next morning. The task at hand was to decide if the Pakistani government should accede to the demands made by the United States in the aftermath of the September 11 tragedies, demands related to the still-emerging U.S. policy toward Afghanistan, accused of harboring prime suspect Osama bin Laden. The U.S. request came in the form of a virtual threat. Media reports tell us that the Pakistani government has been asked to restrict the movements of goods and supplies to Afghanistan, seize the assets of Afghan/Taliban leaders, provide logistical support to the U.S. armed forces along with the use of Pakistani airspace if the need arises and, most importantly, share up-to-date intelligence on bin Laden and his followers in Afghanistan.

In the late 1970s, another Pakistani general, Zia ul Haq, must have convened a meeting similar to Musharraf's. Then, the military junta was asked to play a crucial role in support of the U.S.-financed resistance to the Soviet forces occupying Afghanistan. That decision was undoubtedly an easier one for the dictator Zia ul Haq and his advisers. The general had been in power for two years, and his religiously conservative regime was already unpopular at home and abroad. Supporting the U.S. would grant his government badly needed legitimacy on the world stage. Zia ul Haq also anticipated a U.S. aid package to help the Pakistani state address its perpetual social and economic problems.

To the skeptical Pakistani population, the military regime portrayed its intervention in Afghan affairs as humanitarian and political assistance to fellow Muslims. But the junta's decision to play ball with the U.S. was also taken for geostrategic reasons. Since Pakistan's independence in 1947, relations between Afghanistan and Pakistan had been strained, due to boundary disputes and the feared spillage of Pashtun nationalism across the border. Afghan rulers and elements of Pakistan's Pashtun population in the North West Frontier Province (NWFP) bordering Afghanistan periodically questioned the artificial line that the British had drawn to divide a culturally and ethnically continuous area into parts of British India and Afghanistan in the mid-nineteenth century. On occasion Afghanistan presented arguments for a greater Pashtun state, to include parts of Pakistan's northern territory.

Hence, with openly hostile India on their eastern flank, Pakistani military strategists have also regarded their not-so-friendly western neighbor with anxiety. This state of affairs was aggravated by the communist-led coup in Afghanistan in 1978, and the subsequent Soviet invasion of that country in the winter of 1979. The U.S.-backed resistance to the Afghan regime guaranteed, at least in the minds of the

Pakistani military leaders, a somewhat concrete resolution of their Afghan problem.

The mass displacement of the Afghan population, the destruction of their homes and villages, and the loss of 1.5 million Afghan lives during that country's long civil war have somehow been erased from the consciousness of the Western media. Nor do many outside Pakistan remember the Afghan war's impact on Pakistani civil, cultural, and political life.

The Pakistani military used the infusion of international aid to strengthen its Inter-Services Intelligence Directorate (ISI), which became the principal liaison between U.S. intelligence agencies and the varied factions of the Afghan resistance movement known as the mujahedeen. The ISI assumed a lead role in suppressing democratic dissent within Pakistan. With well over 90,000 men under its aegis, the ISI remains an independent power base within Pakistan's government structure. There are no constitutional checks and balances on its operations. Its leadership consists of highly motivated and, in most cases, religiously zealous officers who are concerned with safeguarding what they consider to be the spatial and ideological boundaries of the Pakistani state. Hence, the ISI has been directly or indirectly involved in all major domestic and international decisions made by successive military and civilian governments over the last two decades.

On the political level, the economic and development aid helped Zia ul Haq to consolidate his plan for Islamization of the country. Some of the legacies of this era are evidentiary laws based on the Koranic law or sharia, the creation of sharia courts, laws that discriminate against minorities and women, and the dreaded blasphemy laws which continue to restrict the civil and political rights of Pakistani citizens. Development funds were also used to establish and maintain madrassas (religious schools) in different parts of the country. Zia ul Haq and his junta considered the students and graduates of these schools the foot soldiers who would support the dictator as he pressed ahead with his agenda to build an Islamic polity and a theocratic state. Another legacy of the war was the unprecedented infiltration of Pakistani society by drugs and arms. Profits from drug and weapons trafficking helped finance the covert war in Afghanistan, while funneling enormous wealth to a section of the Pakistani military brass.

But the triumph of the Afghan resistance forces in 1992 did not result in what the Pakistani military had always desired: a stable Afghanistan following the dictates of Islamabad. With the Cold War already a fading memory, the U.S. and other Western countries virtually abandoned the victorious mujahedeen, making only vague promises of development aid to rebuild war-ravished Afghanistan. In subsequent years, infighting among the new Afghan leadership—and their growing independence from the ISI—led Pakistan to intensify its involvement in the affairs of this struggling state. The Taliban, a radical faction of madrassa students under the guidance of Mullah Mohammed Omar of Kandahar, were bankrolled by the Pakistani military on their path to victory in 1995–1996.

From the perspective of the generals in Islamabad, the Taliban's loyalty to and dependence on them, at least, would guarantee a safer and less volatile western border. In addition, the Pakistanis were interested in secure routes to the landlocked Central Asian states. A stable Taliban-led Afghanistan would contribute to a larger geopolitical strategy wherein Pakistan, the U.S., and international petroleum companies envisioned multiple pipelines transporting oil and natural gas from the mineral-rich Central Asian countries to Pakistani ports on the Persian Gulf. But the strongly independent and unpredictable nature of the Taliban regime, and the continuing war in northern Afghanistan, have over the last two few years dampened the initial excitement that these schemes had generated in Pakistan and elsewhere.

More than a decade after his death in an airplane explosion, Zia ul Haq's ghost lingers on, as Pakistani cultural life shifts toward embracing orthodox Islamic values in both public and private spaces. Further, as the state has forsaken the task of providing systematic educational and employment opportunities to its constituents, the madrassa system has become an avenue for a large percentage of the rural and urban poor seeking social and cultural advancement. The millions trained in the madrassas have emerged as highly organized and violent power brokers who can destabilize any regime that manages to take power. The Pakistani state and military have cynically deployed these forces against internal opposition and recruited them for the state's other covert war, in Kashmir. The price of such manipulation is that, a decade after Zia's death, Pakistan remains today a politically unstable place, rife with growing ethnic and sectarian violence.

The differences between the late 1970s and September 2001 far outweigh the similarities. Musharraf has also been in power for two years, and he is also unpopular domestically and internationally. But Musharraf's military junta may not be able to push its new Afghan policy as easily as the previous dictator did. The same madrassa-trained forces that were nurtured by Zia ul Haq, and used to bolster the rule of governments since he died, could now meet Musharraf with sharp and violent resistance.

Meanwhile, the indices for health and education in Pakistan are among the lowest in the world. Violence and lawlessness are endemic, and most people eke out a living under the official poverty line. Combined with religious militancy and the easy availability of weapons, this puts Pakistan in a socially explosive situation. By accepting the U.S. demands in exchange for fresh promises of international largesse, the Pakistani military may be saving its own skin from the wrath of a U.S.-led coalition. But in the process, the regime once more appears willing to plunge Pakistan into an uncharted future, with no regard for such stability as remains in Pakistani social life.

Among most Pakistanis and Afghanis, the promise of U.S. assistance in exchange for strategic support falls on deaf ears. These people remember a series of broken Western promises, most recently when the U.S. and its allies did not provide much-needed development assistance in the early 1990s. When the Berlin Wall fell, it seems, so did U.S. and Western interest in countries which had done the West's bidding to accelerate the Cold War's demise. One hopes against reason that in its current high-stakes game the Pakistani military does not take the long-suffering populations of Pakistan and Afghanistan on yet another disastrous ride.

SUGGESTION FOR FURTHER READING

Ali, Kamran Asdar
    2002   *Planning the Family in Egypt: New Bodies, New Selves.* Austin: University of Texas Press.

CHAPTER 40

WAR DESTROYED CHECHNYA'S CLAN STRUCTURE

Middle East News Online, January 5, 2002

FRANCESCA
MEREU, *with*
Sergei Arutyunov
and Ian Chesnov

The people of Chechnya, in the Northern Caucus region, have been seeking independence from Russia since the dissolution of the Soviet Union more than a decade ago. In an effort to maintain control over Chechnya, Russia has engaged rebel fighters in a bloody war that has devastated the predominantly Muslim society.

This article by Francesca Mereu appeared two months after Russian president Vladimir Putin announced that the war in Chechnya was also a "war on terrorism." The piece contains a great deal of information about the disintegration of Chechen social structures, which is described by Russian anthropologists Sergei Arutyunov and Ian Chesnov. According to Arutyunov, the destruction of traditional clans, or taips, has increased the influence of Wahhabi leaders advocating an extremely strict form of Islam.

With the world's attention largely focused on the U.S-led military campaign in Afghanistan, Russia's two-year-old war in the breakaway republic of Chechnya—which it defends as a battle against terrorism—continues unabated. The Russian military said on 3 January that it had killed more than 100 rebels in a special operation that ended a week of fierce fighting.

The war—Chechnya's second such conflict with Russia in a decade—has claimed thousands of lives and has irreparably altered the traditional bonds of religion and family structure that shape Chechen society . . .

The Chechens of Russia's North Caucasus region are a tight-knit society based on extended families, or clans, guided by a council of elders. These clans, which traditionally lived together in a single village, are called *taips*. During Stalin's infamous deportation of Chechens to Central Asia, the links remained strong between members of a single taip; and even now, as war and social unrest have forced thousands of Chechens to leave their home villages and scatter throughout the republic or abandon the region altogether, the links continue to endure.

There are more than 150 taips in Chechnya, each with its own traditions and council of elders. Respect for elders is paramount in Chechnya, where a clan's oldest members traditionally have the final say. But in recent years, the elders' absolute authority has given way to an arrangement of making recommendations to the taip that can be, but are not always, followed.

According to Sergei Arutyunov, a member of the Russian Academy of Sciences and the head of the Caucasus department at Moscow's Ethnology Institute:

> [A] clan may have more or less informal elders. These elders may form a kind of council—a clan council—which may give non-obligatory recommendations. [The elders] have no power to enforce these recommendations. But they may give some valid recommendations, which will probably be more or less followed by the majority of clan members.

Ian Chesnov, an anthropology professor at Russia's State Humanitarian University in Moscow, has spent several years in Chechnya studying cultural traits. Chesnov says that according to Caucasus tradition, a member of a taip is never abandoned in time of trouble. To the contrary, a taip acts as a kind of family network that makes sure all members have the support they need.

The taip forms the core of Chechen society—and, many Chechens believe, predetermines the characteristics and personalities of its members. The perceived link between clan and character type is so strong that taips are considered a key aspect of the region's political life as well.

Chechen warlord Salman Raduev, who in late December was sentenced to life in prison for terrorism and murder, is a member of the Gordaloy taip. His crimes, including a 1996 raid on the southern Russian town of Kizlyar in which 78 people were killed, dishonored all the members of the taip—including Chechen president Aslan Maskhadov, whose wife is a member of the Gordaloy taip.

Valery Batuev, a reporter on Caucasus issues for the *Vremya MN*, a Russian daily, says Maskhadov—often criticized for what is seen as an inability to maintain control over rival factions within Chechnya—was unable to arrest or condemn Raduev, since doing so would have meant conflicts within the taip.

Chechnya's taips fall into nine distinct "tukums," or tribes. Legend holds that all Chechens descend from an original family of nine brothers, a belief represented by the Chechen symbol, which depicts a wolf encircled by nine stars. Batuev describes the tukums' function:

> The taips are organized into nine tukums. A tukum is a political-military union meant to function in cases of [outside] threats or aggression. [The tukums] used to unify all the [Chechen] nation and the taips.

A tukum has no leader and is composed of a loose group of clans that share a common ancestry. Batuev says that although in the past tukums were able to organize fighting in case of war, in recent times they have played a role that is more symbolic than military. During Chechnya's two latest military conflicts, the tukums had little influence over events.

Together, Chechnya's two wars with Russia have cut its population by half. Many Chechens have fled their homes to escape the bloody conflict, and many have died—some 50,000 in the 1994–1996 war alone. Before that war, Chechnya's population stood at some 1.2 million. By 1999, estimates had dropped to between 600,000 and 780,000 people. The capital city of Grozny once had 400,000 residents. Now, analysts say, there are fewer than 40,000 people remaining.

Such drastic demographic shifts have inevitably left their mark on Chechnya's tukum and taip structures. According to Arutyunov, the republic is undergoing a severe identity crisis.

Just 10 years ago, he says, Chechnya's younger generations had every reason to expect that their lives would progress much as their parents' had—with marriage, children, and the building of a career. This meant that young people still turned to their fathers or taip elders for advice, and the clan's older generations helped arrange good marriages and interesting, well-paid jobs for the young. But now, Arutyunov says, Chechen society has changed:

> Now, in most cases, the influence of [older] people is lost, and as a rule—except for some very rich and influential people—a father is hardly in a position to arrange a decent and profitable marriage for

his son. He is in no position to put him into any good job. And so the authority, the prestige, the influence of this elder generation is destroyed.

Chechnya's younger people, Arutyunov continues, are disoriented, and are now looking for new authority figures—a search that in many instances leads them to the radical Wahhabi Islamic sect or leaders of criminal rings. The generation gap has gotten so severe, Arutyunov says, that there have been several reported cases of young Chechen men beating their fathers to death. Just a few years ago, this was the strictest taboo in the Chechen social code.

. . . Islam was introduced into Chechnya over a period of centuries, gaining a number of converts by the fifteenth and sixteenth centuries but not taking firm root until well into the eighteenth and mid-nineteenth centuries.

The Chechens were converted to the Sunni branch of Islam, with particular emphasis on its mystic Sufi form. Sufism has come to mean those who are interested in finding a way or practice toward inner awakening and enlightenment . . .

More than 800 mosques and numerous Islamic schools were located in Chechnya at the turn of the twentieth century. But from 1928 to 1941, Soviet dictator Josef Stalin tried to eliminate the country's Islamic traditions. Most mosques were closed, and Muslim clerics and believers in the Chechen and Ingush republics were arrested, deported, or executed—in all, some 14,000 people. Sufi spiritual leaders and believers were labeled "counterrevolutionaries" . . .

In Chechnya and Ingushetia, the control of the organs of Soviet power remained in Russian hands, with no concessions to local authorities, as in other Soviet Muslim republics. Only in 1979 did Soviet authorities allow the opening of a few mosques, to stop the growth of clandestine Sufi brotherhoods. Indeed, the orders themselves organized their own clandestine Arabic classes and schools where the Koran was taught. In Chechnya and Ingushetia, there were 5 legal and 292 clandestine mosques.

When Mikhail Gorbachev's program of economic, political, and social restructuring, or perestroika, began in 1986, it also brought about wage cuts, price hikes, food shortages, and unemployment. The North Caucasus republics were not spared. On the one hand, massive unemployment caused the rise of criminal structures, destabilizing Chechen society. On the other hand, people enjoyed more religious freedom.

. . . Sufi brotherhoods were unable to function in the new conditions. The sheiks were able to exercise their moral authority only in conditions of relative social peace. But from the start of perestroika, that peace was under threat. This situation encouraged the spreading of a fundamentalist movement called Wahhabism.

Said Yakhyev is a Sufi spiritual leader who teaches Islam at Moscow State University. Yakhyev lived in Chechnya during perestroika. He explains how and why this radical Islamic religious movement took easy root in Chechnya:

Wahhabism in Chechnya began to spread in the 1980s in the period of glasnost, when [new] things were allowed. And people who got freedom [for the first time] began to think about a new kind of religion, about new ideas. It was very fashionable at the time. Wahhabism was able to spread in Chechnya because at the time nobody was able to face it and to negate its false dogmas. There was no real religious opposition to it, and now it is the same . . .

The Wahhabis' influence became stronger in Chechnya after the Russian military campaigns in the republic. Many years of war impoverished and destabilized Chechen society, and the Wahhabis used this situation to their advantage . . .

Today, many families have lost everything in the wars. Few can afford to continue the burial tradition. Some families are forced to borrow money for funeral banquets. According to Arutyunov, it is now common for young members of a family to tell people who arrive for a funeral to leave. And these impressionable young people, after listening to Wahhabi leaders, begin to believe that the burial tradition is wrong and in opposition to real Muslim principles. According to the Wahhabis, Islamic law forbids rejoicing or eating at the funeral of a fellow Muslim.

Arutyunov says many young people are beginning to think the Wahhabis teach principles that have more relevance to current life in Chechnya.

It is strongly contrary to [Chechen] customary laws and habits, but many people will listen and say, "This guy [a Wahhabi leader] is right." He has reasons to talk so. Indeed, the custom is bad, because fulfilling the custom means to ruin his family.

In 1999, correspondent Oleg Kusov interviewed young people in Gudermes, the second-largest town in Chechnya. They told him they would follow the Wahhabi principles because the Wahhabis gave them $100 a month—a large amount of money the traditional Sufi orders are unlikely to be able to pay.

. . . The differences between the Wahhabi followers and the Sufi can best be understood in their differing concepts of the jihad:

> Wahhabis follow the old concept of jihad, meaning the holy war to convert the infidels. The Sufis have another interpretation of jihad. They see it not as a war against the infidels, but as a war that a Muslim has to fight against his own defects to try to reach perfection.

The Russian military refers to Chechen field commanders as Wahhabis. But Anna Politkovskaya, a journalist with *Novaya Gazeta* who has covered the Russian-Chechen conflict, contends that this is a mistake.

According to Politkovskaya, Chechen field commanders loyal to Chechen leader Aslan Maskhadov defend Chechen national traditions and oppose fundamentalist groups like the Wahhabis, since they believe they will destabilize Chechen national unity. Another group, according to Politkovskaya, consists of those who surround field commanders like Shamil Basaev and Khattab. This group seeks an Arab-style Islamization of Chechnya.

The Sufi brotherhoods try to keep their distance from the conflict. With no end to the war in sight, many believers and spiritual leaders have left Chechnya for neighboring Ingushetia or Russia . . .

SUGGESTIONS FOR FURTHER READING

Holloman, Regina E., and S. Arutyunov, eds.
    1978   *Perspectives on Ethnicity.* The Hague: Mouton.
Wehling, Fred, and S. Arutyunov, eds.
    1995   *Ethnic Conflict and Russian Intervention in the Caucasus.* La Jolla: University of California, San Diego Institute on Conflict and Cooperation.

PART VI

EXAMINING MILITARISM AND THE "WAR ON TERROR"

CHAPTER 41

U.S. ANTI-TERRORIST MESSAGE WON'T FLY IN ISLAMIC WORLD

Pacific News Service, October 11, 2001
www.pacificnews.org

WILLIAM O.
BEEMAN

Many anthropologists use historical analysis to help understand contemporary human cultures and societies. In this article, William O. Beeman explains that for many people in the Islamic world—particularly in the Middle East—the "war on terror" declared by George W. Bush in the days following the September 11 attacks may appear continuous with centuries of colonial domination at the hands of British, French, Russian, and American empires.

President George W. Bush has stated that the United States is fighting terrorism—not Islam—in its military response to the September 11 attacks. But Muslims throughout the world dismiss this admirable notion, perceiving America's deeds to be at odds with its words. They say the United States is continuing a familiar pattern of exploitation by Western nations in the Middle East.

The colonial powers of Europe—Great Britain, France, and Russia—began their exploitation of the Islamic world shortly after the establishment of the industrial revolution in the eighteenth and nineteenth centuries. Before that time, Middle Eastern nations had an arguably superior civilization to that of Europe. But the industrializing Europeans suddenly leapfrogged over the rest of the world with superior transportation, military power, and economic institutions. They made incursions into the Islamic world, gobbling up territory and bankrupting traditional manufacturing, such as textiles. With faster ships and advanced financial institutions, they bypassed Middle Eastern middlemen in trading with East and Southeast Asia.

The Middle Eastern rulers were desperate for cash to modernize their nations. They therefore entered into a devil's bargain with Europeans, selling "concessions" to the agricultural, mineral, financial, and transportation rights of their nations. The rulers were enriched in these deals, and so were the Europeans.

However, the people of these countries lost their patrimony.

This touched off two great Islamic anticolonial movements. One was led by Jamal al-Din al-Afghani, an Iranian, who preached Islamic reform and resistance to colonial powers in the late-nineteenth century. The other movement was led by the Jadidists—intellectuals in Tataristan, a Turkic region in southern Russia, who encouraged the peoples of the Caucasus and Central Asia to break away from Europe and establish their own national identities.

The Islamic resistance did not stop the Europeans from pursuing military and economic dominance in the Middle East until the end of World War II. Adding insult to injury was a perceived contempt on the part of Europeans for Middle Eastern civilization.

Following World War II, a series of coups and revolutions brought nationalist governments to the fore throughout the region. The Islamic resistance had begun. The West reacted by identifying compliant rulers with a talent for autocratic rule and propping them up with guns and financial support. This seemed to perpetuate the nineteenth century pattern of alliance between Europeans and corrupt local rulers with the aim of exploiting local people.

After 1972 Great Britain withdrew entirely from the region, and the United States, fearful of Soviet influence, stepped up its presence with military, political, and economic support for local rulers in Iran, Egypt, Saudi Arabia, and Kuwait, among others.

Now in America's fight against terrorism, its principal partners are again Great Britain and Russia. People in the Islamic world look at this current alliance and immediately see the same nineteenth-century actors carrying out the same pattern of damaging behavior. Even the current rulers of the region realize this, and have backpedaled and equivocated to avoid appearing to be pawns of the United States. No matter how much President Bush protests that we are not attacking Islam, his credibility in the Middle East is zero.

To make the American message believable, Washington must at least acknowledge the unfortunate historic pattern of colonialist exploitation, with which it has become linked, and make a plausible declaration of a break with the past. The people of the region would greet an appeal for a new era in U.S.-Middle East relations with understandable skepticism at first. However, if America followed these words with credible deeds—such as full internationalization of military forces in the Gulf region, and provision of strong leadership to solve the dilemma of Israeli-Palestinian relations—President Bush might be able to persuade the Islamic world to believe his sentiments.

SUGGESTION FOR FURTHER READING

Beeman, William O.
　1986　*Language, Status, and Power in Iran.* Bloomington: University of Indiana Press.

CHAPTER 42

TERROR AND INDIGENOUS PEOPLES: WAR WITHOUT END

CounterPunch, November 3, 2001
www.counterpunch.org

DAVID PRICE   After George W. Bush declared a vaguely defined "war on terrorism," he immediately began seeking new international allies. Russia, China, and Israel quickly adopted the language of antiterrorism to condemn the self-determination struggles of the Chechens, Uighurs, and Palestinians, respectively—all groups that have legitimate territorial disputes with the nation-states that rule them.

In this selection David Price warns that some nation-states could use the war on terrorism as a pretext to initiate or intensify the repression of indigenous people and ethnic and religious minorities around the world.

When President Bush declared war on terrorism with his neo-McCarthyistic threat to the world that "you are either with us or with the terrorists," he struck a chord with many frightened Americans, but other peoples around the world heard other important harmonics within this chord. For many of the world's indigenous peoples, these words brought terror and anticipation of new levels of outright oppression from the nation-states that repressively surround and manage them.

In the time since this declaration, the president has not clarified who these new terrorist enemies are, and the administration and its allies have since carefully avoided defining just who is and who isn't a terrorist—beyond this initial defining claim that they are those who are against "us." The administration understands that any behavioral definition of terrorism risks exposing the nonsense of behaviorally distinguishing between such categories of actors as terrorists, freedom fighters, and military forces. The relativist adage that the difference between a terrorist and a freedom fighter depends on who owns the newspaper that reports on their actions, seems to be forgotten by many on the American left who watched Washington play roughshod with the self-determination of peoples of Central America in the 1980s. While a few pundits note the dangers of engaging in a war without any identifiable landmark of victory, there are equally real dangers to many minority populations around the world if the governments managing their native lands are given the green light to repress them as "terrorists."

As the United Nations supports new antiterrorist policies, we find new levels of cooperation and agreement among member nations, though these talks occur with an explicit agreement that terrorism shall remain undefined. Concerns are being raised by international human rights groups and the German foreign minister that these policies will usher in high levels of state terrorism against minority populations, but for the most part these objections have been suppressed in the interest of a newfound unity of purpose.

There are growing fears among anthropologists and others who work with indigenous peoples around the world that this new secret war on terrorism will have devastating effects on indigenous peoples' struggles for human rights and political recognition. Many fear that Secretary of State Powell, the coalition builder, will purchase the cooperation and approval of national leaders around the world by adopting policies in which the United States will not protest or intervene when these states suppress and annihilate their own ethnic minority populations. When police and military units use force against these groups, their actions are "legitimate," while the use of these same tactics—even defensively—by indigenous groups, minority populations or separatist groups, become "terrorism."

As Powell signals Russia that the U.S. can learn to see their bloody war in Chechnya as part of the global war on terrorism, this signal is welcomed by other world leaders wishing a free hand to deal with their own domestic indigenous troubles. Most of the world's nation-states maintain hostile relations with one or more troublesome domestic groups contesting power relations; these hostile relations are frequently marked by violence and counterviolence. The idiom of power dictates that the violence of the state is legitimized as peace keeping, while that of the dispossessed becomes terrorism. But acts of "terrorism" are not limited to acts of violence. The range of nonviolent actions that have in the past been defined as terrorism is disturbing and has included teaching native languages and engaging in outlawed religious or cultural ceremonies.

The world is filled with peoples who have legitimate, historical disputes with the nation-states that rule them. Whether it is the Basques in Spain, the Irish in the United Kingdom, the Tamils in Sri Lanka, Zapatistas in Mexico, Chechens in Russia, or hundreds of other groups of native peoples, there are contentious battles for power that will rapidly become even more lopsided if the current hysteria of ill-defined antiterrorism is allowed to continue. The postcolonial wars of Africa smolder along ethnic lines in which minorities and the lesser-armed are freely defined as terrorists. We need to demand that our government clarify what deals have been made with other governments regarding their treatment of native peoples.

While many of the payoffs to client nations for joining the U.S.-led coalition before the [1991] Gulf War were monetary (for example, the U.S. forgave half of Egypt's crippling $60 billion dollar debt for symbolically joining the Western coalition), there are signs that one currency of payoff in the war on "terrorism" will be the granting of a new degree of latitude for coalition members to oppress their troublesome internal resistance groups. Powell seems willing to encourage such potentially genocidal tit-for-tat arrangements if this will buy him a coalition willing to risk the wrath of this new yet-to-be-named enemy.

While the current military focus is on Afghanistan and the surrounding region, the Bush administration's suggestion that this could be a 40-year war on terrorism, much like the Cold War, threatens to bring harm to hundreds of indigenous groups around the world. Currently, many on the American left appear divided in their opposition to and support for this new Afghan war. Be this as it may, the left must resist the temptation to transfer this newfound fear of "terrorism" into support for the oppression of indigenous peoples around the globe.

SUGGESTIONS FOR FURTHER READING

Price, David
    2002   "Past Wars, Present Dangers, Future Anthropologies." *Anthropology Today* 18, no. 1: 3–6.
Sluka, Jeffrey A. (ed.)
    2000   *Death Squad: The Anthropology of State Terror.* Philadelphia: University of Pennsylvania Press.

CHAPTER 43

AFGHAN WAR COULD BE RECRUITING TOOL FOR TERRORISTS

Syracuse Post-Standard, November 8, 2001

JOHN
BURDICK

This piece, written by John Burdick in the weeks fol- lowing the U.S. air attacks over Afghanistan, sounds a warning call. He argues that if the Afghan conflict re- sults in civilian casualties and exacerbates humanitarian crises, it could help extremists find new recruits among those suffering the consequences of war. The same might be said of the broader international "war on terror" spear- headed by the United States.

Although the demise of the Taliban occurred relatively rapidly (by No- vember 2001 they had abandoned all major Afghan cities), U.S. bombing over targets in Afghanistan—and the resulting civilian casualties—continues as this book goes to press, and political instability bordering on lawlessness plagues much of the country's territory.[1]

When I watch the news of U.S. military action in Afghanistan, my biggest question is: How does this action make the world safer for my two elementary-school-aged children?

Unfortunately, the more I learn about the situation, the more I be- lieve that attacking Afghanistan is making the world a more, not less, dangerous place, and making terrorist attacks more, not less, likely on U.S. citizens here and abroad.

When I listen carefully to our leaders, the message I hear is that this military action cannot really reduce the power of al-Qaeda itself. They have told us that we are dealing with a loose network of cells with operatives in up to 60 countries who can work independently from multiple locations, and that even as communications are cut from Af- ghanistan, threats to U.S. citizens are so real and constant that we must learn to live with them "indefinitely." Our own secretary of defense has said the aim is no longer to get Osama bin Laden, and that he doubts we will ever catch him. We are dealing with a multiple-headed Hydra—hit it in one place and it pops up in another.

Meanwhile, the longer it takes to overthrow the Taliban, the more dangerous this military strategy becomes. Our leaders are telling us that replacing the Taliban may take a very long time indeed. If the fight is going to be long, that means civilian casualties will mount, and the likelihood of many Afghans dying from starvation increases. As the war drags on, more and more people throughout the world are likely to become convinced that this is a war against Muslims. They will respond as they already are doing, by entering a jihad against the United States.

I have read reports that there are thousands of Muslims congregating on the border with Afghanistan, ready to fight the United States; thousands more are signing up in countries like Indonesia, the largest Muslim nation in the world.

The U.S. response so far has simply been to threaten yet more military action, against yet more countries. Do we intend to threaten, simultaneously, up to 60 countries with military action? Even though all the evidence we have is that there is no quicker way to shore up shaky authoritarian regimes than by attacking them—as we have learned in Iraq and Libya, for example? And as civilians die in any such attacks, that the United States is only increasing the will of others to fight against us, expanding the pool of people throughout the world who are so enraged that they line up to enter into terrorist cells?

Our leaders tell us that one of the most important ways to combat terrorism is to "dry up the swamp" in which they operate. That makes sense to me. But that must mean more than cutting off their financial lifelines. It should mean draining the motivations from the people who are now ready and willing to march as recruits in their shadowy armies.

There is a realistic alternative to the present policy. Before October 7, the United States was leading a broad-based effort to form an international coalition that could endure the test of time. Never before had the United States enjoyed so much international sympathy—a sentiment fast disappearing as bombs fall on Kabul. With that sympathy, the United States had already won two unprecedented victories: the withdrawal of many millions of dollars in aid to the Taliban from Saudi Arabia and Pakistan. By freezing bin Laden's assets and gaining high-quality intelligence from nearby countries, we would have denied the Taliban their main incentive for protecting bin Laden: millions in protection money.

By launching a campaign of words that separated bin Laden as Saudi from the Afghan people, that separated him as a fanatic from peace-loving Muslims everywhere, we could have "drained the swamp" of his supporters and demonstrated to the world that pluralistic democracy, not fundamentalism, enjoys the moral high ground in the world. Backed by a genuine, strong coalition to provide intelligence and cooperation on cutting off aid from the Taliban, and turning to the United Nations for the possible enforcement of international law, we could have pressured the Taliban to turn over bin Laden.

Of course, such a policy would have been slow. But our leaders have urged us to be patient. I take them at their word. If we can be patient while thousands of people are being killed and dying, we certainly can be patient while they are not. If we can be patient while the world is becoming a more dangerous place for ourselves and our children, certainly we can be patient while they are not.

EDITOR'S NOTE

1. See Dexter Filkins, "Flaws in U.S. Air War Left Hundreds of Civilians Dead," *New York Times*, July 21, 2002. See also Robert Fisk, "Afghanistan Is on the Brink of Another Disaster," *The Independent*, August 14, 2002.

CHAPTER 44

FIRST, KNOW THE ENEMY, THEN ACT

Los Angeles Times, December 9, 2001

DALE F.
EICKELMAN

Following the attacks of September 11, the mass media, U.S. policy makers, and others began to focus on a possible culprit: a decentralized international network known as Al Qaeda, with roots in Afghanistan among the multinational force of mujahedeen fighters once supported by the CIA. In this article, Dale F. Eickelman argues against the "fundamentalist" stereotypes often associated with terrorist attacks against U.S. targets. He maintains that Al Qaeda is thoroughly modern and makes effective use of new media to communicate with millions of people across the Middle East and beyond.

Eickelman concludes with a point emphasized in many of the commentaries in this volume—that the best long-term counterterrorism strategy for the United States would involve encouraging Middle Eastern countries to respond to their populations' demands for political self-determination.

In retrospect, the December 2000 report of the U.S. National Intelligence Council, *Global Trends 2015,* was chillingly prescient. It predicted that "terrorist tactics will become increasingly sophisticated and designed to achieve mass casualties." At the same time, it envisioned a trend away from state-supported political terrorism and toward "more diverse, free-wheeling, transnational networks—enabled by information technology." It forecast attacks "on U.S. soil."

Now that those attacks have come, America will have to devise strategies to cope with terrorism—as have, to greater and lesser effect, England, Northern Ireland, France, Spain, Colombia, Peru, Sri Lanka, Japan, Algeria, Turkey, and Israel.

As each of those countries has come to realize, the first step is to know one's enemy. Al Qaeda differs from other terrorist movements in selecting targets on a global rather than a regional or local scale and in using tactics that initially defied the imaginations of the most experienced counterterrorist specialists. Al Qaeda is also thoroughly modern, representing the dark side of globalization. Its membership transcends national boundaries, drawing from Muslim countries throughout the Middle East and South Asia.

In a strange irony, the group's multinational makeup has its roots in the U.S. and Saudi-approved recruitment of transnational Arab and other foreign fighters to the cause of expelling the Soviets from Afghanistan after they invaded in 1979. Al Qaeda, whose leadership includes many first drawn to Afghanistan in support of the anti-Soviet cause, has developed into a flexible multinational organization. Despite determined international surveillance, it has moved cash, people, and weapons across frontiers.

Like the drug lords of Colombia in the 1980s, Al Qaeda is defensively organized. Its chain of command is not formal and hierarchical, so it is less open to destruction and interdiction. The Colombian drug lords offered *plata o plomo*—silver or lead, a bribe or a bullet—to induce cooperation or acquiescence. Al Qaeda, claiming to act in the name of Islam, pays out less than the drug barons because it makes stronger ideological claims. Its message may appeal only to a tiny minority, but, for that minority, Al Qaeda's ideological appeals, calls to action, and track record are convincing.

In part, the group's success can be traced to its ability to effectively use the tools of the pop culture it rejects. An Al Qaeda recruitment video that circulated widely in the Middle East prior to September 11 demonstrated that the group's propaganda skills reached the "Arab street"—its target audience—more effectively than the Western superpowers or many Arab governments. The video begins with the attack on the USS *Cole*. It then moves to a quick-cut montage of aggression against Muslims in Palestine, Jerusalem, Lebanon, Chechnya, Kashmir, and Indonesia. Many of the images are from Western news clips that still bear the BBC or CNN logos. The scenes are juxtaposed with images of a scholarly bin Laden, posing in front of bookshelves or seated on the ground like a religious scholar. Then, putting to rest any thought that this is an organization of wimps, come clips of Al Qaeda military training in Afghanistan, including target practice on a projected image of Bill Clinton.

So, knowing the enemy, how do we devise strategies for managing the risk of living in a world with Al Qaeda? The war against terrorism has already brought short-term abridgements of human rights and political liberties, both domestically and internationally—especially in Central Asia and the Middle East. But these are not long-term solutions to reducing the threat posed by Al Qaeda and like-minded groups and may even be counterproductive.

Addressing underlying issues of poverty, unemployment, and global economic imbalances—however desirable—is also not sufficient. Poverty and unemployment do not in themselves breed terrorism. Many of the most dedicated terrorists and advocates of extreme violence are affluent professionals or scions of the middle class. And some members of Al Qaeda's top leadership—including bin Laden and his Egyptian colleague, medical doctor Ayman Zawahiri—come from the wealthiest stratum of society.

Yet, they have grasped what the U.S. and its allies have not: how to appeal to disaffected elements of the Arab street, an increasingly educated public that today has access to a wide range of uncensored media and information that creates a desire for accountability from governments. In villages and small towns in Egypt and Iraq in the late 1960s, I frequently saw men at coffee shops or seated in circles, with one of the few literates reading aloud to the others. In Morocco in the early 1970s, rural people sometimes asked me to "translate" newscasts from the standard transnational Arabic of the state radio into their colloquial Arabic. Today this is no longer required. Mass education and new communications technologies enable large numbers of Arabs to hear and see Al Qaeda's message directly.

The growth—and challenge—of this new public was widely recognized in U.S. policy circles well before September 11. In testimony before the Senate Select Committee on Intelligence in February 2001, CIA Director George J. Tenet cited the Arab street, in explaining that "the right catalyst—such as the outbreak of Israeli-Palestinian violence—can move people to act. Through access to the Internet and other means of communication, a restive public is increasingly capable of taking action without any identifiable leadership or organizational structure."

Because many governments in the Middle East are deeply suspicious of an open press, nongovernmental organizations, and open expression, it is no surprise that the public is increasingly influenced by the often extreme and hard-to-censor "new media." Leadership can remain anonymous, an advantage in the Middle East, which, in general, has a democracy deficit and a demonstrated propensity for cracking down on critics.

One consequence of this democracy deficit is to magnify the power of the street in the Arab world. Bin Laden speaks in the vivid language of popular Islamic preachers and builds on a deep and widespread resentment against the West and local ruling elites identified with it. The lack of formal outlets to express diverse political opinions makes it easier for terrorists like bin Laden, who cloaks himself in religion, to hijack some in his audience and motivate a lethal few to action.

We must accept that there will always be ideas available to justify intolerance and violence, and there will also always be ways for terrorists to manipulate open societies for their own nefarious ends. Countering radical ideologies and theologies of violence is not easy. Yet, the very proliferation of voices arguing in open debate about the role of Islam in the modern world and in contemporary society can contribute significantly to defusing terrorist appeals to the street. Public opinion is easier to hijack in the absence of full debate. Without public discussion, ideas are reduced to their simplest and starkest terms. That is why British prime minister Tony Blair's response to Al Qaeda videotaped propaganda on Qatar's Al Jazeera satellite TV last October—he immediately asked Al Jazeera for equal time to reply—was more appropriate than the first U.S. response, which was to call for censoring the broadcast of Al Qaeda tapes.

The best long-term way to mitigate the continuing threat of terrorism is to encourage Middle Eastern states to be more responsive to their populations' demands for participation. Some countries, including some of our allies, see such "open society" activities as subversive—as Egypt demonstrated in May when a security court sentenced civil rights activist Saad Eddin Ibrahim to seven years of hard labor for criticizing the regime and calling into question the fairness of recent elections.

It is no easy job to convince Arab states that it is in their interest to create open societies. But they must recognize that increasing levels of education, greater ease of travel, and the rise of new communications media are turning the Arab street into a public sphere in which large numbers of people—and not just a political and economic elite—want a say in governance and public issues. Some countries, like Morocco, have been moving steadily in that direction. The terrorist option has no appeal to Moroccans. They have a greater stake in their society. The example of neighboring Algeria offers Moroccans a harrowing example of the alternative, and the Moroccan street speaks of it often.

There are liberal as well as illiberal voices in the Middle East and multiple contenders for the guardianship and interpretation of Islamic beliefs and values. Giving larger numbers of people a greater stake in decision-making in their societies and the opportunity to express their views will undermine the appeal of the terrorist alternative—and diminish its appeal to the street.

CHAPTER 45

SEPT. 11 EXPOSES FUTILE SEARCH FOR "PERFECT" MISSILE DEFENSE

Syracuse Post-Standard, December 18, 2001

JOHN
BURDICK

In this article, John Burdick exposes the folly of George W. Bush's abandonment of the international Anti-Ballistic Missile Treaty in order to pursue the development of a missile defense shield. He reminds us that the events of September 11 demonstrate that low-tech weapons may be deployed with devastating effects, and that the creation of a missile defense program would only encourage China, India, and Pakistan to build up their nuclear stockpiles.

When placed in the context of Bush's opposition to the Comprehensive Test Ban Treaty (see Chapter 21) and the "Nuclear Posture Review" recently prepared by the Bush administration, which recommends research and possible development of "mini-nukes," Burdick's message is all the more urgent.

President George Bush's declaration that the United States will withdraw from the Anti-Ballistic Missile Treaty in six months' time is a grave mistake that will have very negative, unanticipated consequences. The president says the United States needs a free hand to develop its missile-defense shield. Many Americans see the attacks of September 11 as justifying missile defense more than ever. Upon more careful consideration, however, I hope they will realize that going ahead with missile defense is wrong.

Is it possible to build an impenetrable missile-defense shield? Some think we could pull it off. After all, if we split the atom and put a man on the moon, why shouldn't we be able to create a system that will distinguish, in a split second, dummy from real missiles thousands of miles away, target them with pinpoint accuracy and destroy them? Maybe we can. The problem is that the task is not just to create a system that can do this, but that can do it flawlessly.

In the history of inventions, there has never been the need to create

a perfect system. Putting men on the moon, even splitting atoms, are accomplishments that allow for margins of error. If a moon-ship lands 10 feet off of the bull's-eye, or atoms in an atom-smasher escape being smashed, no cities are thereby incinerated. Never before have scientists and engineers been asked to create a system in which a tiny imperfection could result in the deaths of millions.

So heavy is this weight that last year, 50 Nobel prize-winning physicists from around the world signed a letter to the president stating their judgment that a perfect shield could not be built, and that therefore no such system should be pursued. Even Secretary of Defense Donald Rumsfeld agrees a perfect system cannot be built; but his conclusion is that "even an imperfect shield can serve as a deterrent."

But is it? Why, in the end, would countries with nuclear capabilities be deterred from shooting an ICBM at us? Quite simply, because of our capacity to retaliate immediately with overwhelming force to easily traced missile launch pads. Some countries might be headed up by madmen willing to sacrifice their people for the joy of seeing a mushroom cloud over the United States. But one cannot have it both ways. If we are dealing with madmen, then why should we expect an imperfect shield would deter them? If we accept that they may be deterred at all, then we should simply rely on the strongest kind of deterrence—the threat of retaliation. That is, we should rely on the basic principles of the ABM Treaty, as we have for the last 30 years.

Now it is said the real threat may in fact no longer be "rogue" states; it is, rather, groups such as al-Qaeda. If Osama bin Laden and his followers were willing to kill thousands, wouldn't they be willing to kill millions? Certainly. But being willing and being able are entirely different things. Terrorists cannot launch intercontinental missiles; they wreak havoc with low-cost attacks, such as flying airplanes into buildings or releasing biological or "dirty radiation" bombs. The attacks of September 11 have demonstrated that the United States was looking in the wrong place for what threatens us. Low-tech, nonnuclear attacks are the most clear and present danger facing the United States, not nuclear-tipped rockets.

Missile defense could be chalked up as simple misallocation of funds, were not its international consequences so grave. China has already stated that if we start building a defense shield, it will increase its nuclear arsenal in order to overwhelm it. If China does this, India and then Pakistan will feel pressured to follow suit. Russia, in turn, has stated that, faced with the new U.S. policy, it will stop reducing, and may increase its own nuclear arsenal.

In such a world, no country will have an incentive to invest resources in nonproliferation of nuclear materials, making the likelihood of these materials ending up in the hands of terrorists (in the form of "dirty bombs" deliverable in the back of pickup trucks) all the more likely.

A world in which the United States has withdrawn from the ABM Treaty is thus inherently a more dangerous world. It is more urgent than ever that Bush reconsider his stand that the treaty is a relic of the past. It just may be the safeguard of the future.

CHAPTER 46

IGNORANCE IS NOT BLISS

San Francisco Chronicle, January 2, 2002

ROBERTO J. Throughout the U.S. military campaign in Afghani-
GONZÁLEZ stan (which began in October 2001), the mainstream
media in the United States effectively ignored the
question of civilian casualties—euphemistically called "collateral damage"
by Pentagon and Defense Department officials. As in the case of the [1991]
Persian Gulf War, the Pentagon maintained strict control over access to
battle zones and asked reporters to submit materials for review. But by
December 2001, credible reports of high numbers of civilian casualties began
to appear in the alternative and European media.[1]

In this article, Roberto J. González draws attention to the issue of civilian
casualties and the complacent role played by the corporate media cartel. His
piece was published following a U.S. air attack over a village in Afghanistan's
Paktia province, in which approximately fifty civilians were killed.

Since the publication of this article, U.S. attacks on civilians have continued, including most recently a July 2002 bombing raid on a wedding party
in the village of Kakrak, in which more than fifty people were killed.

For the past three months, Pentagon officials have veiled an essential aspect of the "war on terrorism": civilian casualties in Afghanistan. Blocking access to information about the human costs of U.S.
bombing—and its consequences—might create a dangerous future for
Americans.

Such restrictions keep us from understanding how the rest of the
world views the war, and why it might provoke future attacks on the
United States. They may also breed complacency, ignorance, and national insecurity.

Measures taken by military officials obscure information about the
effects of U.S. bombing.

For example, since October 11, the Pentagon has purchased exclusive rights to all satellite images from Space Imaging, a U.S. company that produces accurate pictures that might allow independent media to survey bomb damage.

In addition, U.S. bombs destroyed Al-Jazeera's television station in Kabul in October. The Qatar-based independent network reaches much of the Arab world and frequently broadcasts images from Afghanistan.

Official acknowledgment of civilian deaths has been minimal.

Descriptions of heavily bombed frontline positions never mention that they sometimes traverse densely populated neighborhoods. Frequently, officials claim that civilian deaths "cannot be independently confirmed."

Yet, according to a recent report by Professor Marc Herold, an economist at the University of New Hampshire, the number of Afghan civilians killed by American bombs has surpassed casualties from September 11.

Herold's report—the first independent survey of its kind—claims that 3,767 civilian deaths were caused by U.S. bombing between October 7 and December 10. Not included are indirect deaths caused by land mines or lack of water, food, or medicine.

The data, drawn from independent news sources and firsthand accounts, include: dates, locations, types of munitions used, and sources. Much of it is based upon mainstream British, French, and Indian press agencies such as the BBC and the *India Times*.

While respected news agencies abroad have reviewed Herold's report, the American media have largely ignored it. Only a few journals and Internet sites and the radio program *Democracy Now!* have analyzed it.

Why have the U.S. media missed the story?

Part of the explanation may be related to the industry itself. Recent mergers between media corporations have homogenized news, especially television news. AOL/Time Warner, Viacom, News Corporation, Disney, and GE own CNN, CBS News, Fox News, ABC News and NBC, respectively.

Many Americans rely exclusively upon this cartel for information on the "war on terrorism," which is presented more as entertainment than news.

Broadcasts include repetitive accounts of the search for Osama bin Laden, trivia about weapons, war images that resemble video games, and footage of cheerful Afghans trimming their beards and playing music.

These pictures are punctuated by angry pundits and politicians who reduce complex events to simplified formulas ("good versus evil") using language reminiscent of Hollywood Westerns ("dead or alive").

Whether such misinformation stems from Pentagon pressure, fear of offending advertisers, or shabby journalism is largely irrelevant. The effect is the same: Warfare is presented as light entertainment.

While American viewers remain oblivious, Europeans, Asians, and others have access to information about the catastrophic effects of U.S. bombing. They have seen images of dead and wounded civilians and the many widows, widowers, and orphans created by Operation Enduring Freedom.

Many are convinced that this is a U.S. crusade against Islam, and with each passing week, violent "blowback"—the CIA's term for unintended foreign policy consequences—appears more likely.

Ignorance may be dangerous in the current climate.

Murky official statements and a distracted mass media deny us information which might help prevent future attacks.

George Orwell once noted that in free societies, censorship is more sophisticated and thorough than in dictatorships because "unpopular ideas can be silenced, and inconvenient facts kept dark, without any need for an official ban."

But keeping Americans in the dark about inconvenient facts in Afghanistan is reckless at best, and potentially dangerous.

Civilian deaths should be openly acknowledged by the Pentagon and reported by the mass media if we wish to minimize the possibility of future attacks on American soil.

EDITOR'S NOTE

1. See "Afghan Civilian Death Toll Rises," *Financial Times,* December 24, 2001. See also Seumas Milne, "The Innocent Dead in a Coward's War," *The Guardian,* December 20, 2001.

SUGGESTION FOR FURTHER READING

Herman, Edward S., and Noam Chomsky
    1988   *Manufacturing Consent: The Political Economy of the Mass Media.*
        New York: Pantheon.

CHAPTER 47

**TURN OFF YOUR
TUNNEL VISION**

Washington Post, January 6, 2002

MAHMOOD
MAMDANI

By the beginning of 2002, the U.S. "war on terror"
had expanded to many countries, including the Philippines, Georgia, Afghanistan, Pakistan, Yemen, and
Somalia, among others. Professor Mahmood Mamdani cautions that an
overly zealous search for Al Qaeda members could negatively affect U.S.-
African relations if it leads to repression or state terrorism directed against
Africans. He recalls the "American embrace of terrorism" in Angola, Mozambique, and other countries throughout the Cold War, and U.S. complacency
in the years following.

The Pentagon's search for al Qaeda members in Somalia is the latest
indication that September 11 could have an adverse effect on U.S. relations with African nations. To understand why, think back to 1975,
when the United States was defeated in Indochina and the Portuguese
empire collapsed in Africa. The same events that Africans celebrated as
ushering in the end of European colonialism opened a new phase in the
Cold War: There was a shift, not only in the Cold War's center of gravity
from Indochina to southern Africa, but also in the methods of waging it.
Official America harnessed, even cultivated, terrorism in the struggle
against movements it saw as Soviet proxies. Yes, I do mean "terrorism,"
which Washington supports when it backs groups for whom the preferred method of operation is destroying the infrastructure of civilian
life.

The post-Vietnam embrace of terrorism did not end with the Cold
War. Right up until September 11, America counseled African governments to "reconcile" with terrorist groups. Since then, that has given
way to a demand for justice. But just as reconciliation became a code
word for impunity, the danger now is that "justice" will mean bloody
revenge.

Reconciliation became a strategy to undermine newly won state independence; the campaign against terrorism risks demonizing dissent.

I was a young lecturer at the University of Dar-es-Salaam in Tanzania in 1975, and I remember well the U.S. approach to southern Africa then and in the years that followed. Faced with the possibility of a decisive victory in Angola by the MPLA, the Popular Movement for the Liberation of Angola, which it saw as a Soviet proxy, Washington encouraged South Africa to intervene militarily in support of UNITA, the National Union for the Total Independence of Angola. But South African military assistance only tarnished UNITA with the brush of apartheid and weakened it. Preoccupied with how to bring South Africa out of political isolation to contain movements such as the MPLA, the Reagan administration announced a major policy shift: "constructive engagement" with the apartheid regime.

The American embrace of terrorism was global—in Angola; in Mozambique, where it supported RENAMO, the Mozambique National Resistance; in Nicaragua (the contras); and in Afghanistan (the mujahedeen). Terrorism distinguished itself from guerrilla war by making civilians its preferred target. What official America today calls collateral damage was not an unfortunate byproduct of war; it was the very point of terrorism. And the point of collateral damage was never military, always political.

When South Africa curtailed assistance to UNITA in 1991, U.S. aid was stepped up. The hope was that terrorism would deliver a political victory in Angola, as it had indeed in Nicaragua. The logic was simple: If the level of collateral damage could be made unacceptably high, the people would surely vote the terrorists into power.

Even after the Cold War, the tolerance for terror remained high. The callous Western response to the 1994 genocide in Rwanda was no exception. Nor was January 6, 1999, when Revolutionary United Front gunmen maimed and raped their way across Freetown, Sierra Leone, killing more than 5,000 civilians in a day. The U.S. response was to pressure the government to share power with the rebels.

If the Cold War was an umbrella under which America sheltered right-wing dictators in power and embraced terrorists out of power, the danger is now the temptation to view Africa while preoccupied with a single overriding concern—this time terrorism—and to once again ignore African realities.

SUGGESTIONS FOR FURTHER READING

Mamdani, Mahmood
  1996   *Citizen and Subject: Contemporary Africa and the Legacy of Late Colonialism.* Princeton: Princeton University Press.
  2001   *When Victims Become Killers: Colonialism, Nativism, and the Genocide in Rwanda.* Princeton: Princeton University Press.
Mamdani, Mahmood, ed.
  2000   *Beyond Culture Talk and Rights Talk: Comparative Essays on the Politics of Rights and Culture.* New York: St. Martin's Press.

CHAPTER 48

THE ROOTS OF
MUSLIM SEPARATISM
IN THE PHILIPPINES

AsiaSource, January 2002
www.asiasource.org

THOMAS
MCKENNA,
interviewed by
Nermeen Shaikh

In January 2001, the United States announced that it would send six hundred military "advisers" to help train Philippine troops for battle with armed Muslim separatists on the southern island of Mindanao. Critics immediately charged that the "war on terror" might take the form of an American-led worldwide crackdown on separatists challenging the hegemony of U.S. allies, no matter how corrupt or repressive they might be. In the following interview, Thomas McKenna discusses the history of Muslim separatism in the Philippines and also analyzes the effects of Spanish and American colonialism on Muslim identity.

NERMEEN SHAIKH: The South of the Philippines, where the minority Muslim population is concentrated, managed to evade Spanish colonialism for 300 years. Could you please explain the significance of this, if any, for Muslim-Christian relations in the postcolonial context?

THOMAS MCKENNA: Because of their evasion of Spanish colonialism, Philippine Muslims comprise the largest category of unhispanicized inhabitants of the Philippines. Although they live in the only predominately Christian country in Southeast Asia, they share their religious culture with the neighboring majority Muslim nations of Indonesia and Malaysia. They also retain aspects of an indigenous pre-Islamic and precolonial Philippine culture— expressed in dress, music, political traditions, and a variety of folk beliefs and practices—that are similar to those found elsewhere in island Southeast Asia but are today almost entirely absent among Christian Filipinos. Thus, while Philippine Christians and Muslims inhabit the same state and are linked together by various attachments, they are separated by a significant cultural gulf as the result of historical circumstances. I argue in my book that cultural differences do not by themselves create ethnic conflict. However, Christian Filipinos, including representatives of the Philippine state, have often tended to view Philippine Muslims as socially backward and untrustworthy precisely because of their history of resistance to hispanicization. For their part, Philippine Muslims have tended to be highly suspicious of the intentions of the Philippine government and generally wary of Christian Filipinos. These prejudices and suspicions notwithstanding, Muslims and Christians have been able to coexist peacefully in the southern Philippines for most of the time they have lived together.

NS: You suggest in your book, *Muslim Rulers and Rebels*, that the Muslim nationalist movement emerged out of the period of American colonialism (1899–1946), and not Spanish colonialism, and, in fact, that the American colonial authorities actively encouraged its development. Could you please elaborate on this?

TM: I state in my book that American colonial authorities encouraged the development of a transcendent ethnoreligious identity among Philippine Muslims. That unified identity then formed the basis of the nationalist "Bangsamoro" identity of the Muslim separatist movement, begun in the late 1960s. Philippine Muslim armed resistance to Spanish aggression was very real and obviously effective, but it was not a unified Islamic resistance in the sense sometimes imagined. As elsewhere in Southeast Asia, sultanates just as often fought with one another, sometimes forging temporary alliances with the Spaniards to do so. Nevertheless, the ability of southern sultanates individually to withstand Spanish hegemony for more than 300 years is a testament to their military and diplomatic prowess. As stated in my book, certain perceptive American colonial agents realized that the "Moros" were not unified and thought it would be a good thing to unite them under leaders the Americans regarded as "enlightened" (i.e., Westernized). American colonial intentions were complex, but a primary intention seems to have been to prepare Philippine Muslims for the eventual end of American colonialism and their inclusion in an independent Philippine republic as a consolidated and relatively progressive ethnic minority. It was a naive intention, and events, of course, didn't work out that way. But colonial practices did have the effect of encouraging the development of a unified Philippine Muslim (or Bangsamoro) identity. Not incidentally, American colonialism also provided a lingua franca—English—for contemporary Muslim separatists. Philippine Muslims are linguistically diverse and, as is the case with Christian Filipinos, English has provided a neutral political language.

NS: You also mention that the Muslim nationalist movement in the Philippines describes itself as both Islamic and anticolonial. Could you explain how this self-conception emerged and whether it is shared by the different factions of the separatist movement today?

TM: The Muslim nationalist movement is anticolonial in the same sense as any other nationalist movement in Southeast Asia, including Philippine nationalism. The difference is that Muslim separatists see Spanish and American colonialism in the Muslim Philippines as having been supplanted by colonial rule from Manila under the Philippine republic. The Islamic aspect is far more complicated, primarily because there are differing interpretations of what it means to be Islamic. The Muslim separatist movement is a self-consciously Islamic movement in the sense that its political fronts, to various degrees, envision that a Philippine Muslim nation (or autonomous region) will be influenced by an Islamic model of governance. To my knowledge neither the MNLF nor the MILF has articulated a detailed plan for governing an autonomous region or independent nation based on an Islamic model.[1] There is no clear model from the history of the Muslim Philippines. None of the Philippine sultanates complied at all closely to Quranic (shariah) law in their legal codes. I have suggested in my book that statements by the leadership of the MNLF and the MILF about the "Islamic" nature of their movement should be interpreted quite generally to refer to the defense of Philippine Muslim territory and traditions, as a response to Philippine Christian chauvinism, and as a desire to strengthen social and political connections between Philippine Muslims and the Islamic world. What [the armed Muslim separatist group] Abu Sayyaf means by "Islamic" is difficult for observers (or at least this observer) to ascertain.

NS: In your book you argue that the remote causes of Muslim separatism in the Philippines may be traced to Western colonizers but the more proximate cause can be found in the policies of the post-1946, Christian-dominated Philippine state. Can you outline

some of the policies and practices that may have either exacer-
bated or created antagonisms between the Muslim minority and
the Christian majority?

TM: Until the 1950s, Muslims formed the majority population of
almost every region of the southern Philippines. Soon after the
founding of the republic in 1946, the Philippine government began
to sponsor large-scale migration from the poor and politically
troublesome regions of the north and central parts of the country to the agricultural frontiers of the lightly populated southern
islands. The large, fertile, and underpopulated island of Mindanao
became the primary destination for Christian migration to the
southern Philippines, and by the late 1960s Mindanao Muslims
found themselves a relatively impoverished minority in their own
homeland. While the scale of Christian immigration to Mindanao
itself caused inevitable dislocations, the manner of its occurrence
also produced glaring disparities between Christian settlers and
Muslim farmers. From 1946 onward, the government provided
steadily more opportunities and assistance to settlers from the
North. By contrast, government services available to Muslims
were not only meager, compared to those obtained by immigrant
Christians, but were also fewer than they had received under the
colonial regime. The new Christian communities became linked
to trade centers and to one another by networks of roads, while
Muslim communities remained relatively isolated. The late 1960s
also saw an unusually antagonistic stance toward Muslims on the
part of the new national administration of Ferdinand Marcos.

NS: Could you briefly explain the distinctions between the three
principal groups representing Muslim grievances in the present-
day Philippines: the Moro National Liberation Front (MNLF), the
Moro Islamic Liberation Front (MILF), and Abu Sayyaf?

TM: The MNLF, founded and led by Nur Misuari, is the original
underground political front of the Muslim separatist rebellion.
Misuari is a signatory to the Tripoli Agreement of 1976, the first
peace agreement signed between Muslim separatists and the Philippine government. Until fairly recently, the MNLF was the only
separatist armed organization with which the government was
willing to negotiate in any substantive way. The MILF dates from
1984 as a separate organization but can trace its roots back to
the beginnings of modern Muslim separatism. Its leader, Hashim
Salamat, was second in command of the MNLF until 1979. The

MILF is headquartered in central Mindanao, is well organized, and has thousands of fighters and broad popular support in rural villages. Although the MILF has stressed the Islamic aspect of the separatist movement, and has somewhat more Islamic clerics in leadership positions (Salamat himself is a cleric), the stated goals and policies of the two groups do not differ significantly. The Abu Sayyaf faction is of relatively recent origin, appearing only in 1995, and is centered on the island of Basilan. They are a small, radical, and somewhat mysterious group with limited popular support. While the Abu Sayyaf faction has garnered more headlines in the past five years with its killings and kidnappings of Christians, it is by far the smallest of the three groups. Both the MNLF and the MILF have condemned the activities of the Abu Sayyaf.

NS: It has been suggested that Abu Sayyaf, the most militant of these organizations, was initially supported by the Philippine military to discredit the separatist movement and create divisions between Muslims. Do you think there is any truth to these claims?

TM: I have heard these sorts of claims myself from Philippine Muslims since 1995, although I haven't seen any credible evidence to support them. It is not surprising that such suggestions have been made. Abu Sayyaf is a very mysterious and perplexing group, and some of the activities credited to or claimed by them seem highly irrational and counterproductive.

NS: In 1996 the Moro National Liberation Front reached an agreement with the government, and the group laid down its arms. Could you explain what became of this agreement and why it is that the Philippine Congress never ratified it? Analysts have suggested that the Autonomous Region in Muslim Mindanao (ARMM), which was established following the agreement, is not working at all. Do you agree with this claim, and if so, why do you think this has been the case?

TM: The 1996 Peace Agreement between the Republic of the Philippines and the MNLF did not require ratification by the Philippine Congress. However, many Philippine legislators did not support the agreement and were able to take a number of steps to limit or eliminate funding for implementation and to pressure the administration to water down the provisions of the final agreement. Opposition in congress to the peace agreement seems to have been led by Christian senators and representatives from Mindanao. The 1996 Peace Agreement arranged for the implementation of the original Tripoli Agreement in two phases. First, it created a transitional administrative structure known as the Southern Philippines Council for Peace and Development (SPCPD). Nur Misuari, the founder and chairman of the MNLF, was made chairman of the SPCPD and won election as governor of the ARMM. The second phase of the 1996 Peace Agreement, which was originally scheduled to begin in September 1999, called for the establishment of a new regional autonomous government.

Despite the initial promise of the 1996 Peace Agreement, it has stalled badly in its implementation and is in serious danger of unraveling altogether. The September 1999 deadline for initiating the second phase of the agreement has come and gone. The autonomy agreement is stuck in its initial transition phase and has made very little progress in achieving either peace or development in the Muslim South. While the reasons for the failure of the most recent attempt to achieve meaningful autonomy for Philippine Muslims are complex, two particular (and indirectly related) problems stand out. First, due in part to congressional opposition, the SPCPD was provided entirely inadequate levels of power and resources. Not only was the SPCPD deprived of any internal taxation authority, its overall authority was severely restricted.

The second particular problem is that the 1996 Peace Agreement has not brought peace to Muslim Mindanao. The Philippine government decided to negotiate only with the main Muslim separatist faction—the MNLF led by Nur Misuari, a signatory to the original Tripoli Agreement. The MILF had sufficient military might and civilian support to wage war against the government but was ignored. After some initial armed encounters with government troops shortly after the 1996 Peace Agreement was signed, the MILF signed a ceasefire agreement with the government, in 1997, and entered into peace talks. Negotiations proceeded slowly and were interrupted by occasional skirmishes. Since late 1999, however, fighting has intensified, and in early 2000 the MILF withdrew from peace talks. At this moment (June 2000), fighting between the MILF and government troops is more intense and widespread than at any time since the signing of the Tripoli Agreement and threatens to erupt into a resumption of war.

NS: What international factors have contributed to the conflict between Muslim separatists and the Philippine state?

TM: Muammar Kadaffi has been involved in various ways, some of them quite positive in terms of seeking a settlement. The original 1976 peace agreement was signed in Libya. Libya has also sheltered and supported MNLF fighters at various times. So have Pakistan and Saudi Arabia. I think, however, that the most substantive and positive contribution has come from the Organization of the Islamic Conference of Foreign Ministers (OIC, for short), a very influential international body made up of foreign ministers of Muslim states. The OIC publicized the grievances of the separatists very early on. It pressured the Philippine government to negotiate with the MNLF and threatened a reduction of oil supplies to Manila. It arranged the first peace agreement and has been very active in facilitating negotiations and arranging agreements, including the most recent, ever since.

EDITOR'S NOTE

1. The MNLF and the MILF are the Moro National Liberation Front and the Moro Islamic Liberation Front, respectively.

SUGGESTION FOR FURTHER READING

McKenna, Thomas
    1998   *Muslim Rulers and Rebels: Everyday Politics and Armed Separatism in the Southern Philippines.* Berkeley and Los Angeles: University of California Press.

PART VII

ACADEMIC FREEDOM AND CIVIL LIBERTIES

CHAPTER 49

LYNNE CHENEY— JOE LIEBERMAN GROUP PUTS OUT A BLACKLIST

San Jose Mercury News, December 13, 2001

ROBERTO J.
GONZÁLEZ

In October 2001, members of an influential Washington-based organization called the American Council
of Trustees and Alumni (ACTA) issued a thirty-eight-
page document entitled *Defending Civilization,* which accused U.S. universities of "failing America." As evidence, its authors listed more than one
hundred allegedly unpatriotic campus incidents. The document accused
more than forty professors of engaging in what ACTA called anti-American
activities.

The chilling effect of post–September 11 censorship was not limited to
the academy. Television comedy shows, books, and even cartoons were subjected to censorship, including Aaron McGruder's comic strip *The Boondocks*
(see page 240), which editors pulled from several newspapers.

In this piece, Roberto J. González responds to the ACTA report by arguing that universities are among the few remaining institutions in American
society in which ideas may be openly exchanged. He argues that debate,
critique, and dissent have been vital elements in American democracy.

An aggressive attack on freedom has been launched upon America's
college campuses. Its perpetrators seek the elimination of ideas and activities that place September 11 in historical context, or critique the
so-called war on terrorism.

The offensive, spearheaded by the American Council of Trustees
and Alumni, a Washington-based group, threatens free speech, democratic debate and the integrity of higher education. In an incendiary report, *Defending Civilization: How Our Universities Are Failing America,* the American Council claims that "college and university faculty
have been the weak link in America's response" to September 11. It also

THE BOONDOCKS   by AARON MCGRUDER

asserts that "when a nation's intellectuals are unwilling to defend its civilization, they give comfort to its adversaries."

The report documents 117 campus incidents as "evidence" of anti-Americanism. More than 40 professors are named, including the president of Wesleyan University, who suggested in an open letter that "disparities and injustices" in American society and the world can lead to hatred and violence.

Other examples abound. A Yale professor is criticized for saying, "It is from the desperate, angry and bereaved that these suicide pilots came." A professor emeritus from the University of Oregon is listed for recommending that "we need to understand the reasons behind the terrifying hatred directed against the U.S. and find ways to act that will not foment more hatred for generations to come."

Dozens more comments, taken out of context and culled from secondary sources, are presented as examples of an unpatriotic academy.

The American Council of Trustees and Alumni was founded in 1995 by Lynne Cheney, the vice president's wife, and Senator Joseph Lieberman. Its web site claims that it contributed $3.4 billion to colleges and universities last year, making it "the largest private source of support for higher education." Cheney is cited several times in the report, and is reportedly a close associate of its authors, Jerry Martin and Anne Neal.

Although the council's stated objectives include the protection of academic freedom, the report resembles a blacklist. In a chilling use of doublespeak, it affirms the right of professors to speak out, yet condemns those who have attempted to give context to September 11, encourage critical thinking, or share knowledge about other cultures. Faculty are accused of being "short on patriotism" for attempting to give students the analytical tools they need to become informed citizens.

Many of those blacklisted are top scholars in their fields, and it appears that the report represents a kind of academic terrorism designed to strike fear into other academics by making examples of respected professors.

The report might also function to extend control over sites of democratic debate—our universities—where freedom of expression is not only permitted but encouraged.

At my campus, symposiums, teach-ins, and lectures about religion, terrorism, Central Asia, the Middle East, and U.S. foreign policy have been organized recently. A teach-in entitled "Background for Understanding" drew hundreds of students, faculty, and citizens from many political and intellectual perspectives. The audience had the opportunity to ask questions and comment freely. The discussion was lively and at times contentious.

As a microcosm of society, the university is a place where people of different ethnicities, religions, generations, and class backgrounds exchange ideas and opinions. Anyone who has visited Bay Area colleges knows that they are especially rich places for intercultural exchange.

The vigorous and often heated debates typical of such encounters are a hallmark of democratic processes. On most campuses this can still be done freely, but official accusations of anti-Americanism might intimidate and silence some voices.

That is not patriotism, but fascism. The American Council's position is inaccurate and irresponsible. Critique, debate, and exchange— not blind consensus or self-censorship—have characterized America since its inception.

Our universities are not failing America. On the contrary, they are among the few institutions offering alternatives to canned mainstream media reports.

The targeting of scholars who participate in civic debates might signal the emergence of a new McCarthyism directed at the academy. Before it escalates into a full-blown witch hunt in the name of "defending civilization," faculty, students, and citizens should speak out against these acts of academic terrorism.

CHAPTER 50

ACADEMIA UNDER ATTACK
SKETCHES FOR A
NEW BLACKLIST

CounterPunch, November 21, 2001
www.counterpunch.org

DAVID PRICE   In this commentary, David Price links the ACTA report
Defending Civilization to a pattern of censorship that
has appeared in various moments in U.S. history, most notably in the early
1950s when Senator Joseph McCarthy directed a political witch hunt against
suspected communist collaborators.

Price's piece describes how the champions of "civilization" typically claim
that "the institutions and practices of the ruling classes and the state are
desirable" while condemning other points of view. He notes that the critiques expressed by some academics are contemporary examples of points
of view upsetting to those in the higher circles of power.

My office is cluttered with over 20,000 pages of FBI files chronicling
the damage inflicted on academic freedom in America by McCarthyism. These hundreds of different files tell divergent stories with various twists, turns, and morals, but most of them are bound together
by a simple feature: the names of these individuals whose lives were
invaded and altered appeared somewhere, sometime, on lists of subversives, and the FBI read these lists and opened investigatory files
(or added to existing files) on these individuals. There were countless
lists of suspect academics printed in publications such as the *American Mercury, Readers Digest,* and newsletters of the American Legion
and various religious denominations. Most often these individuals had
taken public stands on unpopular issues such as peace and racial, economic, and gender equality.

These lists are making a comeback, as once again intellectuals with
minority views are being identified and tracked by censorial groups.
One such group is the American Council of Trustees and Alumni

(ACTA). The ACTA is a Washington, D.C.–based organization with the proclaimed mission of being "dedicated to academic freedom, quality and accountability." Oddly enough, its primary means of reaching this stated goal is by intimidating scholars who assert these principles of academic freedom in ways that run counter to the ACTA's narrow views of the past and present.

The ACTA recently produced a 38-page pamphlet that in many ways reads like a prototype of a neo-McCarthyist blacklist for our new hot war. The pamphlet, *Defending Civilization: How our Universities Are Failing America and What Can Be Done About It*, compiles 117 quotes from respected American academicians critical of current U.S. policies. These quotes range from gentle questions concerning the propriety of specific actions to radical critiques of American policies and practices, but the quotes lead the ACTA to make the charge that "college and university faculty have been the weak link in America's response to the attack" of September 11.

ACTA chairwoman emerita and national "Second Lady," Lynne Cheney, is quoted on the pamphlet's cover endorsing the need for Americans to study the past—though the envisioned past she'd have us study is clearly compartmentalized in ways that serve hegemonic interpretations of the current crisis. Cheney tells us that "living in liberty is such a precious thing" as the pamphlet compiles a list of Americans whose liberties the ACTA would like to see reduced. But Republicans like Cheney are not alone to blame for this pamphlet designed to threaten those who would actually practice academic freedom.

Besides Cheney, the remaining members of the ACTA governing board are two of Cheney's National Endowment for the Humanities colleagues, Jerry Martin and Anne Neal, and two conservative Democrats, Joseph Lieberman and Richard Lamm.

The pamphlet has a few tantalizingly strident quotes, such as the widely publicized (and later apologized for) quote by University of New Mexico historian Richard Berthold that "anyone who can blow up the Pentagon gets my vote," but most of the quotes are moderate in their view and tenor. In fact, one of the remarkable things about this pamphlet is how relatively tame or even commonsensical many of the quotes are, for example, CCNY sophomore Nuriel Heckler's observation "We don't feel military action will stop terrorism, but it will lead to racism and hate" or Jesse Jackson's statement that we should "build bridges and relationships, not simply bombs and walls."

To the ACTA, such moderate suggestions are too much and must be shouted down.

This pamphlet title's use of the term "civilization" is significant. As anthropologist Thomas Patterson recognizes, traditionally "civilization's champions have claimed that the institutions and practices of the ruling classes and the state are desirable and necessary in that they maintain order and underwrite the conquest of nature." That academics are not choosing to engage in supporting this modern conquest is indeed disappointing to the ACTA.

That American intellectuals would raise the ire of censor-prone conservatives like those at the ACTA is natural. The refusal of academics to reduce the current war to simplistic analyses of good versus evil, or civilization versus tribalism *should* be upsetting to those who view intellectuals' chief duty as rationalizing the actions of state. The ACTA is opposed to independent thought during this time of war, and it seems to sense no danger in its wish to muzzle and intimidate knowledgeable individuals who are trying to add more information to an ill-informed public during a time a crisis.

The American Association of University Professors (an organization that abandoned many professors during the days of McCarthyism) has thus far come out with strong support for the principles of academic freedom. Last month Mary Burgan, the AAUP general secretary, noted that "a distrust of intellectuals has always lurked beneath the surface of American popular opinion. Now it has begun to leak out again—either through the frontal assault in the partial reporting by the *New York Post* of a forum at the City University of New York, or the sideswipes at campus teach-ins by a respected columnist like Tom Friedman or others such as John Leo." So far the AAUP is standing on the side of academic freedom, but this is a fight in which we must remain ever vigilant.

There is no criticism too strong for those who would intimidate and stifle free thought and expression—especially during times such as these when knowledgeable scholars' access to the public via the media is being curtailed. That members of the ACTA's board are among those who can bend the ear of our new Homeland Security Office should cause us all grave concern, and we must be doubly vigilant in protecting those of us who exercise our right to dissent.

CHAPTER 51

LYNNE CHENEY'S FREE SPEECH BLACKLIST

TomPaine.com, November 18, 2002
www.tompaine.com

HUGH GUSTERSON, *interviewed by Sharon Basco*   Hugh Gusterson was the first academic quoted in the ACTA report *Defending Civilization*. In this interview with Sharon Basco, he considers the ACTA's use of intimidation, scapegoating, and propaganda as techniques of control, and reflects upon the historical link between war and repression of dissenters in U.S. history.

Gusterson also makes a point that resonates strongly with many of the articles in this collection: "The role and the purpose of the university in America is not to cheerlead for whatever the chosen policy of the American government is. The role and purpose of the university is to pursue knowledge and to encourage people to think critically."

SHARON BASCO: Professor Hugh Gusterson, you're the first academic quoted in the report entitled *Defending Civilization: How Our Universities Are Failing America and What Can Be Done About It.*

One of the opening paragraphs of that report says, "While America's elected officials from both parties and media commentators from across the spectrum condemned the attacks and followed the President in calling evil by its rightful name, many faculty demurred. Some refused to make judgments. Many invoked tolerance and diversity as antidotes to evil."

You're the first academic quoted in this report, which states this: "Hugh Gusterson, professor of anthropology and science and technology studies, Massachusetts Institute of Technology: 'Imagine the real suffering and grief of people in other countries. The best way to begin a war on terrorism might be to look in the mirror.'" That's the end of your quote.

HUGH GUSTERSON: One interesting thing I want to observe about that quote is where they chose to begin it. It's a quote from a speech I made at a peace rally at MIT, shortly after September 11. And I took as my theme the difficulty of imagining the real suffering of other people. And just before that quote they select, I talked about how difficult it is for us to imagine the suffering of the people at the World Trade Center as they were dying.

And then I went on from there to invite the audience to try and imagine the suffering of people in Afghanistan if we were to go and declare war on the people in Afghanistan. Of course, the quote is carefully cut so it seems that I only care about the suffering of people in other countries and not about the suffering of Americans as well. That's part of a process of distortion that I think marks the report more generally.

But also more generally I'd like to make a point that universities are not adjuncts of the American government. The role and the purpose of the university in America is not to cheerlead for whatever the chosen policy of the American government is. The role and purpose of the university is to pursue knowledge and to encourage people to think critically. And in my speech at the peace rally I was encouraging students and anyone who was listening to think critically about American foreign policy, about the fact that Americans have not only been victims of violence, but that Americans have often inflicted violence on people in other countries—in El Salvador, Nicaragua, Panama, Vietnam, for example—and the people in those other countries might see U.S. actions as being terrorist actions in their own way.

SB: Have you spoken to anyone at the American Council of Trustees and Alumni about the accusations in the report and about your words being taken out of context?

HG: I haven't spoken to anyone at the American Council of Trustees and Alumni. They never called me to check the quote. And one thing I would like to say. The report makes the argument that political correctness reigns supreme on American campuses today. And the people who do feel inclined to support the U.S. government feel intimidated by the climate of political correctness from giving voice to their true feelings.

And I have to say, looking around me at MIT, this is just complete junk. In their report, they cite five different quotes from people at MIT. Four of those quotes come from the peace rally where I spoke. There's a fifth quote from Noam Chomsky, from a public lecture he gave. And you would think from reading their report that these are the only public statements that have been made about September 11 here at MIT. But it's just not true. There was a whole series of panel discussions organized by the university administration. So, for example, the Center for International Studies did a panel within a few days of September 11. There were four panelists; only one of those panelists in any way criticized American foreign policy. Two of the others called for assassinating Osama bin Laden, or for declaring war on Afghanistan. When that panel was repeated on two subsequent occasions, the person who had criticized U.S. foreign policy was dropped from the panel. There was another panel discussion called "Technology and Terror." There were six panelists, including myself. I was the only one of the panelists on that panel who said anything critical about American foreign policy.

So actually, if you look at MIT, there's a vibrant discussion about the implications of September 11. Many people have called publicly for military action and the people who've criticized military action are actually a minority of the recorded statements. You can go to the MIT news service and check this out.

What the authors of the report did is that they very carefully selected only those comments that were critical of American foreign policy and tried to pretend that those comments represented the entire range of debate at MIT. This is a complete distortion and fabrication.

SB: What do you think they're trying to do with this report? You're an anthropologist, you study human beings and their culture, their relationships. What's your professional viewpoint on this *Defending Civilization* report?

HG: Lynne Cheney has been on a mission for over a decade now to try to clamp down on dissent on campus, and to clamp down on multiculturalist perspectives in education. And I think this fits with a long-term agenda she has. We see at this moment, after September 11, that many groups are opportunistically using the current crisis to try and push an agenda that they had long before September 11. And I think that's part of what Lynne Cheney and this group are up to.

But more than that, I think that any student of American history can tell you that whenever the country is at war, whenever there is a national crisis, it's very clear that the government attempts to clamp down on dissenters, on aliens and so on. This goes all the way back to the Sedition Act shortly after the founding of the Republic—you see it in the mass deportations around the time of World War I, the trial and execution of Sacco and Vanzetti, you see it in the internment of Japanese Americans during World War II and in McCarthyism.

This fits within that pattern. It's an attempt to intimidate internal critics within the United States, to keep them quiet, to say that in a time of crisis there's only one correct opinion, and it's the official orthodox government opinion. And I find it ironic, actually, that Lynne Cheney and the American Council of Trustees and Alumni are calling in this report for more American history on campus, for compulsory classes in American history. Because I think if you study America history you see quite clearly that they fit into this long-standing historical pattern of scapegoating internal critics in times of crisis. It's a very ugly historical pattern.

SB: The report seems to rationalize and anticipate criticisms from people who don't agree with Lynne Cheney's organization. They say in part: "Let us be clear. This is not an argument for limiting free speech on college campuses. Indeed the robust exchange of ideas is essential to a free society. But it is equally important and never more so than in these unsettling times to insist that colleges and universities transmit our history and heritage to the next generation." And then there's an underlined sentence: "Academic freedom does not mean freedom from criticism."

HG: I take strong exception to this comment for two reasons. First of all, as an academic, I live on debate. I thrive on debate. I love people to argue with me about what I've written, what I've said, and I live to debate with other people.

If anyone from the American Council of Trustees and Alumni wants to debate me on my views on the war on Afghanistan, I will be delighted to debate them.

This is not about debate. It's about blacklisting people. It's one thing to do a detailed analysis of someone's written or spoken opinions, and suggest why you think they're wrong. That's not what this report is about. This report is about compiling a list of people who they think are deviants as an attempt to intimidate those people.

The second thing I would say is that the report uses the classic technique of propaganda. In propaganda you impute your own sins to the other side. We saw this with Soviet propaganda, for example. Every time the Soviets invaded a country, they would talk about the other country having committed aggression against the Soviet Union, and the Soviet Union acting out of self-defense.

Cigarette ads do the same thing. They take the perceived weakness of their product, and they turn it around in advertisements. They say that cigarettes make people attractive, cigarettes taste nice, and so on.

And this report uses the classic techniques of advertising and propaganda. They are about intimidation. They are about curtailing the free expression of dissent on campus. Instead, they accuse internal dissenters—who are in a minority in American society—of trying to curtail other people's free speech.

SUGGESTION FOR FURTHER READING

Gusterson, Hugh
    2001   "The McNamara Complex." *Anthropological Quarterly*, Special Section of Social Thought and Commentary (December): 171–177.

CHAPTER 52   HARMONY COERCED IS FREEDOM DENIED

Chronicle of Higher Education, July 13, 2001

LAURA NADER   In this piece, Laura Nader applies anthropological theory and research to an important public issue: the emergence of coercive harmony as an ideology of control in American life. She reminds readers that critique, contention, and dissent have a long history in the United States. Abandoning that tradition might mask repression, or disguise injustice and repression as civility, patriotism, or the American Way.

Although this commentary was written months before September 11, 2001, it is more relevant today than when it initially appeared. News editors, college professors, students, employees, and other citizens have reported coming under fire for expressing views critical of the Bush administration. In light of the rapid changes that have curtailed civil liberties, Nader's words should give us pause.

We have heard a lot recently about the need for consensus, social harmony, and civility. At the end of the presidential election, for instance, both George W. Bush and Al Gore spoke of the importance of unity. But Americans need to remember that our country was founded by dissenters. We need to be reminded periodically of all the good that has come from outrage and indignation, and of what happens to democracy when people don't speak out.

In "Seduced by Civility," a 1996 article in *The Nation,* Benjamin DeMott looks at the current state of political manners and the crisis of democratic values. He points out that in the nineteenth century, people who criticized abolitionists for being uncivil were the ones who were willing to let slavery continue. His conclusion is that we must recognize today's incivility for what it is: a justified rejection of the powers that be, who are more interested in civility than in poverty.

I believe that indignation can make Americans more engaged citizens—and isn't that a basic purpose of most colleges and universities? I am appalled to hear young people speak positively about not being judgmental. (I'm sure that when a student said, in an evaluation of my course, "Dr. Nader is a pretty good professor, except she has opinions," the remark wasn't intended to be a compliment; nonetheless, I took it as one.)

Many college students today were taught dispute resolution in elementary and secondary school, at the cost of trading justice for harmony. Often, what they remember is that they were silenced for the sake of civility. As professors, we ought to encourage our students to express their opinions—with outrage, when it is justified, as it often is. It is our duty to teach students the importance of protest when our society makes the unthinkable appear normal—when we dump nuclear waste on American Indian reservations, broaden the gap between the haves and the have-nots even during a time of plenty, and give Ritalin to millions of American children.

Social scientists are taught to notice patterns that regulate speech or social life. Sometimes we follow such patterns through time and space, to see if we have stumbled upon something of social and cultural significance. In *The History of Manners,* Norbert Elias examined the links between manners, or etiquette, and social control. He was interested in how "civilizing processes," as he called them, take place and how they are interrelated with the organization of Western societies into states. He believed that the standards for human behavior gradually shift over the centuries toward greater restrictions. For example, he found that people in Western societies became less tolerant of spitting in public when they learned that the practice was acceptable in the non-Western societies they saw as less advanced. My interest in manners as a way of controlling behavior came from my work on village law among the Zapotec Indians of Oaxaca, Mexico. I found that the villagers I studied were highly litigious, yet valued harmony and compromise in the courtroom. I came to see their support of harmony as part of a strategy to preserve their autonomy. As long as the village kept its house in order, there was minimal interference from the Mexican government. Five hundred years of colonization had taught the villagers to use harmony for political purposes.

When I looked at legal reform in the United States, I also found harmony being used as a control, this time by the powerful. In the 1970s, something called alternative dispute resolution was born. It was a reform movement in response to the new cases (proponents of the movement called them "garbage cases") that were entering the courts after the social turmoil of the 1960s—cases about civil rights, environmental and consumer rights, Native American and gender issues, and so forth. The movement favored compromise over adversarial procedures, harmony over social justice. Its mandatory mediation and binding arbitration cost us our right to sue. It was a war against the contentious.

Since the 1970s, alternative dispute resolution has gone beyond the law, creeping into our schools, places of work, hospitals, and homes. Tracking the spread of such coercive harmony is not easy. Because it has permeated society over time, most people come to take it for granted or assume it is benign. Conversely, conflicts and disagreement have come to seem bad, to be avoided at all costs. I once received a note from a lumber activist thanking me for coining the term "coercive harmony." It had enabled her to recognize the repression of environmental activism under the banner of consensus and "win-win" solutions in the Clinton administration's policy on logging.

Coercive harmony has often accompanied large-scale social movements, including Western colonialism, Christian missionary work, and globalization. Historians like Jerold Auerbach, at Wellesley College, postulate that in the United States, the use of harmony as a form of social regulation by the government occurs in cycles. Conflict—for example, during the Civil War and the protests of the 1960s—gets out of control, harmony is imposed, and after a time of calm, dissent erupts again.

Europeans today are less concerned about harmony than Americans are. During last year's presidential campaign, many Europeans wondered why the candidates did not seem to know how to debate. One reason is that Americans consider it bad manners to be contentious. In fact, the anthropologist Paul Bohannan notes that Americans have two categories of behavior: polite and rude. The British, he says, add a third: civil, meaning that you pull no punches when you criticize, but that you do so without jeering. As he puts it, an American has to be your close friend before giving you anything but praise when he reviews your manuscript. The British don't make that kind of mistake; they understand that you really want to know the weak points before publication.

The use of coercive harmony in the United States has led us to confuse all criticism with carping and being negative. We don't share the Europeans' zest for controversy. As Robin Lakoff, a linguist at the University of California at Berkeley, says, we want to be perceived as nice. And we put up with circumstances that Europeans would consider outrageous—for example, the absence of universal health care or the fact that fewer than 52 percent of eligible voters cast ballots in the last election.

What should be unacceptable has come to strike us as so normal that when we hear someone speaking frankly, we are startled. Not long ago, in an appearance on *The NewsHour with Jim Lehrer*, Frank Wolak, an economics professor at Stanford University, whitewashed the role of the utilities in the California energy crisis. Not surprising. What did seem surprising was the comment that followed from Bruce Brugmann, editor of the *San Francisco Bay Guardian*, who said that the professor should be working for the utilities rather than Stanford.

Coercive harmony can stifle dissent for a while. But if dissent is too tightly bottled up, it will explode—as happened in the 1960s riots in Watts, Newark, and other places. And the explosions don't all come from members of ethnic minorities: Witness the Oklahoma City bombing in 1995.

Academics should not be party to establishing an ideology of consensus on our increasingly corporatized campuses. Instead, we have a duty to investigate the dangers of coercive harmony and to expose repression when it poses as consensus.

SUGGESTIONS FOR FURTHER READING

Nader, Laura

1997   "Controlling Processes: Tracing the Dynamic Components of Power." *Current Anthropology* 38, no. 5: 711–737.

1997   "The Phantom Factor: Impact of the Cold War on Anthropology." In *The Cold War and the University: Toward an Intellectual History of the Postwar Years*, edited by Andre Schiffrin, pp. 107–146. New York: New Press.

2002   *The Life of the Law: Anthropological Projects*. Berkeley and Los Angeles: University of California Press.

UNCONVENTIONAL ANTHROPOLOGY
CHALLENGING THE MYTHS
OF CONTINUOUS WAR

ROBERTO J.   *The study of man is confronted with an un-*
GONZÁLEZ   *precedented situation: never before have so*
              few, by their actions and inactions, had the
power of life and death over so many of the species.
—LAURA NADER, "UP THE ANTHROPOLOGIST—PERSPECTIVES GAINED FROM
STUDYING UP" (1969)

*We must realize that the discourse of technical rationality is
part of the problem as well as part of the solution and that, unless we ask fundamental political questions about the relationship between the U.S. and the rest of the world, the U.S. will find
the cognitive and technological tools of modernity being used
against it.*
—HUGH GUSTERSON, "THE MCNAMARA COMPLEX" (2001)

Anthropology and American Imperialism

Many of the contributors to this anthology chronicle the emergence of
U.S. global hegemony over the course of the twentieth century and into
the twenty-first. The "American century of war and empire"[1] has had
broad repercussions overseas—and also within our country—as communities, economies, and political systems have been transformed and
often contended with the imperialist dreams of power elites.

While few would dispute such historical facts, within the United
States there are different interpretations of what U.S. imperialism represents. Many neoconservatives wholeheartedly agree that such hegemony exists, yet consider it to be not only justifiable but desirable

on grounds that such a system is essentially benevolent, moral, and progressive. Every imperial project has its ideological justifications; "manifest destiny," "white man's burden," "economic development," and "New World Order" have rationalized civilizing missions in different historical periods. Following an ethnocentric logic, recent attempts by our leaders to encourage "regime change" in such diverse locations as Afghanistan, Iraq, and Venezuela might appear rational and desirable, even when they violate international law.

Where have anthropologists stood on this issue? A generation ago, Kathleen Gough observed that British, French, and American anthropologists had generally not questioned frameworks of colonial power: "Anthropology is a child of Western imperialism . . . We tended to accept the imperialist framework as given, perhaps partly because we were influenced by the dominant theories of our time, and partly because at that time there was little anyone could do to dismantle the empire."[2]

Today, after witnessing struggles for independence in Africa, Asia, and the Americas, many anthropologists would likely be critical of *any* imperial system. Empires have historically denied the right of self-determination to colonized peoples and violently repressed them when they challenged structures of power. When anthropologists conducted ethnographic research or extended fieldwork abroad, the brutal political realities of colonialism often appeared in plain view. After the 1960s, the discipline generally became more attuned to global interconnections and inequalities.[3] The fact that participant observation tended to place the anthropologist in personal relationships with ordinary people probably magnified the effects of imperial systems on small-scale societies. By the nature of their work, anthropologists are positioned to grasp the big picture from the perspectives of individual lives, and consequently many have been outspoken in their critiques of imperialism—including the current U.S. version, which starkly contrasts with the principles upon which our country was founded.

Perhaps this is most clearly visible in U.S. military expansion. In recent months—with alarming speed and no public debate—our leaders have deployed military troops and advisers to parts of the world that were previously off-limits, including the Philippines, Afghanistan, Uzbekistan, Kyrgyzstan, Colombia, Yemen, and Georgia.

The case of Iraq provides us with an alarming example of the new U.S. expansionism. When the Bush administration launched an invasion of Iraq in March and April 2003, it dramatically demonstrated the lengths to which it would go to accelerate the U.S. drive for total global dominance. This was clearly foreshadowed by its *National Security Strategy*, a policy document advocating unilateral military action as the preferred means for projecting U.S. power.

After initially seeking approval from the U.N. Security Council to disarm Iraq (a process which led to the reintroduction of U.N. weapons inspectors to Iraq in late 2002), the U.S. and U.K. eventually abandoned efforts to work within the system of international law. Bush administration officials claimed at various moments that Iraq must be attacked in order to eliminate weapons of mass destruction, for purposes of "regime change," and to bring democracy to the region.

In response, millions of Americans across the country demonstrated their opposition to war in a series of rallies between October 2002 and March 2003—a sight not seen on U.S. streets since the Vietnam era. Tens of millions more demonstrated around the world.

But in spite of popular opposition, the United States and United Kingdom proceeded to attack Iraq, beginning with massive bombing raids over the city of Baghdad in late March 2003 followed by a blitzkrieg-style land invasion. Although it may be many years before we know the full extent of the destruction and death of the second Gulf War, it is clear that thousands of civilians were killed.

As this book goes to press, the U.S. maintains approximately 150,000 troops in Iraq and has imposed the authority of the Pentagon's Office of Reconstruction and Humanitarian Assistance. The military occupation and the Pentagon's rulers resemble a colonial administration in many ways.

In spite of the U.S. troop presence, looters and snipers continue wreaking havoc and instability upon large portions of Baghdad and other Iraqi cities. U.S. troops secured the building housing the Ministry of Oil but allowed thieves (probably members of organized crime rings) to steal thousands of priceless artifacts from the national museum of archaeology. They also allowed arsonists to burn the national library and other buildings containing historic archives and religious texts. The losses are of such significance that eminent scholars have, without hyperbole, compared these events to the burning of the library at Alexandria.

In the political vacuum created by the dismantling of Saddam Hussein's Baath Party, Shiite leaders—some of whom are clerics favoring an Islamic state—are stepping in to fill the void. This is of signal importance, since 60 percent of Iraq's population consists of Shiite Muslims, many of whom were severely limited in expressing their political power (and many of their religious traditions) under Saddam Hussein's secular rule. While the clerics clearly command a great deal of popular support, Bush administration officials have unequivocally stated that they will not accept a theocratic state. Iraq's political future is unclear, but the Bush administration appears determined to maintain tight boundaries around the shape and character of its postwar government. In the meantime, casualties of war mount.

Like the Roman, Spanish, and British Empires of previous eras, the United States has spread its military forces far and wide to maintain global hegemony, but on a scale unprecedented in human history. Today our country spends more each year on the military (approximately $400 billion) than the next nine largest national defense budgets combined. The web of U.S. military bases extends across seventy countries and territories over the globe.

September 11 and the "War on Terror": The Uses of Continuous War

In a recent lecture, MIT linguistics professor Noam Chomsky noted that "the war on terrorism was not declared on September 11; rather, it was *redeclared*, using the same rhetoric as the first declaration 20 years earlier."[4] Mainstream news reports indicate a remarkable continuity in the military actions of the United States and its allies against countries deemed to be supporters of terrorist organizations—actions that have included assassinations, torture, mass murder, atrocities, and war crimes in Algeria, Libya, Turkey, Saudi Arabia, Iraq, Indonesia, the Philippines, Haiti, El Salvador, Guatemala, and many other countries. It is also significant that government officials directing the contemporary "war on terror" include many of the same people charged with fighting "terrorist" threats two decades ago: Donald Rumsfeld, Dick Cheney, Paul Wolfowitz, Colin Powell, John Negroponte, and others. From this perspective, recent events resemble a war without end.

The idea of a society engaged in continuous war—what anthropologist Catherine Lutz has called a "form of peacetime that is in fact war" conducted in faraway lands[5]—is reminiscent of both the totalitarian society envisioned by George Orwell in *1984* and recent statements made by our leaders regarding the "war on terror." By issuing a constant stream of warnings and press releases (some without foundation) about possible terrorist attacks, distorting the truth while subtly and not so subtly threatening dissenters, and directing the fear, wrath, and insecurity of citizens against one another, the leaders of such states sometimes succeed in confounding and manipulating millions of people. This was as true in Nazi Germany as it was in the negative utopia of *1984.* We may be witnessing similar processes at work in our country today.

Orwell linked the continuous war between world powers to the manipulation of reality: "When war is continuous there is no such thing as military necessity . . . the most palpable facts can be denied or disregarded . . . almost any perversion of thought can be safely practiced . . . The rulers of such a state are absolute, as the Pharaohs or the Caesars could not be . . . they can twist reality into whatever shape they choose."[6]

Continuous conflict, together with an insistence that our country is in a state of war against shadowy enemies scattered across dozens of countries, may function as a controlling process creating fear in the minds of citizens. As in the case of Cold War panic over communism in the United States, the widespread selling of fear by members of the Bush cabinet has effectively pried more support from the public and Congress for growing military budgets. Currently, more than half of our government's discretionary spending is dedicated to the military—more than five times the amount dedicated to education. We should bear in mind the January 17, 1961, farewell address of President Dwight D. Eisenhower, in which he cautioned us about how the "military-industrial complex" might threaten freedom, democracy, and cherished American values.

The demonization of non-Western others is undergoing a new phase. In the present context, many groups around the world seeking to assert self-determination in a way that potentially threatens U.S. economic interests or those of its allies are branded with predictable labels by heads of state:

> "Terrorist," like "bandit," designates an enemy of the Western establishment, somebody who stands in the way of Western aims. What Western states do is never banditry or terrorism, even if their actions fit Western definitions of these terms and are declared by Western political entities like the International Court of Justice to be in violation of international law . . . The West remains the repository of civilized values and humane methods, which is being challenged by "barbarians."[7]

This observation is even more compelling when put in the current context: In 2002 our government refused to recognize the legitimacy of the newly formed International Criminal Court, a legal body established to prosecute war crimes, and in 2003 it spearheaded an unprovoked attack, invasion, and occupation of a sovereign nation (Iraq) without U.N. approval—a direct violation of the U.N. Charter.

In Orwell's fictional account, the general public is incapable of distinguishing the government's official versions of history from reality due to direct censorship and manipulation of language. But to what degree do these controls function in our own society—and at what level of popular consciousness?

The Culture Industry and Mainstream Media

A recent report in the London newspaper *The Guardian* sheds light on some of the controls promoted by a continuous "war on terror." The headline is both revelatory and shocking: "U.S. Media Cowed by Patriotic Fever, Says CBS Star." The article features an interview with CBS News anchor Dan Rather, an icon of American television, who comments on the forces of what he calls "patriotism run amok" after September 11:

> It is an obscene comparison . . . but you know there was a time in South Africa that people would put flaming tires around people's necks if they dissented. And in some ways the fear is that you will be necklaced here, you will have a flaming tire of lack of patriotism put around your neck. Now it is that fear that keeps journalists from asking the toughest of the tough questions . . . There has never been an American war, small or large, in which access has been so limited as this one . . . Limiting access, limiting information to cover the backsides of those who are in charge of the war, is extremely dangerous and cannot and should not be accepted.[8]

Rather's comments point to a number of factors: self-censorship, fear of punishment for speaking out against the party line, and limited access to battle zones. That one of the most influential television reporters in our country can be subjected to such pressures should make us stop and think.

For critics of U.S. mainstream media, other mechanisms of information control are well known, particularly those associated with the influence of commercial pressures. Mergers and the consolidation of media firms have linked together television, radio, music, publishing, and Internet providers, which has resulted in a handful of multinational media conglomerates that effectively serve to filter much of the information content of news. Threats from advertisers, sponsors, and organized lobbies occasionally pressure editorial boards, publishers, and producers to reject controversial stories or to frame current events in particular ways or else threaten to withhold underwriting.

Journalists are often subjected to a wide range of filters including press controls, bureaucratic hierarchies, reporting conventions, news organizations, and a set of career rewards and punishments that impact their choice of topics, as well as the style in which they present their reports. The multiplicity of ways in which business interests discipline reporters is the subject of a rich ethnographic account of foreign correspondents by anthropologist Mark Pedelty. He explains that "the ideological content of news texts is representative of the world view of the stockholders, executives, owners, and especially, advertisers who produce, manage, and profit from news production."[9] In a system in which the major news producers are subsidiaries of multinational media corporations, the pressures to conform and self-censor may be overwhelming.

Media watchdog groups such as Fairness and Accuracy in Reporting (FAIR) have extensively documented the effects of such connections and potential conflicts of interest. Their investigations help us understand otherwise confounding phenomena: the portrayal of the September 11 attacks as attacks upon civilians rather than attacks upon symbols of American economic and military power; the omission of international human rights reports critical of U.S. policies from mainstream news broadcasts; and the dearth of reporting on the antiwar movement.

Anthropology's Promise: Exploding the
Myths of "Crackpot Realism"

It appears that a new generation of "crackpot realists"—those who think that the only realistic way of resolving political problems can be found in total war, mass murder, and the use of brute force (even if in violation of international laws)—are in command of our country.[10] The specter of nuclear war once again looms before us, as the current Bush administration has abandoned nuclear test ban treaties, produced a list of countries as potential targets for future attacks, and openly discussed the possible development of "small-scale" nuclear weapons, much to the chagrin of America's closest allies. As if that were not enough, the administration released a document entitled *National Security Strategy* on September 20, 2002, which outlines a new foreign policy doctrine advocating "pre-emption," "first-strikes," and unilateral action as preferred means for maintaining American "unparalleled military strength" and global dominance. The 2003 Gulf War may represent the initial phase of a long-range project to expand U.S. hegemony and project U.S. power across the globe, an idea explicitly promoted by the think tank Project for the New American Century.

The words of Hannah Arendt are particularly relevant: "There are, indeed, few things that are more frightening than the steadily increasing prestige of scientifically minded brain trusters in the councils of government during the last decades. The trouble is not that they are cold-blooded enough to 'think the unthinkable,' but that they do not *think.*"[11] Anthropologists have analyzed a tendency toward irrational rationality among bureaucratic elites in military-industrial settings: Hugh Gusterson calls it "the McNamara complex," while Laura Nader uses the term "institutionalized insanity."

In these unconventional times, anthropologists have a historic role to play in the public arena, detecting general patterns that might lead to a more enlightened U.S. engagement with global politics. Various themes resonate throughout the commentaries: the repeated call for greater U.N. involvement in conflicts, rather than unilateral military actions by our government and its allies; the need for a fuller, more sophisticated U.S. understanding of other cultures—that is, cultural relativism as a political exigency; the importance of our country actively seeking peaceful solutions rather than reacting to violence with heavy-handed retaliatory attacks (preventive diplomacy instead of gunboat diplomacy); the need for democratic governments—with our country in the lead—to make objectives and actions more transparent; and the recognition that lasting peace can only be realized in a world that is more just. What can be more in line with U.S. principles than a world in which justice and the rule of law prevail?

In times of war, anthropologists need to encourage critical thinking. Although some will undoubtedly argue that our discipline should work for government agencies in wartime, the history of U.S. anthropology reveals that such a road is fraught with danger. We should remain cautious and vigilant about how military and intelligence agencies might recruit anthropologists or deploy cultural knowledge in the "war on terror" declared by George W. Bush. During the current period of academic downsizing, career opportunities for anthropologists are shrinking, and new opportunities for employment in the CIA, the Defense Intelligence Agency, and private think tanks as cultural experts might seem particularly appealing to those struggling to find steady employment. Anthropologists should resist temptation as a matter of professional responsibility—at the very least, we should insist on professional autonomy. As David Price has argued, state-managed anthropological wartime research has frequently devastated indigenous cultures: "As social scientists are now being recruited to assist in ethnic and racial 'terrorist profiling' campaigns . . . we have a professional duty to speak out against the futility and bigotry of such abuses."[12] The destructive potential is too great to risk using culture as a weapon.

In the context of the "war on terror," we might begin by taking positive steps to dispel the myths, misunderstandings, and ethnocentrism currently circulating throughout our country, often created by public relations firms and private think tanks and propagated by the corporate mass media. This might serve as an alternative to agency work for those wishing to engage with wider publics. As points of departure, we might consider the following objectives:

1. We could inform the public of the double standard systematically applied to the term "terrorism." In nearly all mainstream reports and in the words of the vast majority of official policy makers, "terrorism" is reserved for those who would challenge the United States or its allies, even when the latter are in violation of international law. "State terrorism" is not a term that is used in the mainstream media, yet violence directed by states against their own people has claimed many more lives than nonstate terrorism during the twentieth century (in Indonesia, Guatemala, Angola, and Nicaragua, to name a few). Typically, such aggression has been ignored or described as "retaliation"—or, more commonly, "self-defense."

2. We could remind the public that "preemptive" attacks and "regime change," directed or supported by our military and the CIA, have not led to regional stability in the Middle East, Latin America, Africa, or other regions. This has also been true in the past, as his-

tory has shown time and time again.[13] Furthermore, history has also shown that air attacks almost always result in civilian casualties, either directly (due to bombing) or indirectly (due to the public health and other humanitarian crises following such raids). The strategy of massive bombing, while perhaps minimizing U.S. war casualties, has frequently led to bitterness, anger, and outright hostility directed toward our country on the part of civilians whose lives have been devastated. The idea that a lasting peace can emerge from a strategy of war and indiscriminate annihilation is unfounded.

3. We could expose the use of euphemisms, doublespeak, and misinformation in Pentagon briefings, presidential speeches, and the mainstream media. Reporters, politicians, and pundits uncritically use such terms as "defense" rather than "war," "freedom fighters" rather than "paramilitary groups," "terrorists" rather than "revolutionaries," "collateral damage" rather than "civilian casualties," "stress and duress" rather than "torture," and "surgical strikes" rather than "missile and bombing attacks," among many others.

4. We could inspire the general public to learn more about other societies, and to recognize that people in many parts of the world have rejected neoliberal models of economic development and certain World Bank and IMF recommendations. For years, media reports have equated "free trade" with (political) freedom, even when the historical record is replete with free-trading dictatorships, such as Marcos' Philippines, Salinas' Mexico, and Suharto's Indonesia.

5. We could describe the emergence and character of the international power elite, and the social and cultural implications of the corporatization of our government. Like the subjects of C. Wright Mills' *The Power Elite*, the contemporary ruling classes may be linked across military, industrial, and political institutions, but today they operate on a truly global scale. For example, the Carlyle Group, a $12 billion private equity firm based in Washington, includes as its advisers former president Fidel Ramos of the Philippines, former South Korean prime minister Park Tae Joon, former British prime minister John Major, former Speaker of the House Thomas Foley, former president George Bush Sr., and former secretary of state James Baker III, among many others. The group represents "a new spin on Washington's revolving door between business and government, where lobbying by former officials is restricted but soliciting investments is not . . . Carlyle has upped

the ante and taken the practice global."[14] Another example comes from the massive contracts for postwar reconstruction in Iraq that the Bush administration awarded to Bechtel and Halliburton. Dick Cheney served as the CEO of Halliburton before becoming vice president.[15] In short, there is still much work to be done in tracing the connections between U.S. foreign policy, the financial interests of multinational corporations, and the revolving doors between government, industry, and the military.

A new politics of responsibility requires that intellectuals in general and anthropologists in particular examine global structures of power and acquiescence affecting us all. It also demands that we break the monopoly of ideas, disseminate critical perspectives, and communicate with broader publics. By establishing connections, an informed and revitalized citizenry may still reclaim their roles as protagonists of history. The United States has given the world a vision of democracy that is worth turning into practice—and we can take a leading role. In the words of one anthropologist,

> I am aware that this discussion is unconventional anthropology; but these are unconventional times. We are all involved in unconventional and portentous military and political events . . . These events have worldwide consequences. It is time that we accepted some unconventional responsibility for our acts, be they acts of commission or of omission.[16]

Accepting this responsibility will help us realize both the potential and the promise of a renewed anthropology.

NOTES

1. Catherine Lutz, *Homefront: A Military City and the American Twentieth Century* (Boston: Beacon Press), p. 4.
2. Kathleen Gough, "New Proposals for Anthropologists," *Current Anthropology* 9, no. 5 (December 1968): 403–407.
3. It is also true that even before World War II, some anthropologists recognized that using cultural knowledge against field subjects—the use of culture as a weapon—was ethically problematic. For a description of Melville Herskovitz's writings about this dilemma, see David Price, "Lessons from Second World War Anthropology," *Anthropology Today* 18, no. 3 (June 2002): 16. For an early anthropological critique of U.S. imperialism, see Franz Boas, "American National-

ism and World War I," in George W. Stocking, ed., *A Franz Boas Reader* (Chicago: University of Chicago Press, 1975), pp. 331–332.

4. Noam Chomsky, "The Journalist from Mars," *Extra!* 15, no. 2 (April 2002): 10.

5. Lutz, p. 8.

6. George Orwell, *1984* (New York: Harcourt Brace Jovanovich, 1949), pp. 163–164.

7. Edward Herman and Gerry O'Sullivan, *The "Terrorism" Industry* (New York: Pantheon Books, 1989), pp. 6–7.

8. Quoted in Matthew Engel, "U.S. Media Cowed by Patriotic Fever, Says CBS Star," *The Guardian,* May 17, 2002.

9. See Mark Pedelty, *War Stories: The Culture of Foreign Correspondents* (London: Routledge, 1995).

10. The term "crackpot realists" was coined by C. Wright Mills in *The Causes of World War Three* (New York: Ballantine Books, 1958).

11. Hannah Arendt, *On Violence* (New York: Harcourt, Brace and World, 1970).

12. David Price, "Lessons from Second World War Anthropology," *Anthropology Today* 18, no. 3 (June 2002): 20.

13. Ramsey Clark pointed this out in an interview with Amy Goodman on *Democracy Now!* (Pacifica Radio), March 20, 2002.

14. Leslie Wayne, "The Carlyle Group: Elder Bush in Big G.O.P. Cast Toiling for Top Equity Firm," *New York Times,* March 5, 2001. See also Dan Briody, *The Iron Triangle: Inside the Secret World of the Carlyle Group* (New York: John Wiley and Sons, 2003).

15. In April 2003, the CBS news program *60 Minutes* reported that the Pentagon awarded a two-year no-bid contract to Halliburton for reconstructing Iraqi oil fields. The contract is worth up to $7 billion. The contract was awarded without competitive bidding. See Steve Kroft, "Halliburton: All in the Family," *60 Minutes,* April 27, 2003.

16. Gerald Berreman, "Is Anthropology Alive?" *Current Anthropology 9,* no. 5 (December 1968): 391–396.

LIST OF CONTRIBUTORS

SERGEI ARUTYUNOV is a member of the Russian Academy of Sciences and Chair of the Caucasus Department at the Institute of Ethnology in Moscow.

TALAL ASAD is Distinguished Professor at the City University of New York Graduate Center, Ph.D. Program in Anthropology.

KAMRAN ASDAR ALI is Assistant Professor in Anthropology and Middle Eastern Studies at the University of Texas at Austin.

WILLIAM O. BEEMAN is Professor of Anthropology at Brown University.

GERALD D. BERREMAN is Professor Emeritus at the University of California, Berkeley.

FRANZ BOAS (1858–1942) was Professor and Chair of the Department of Anthropology at Columbia University.

PIERRE BOURDIEU (1931–2002) was Professor at the College de France.

JOHN BURDICK is Associate Professor of Anthropology at Syracuse University.

ROBERT CANFIELD is Professor of Anthropology at Washington University.

IAN CHESNOV is Professor of Anthropology at Russia's State Humanitarian University in Moscow.

WADE DAVIS is an Explorer-in-Residence at the National Geographic Society.

MARC EDELMAN is Professor of Anthropology at Hunter College and at the City University of New York Graduate Center, Ph.D. Program in Anthropology.

DAVID B. EDWARDS is Associate Professor of Anthropology at Williams College.

DALE F. EICKELMAN is Professor of Anthropology at Dartmouth University.

FADWA EL GUINDI is Adjunct Professor of Anthropology at the University of Southern California.

ROBERT FERNEA is Professor of Anthropology at the University of Texas at Austin.

ASHRAF GHANI is Minister of Finance in the new government of Afghanistan. He is also Adjunct Professor of Anthropology at Johns Hopkins University.

LESLEY GILL is Associate Professor of Anthropology at American University.

ROBERTO J. GONZÁLEZ is Assistant Professor of Anthropology at San Jose State University.

HUGH GUSTERSON is Professor of Anthropology and Science and Technology Studies at the Massachusetts Institute of Technology.

JEFF HALPER is Professor of Anthropology at Ben Gurion University (Israel), and coordinator of the Israeli Committee against House Demolitions.

DAVID HARVEY is Distinguished Professor at the City University of New York Graduate Center, Ph.D. Program in Anthropology.

ROBERT M. HAYDEN is Associate Professor of Anthropology at the University of Pittsburgh.

CINDI KATZ is Professor of Geography at the City University of New York.

CATHERINE LUTZ is Professor of Anthropology at the University of North Carolina at Chapel Hill.

MAHMOOD MAMDANI is Herbert Lehman Professor of Anthropology and Government and director of the Institute of African Studies at Columbia University.

BEATRIZ MANZ is Professor of Geography and Ethnic Studies at the University of California, Berkeley.

JANET MCINTOSH is Assistant Professor of Anthropology at Brandeis University.

THOMAS MCKENNA is Assistant Professor of Anthropology at the University of Alabama at Birmingham.

MARGARET MEAD (1901–1978) was Professor of Social Sciences at Fordham University and Adjunct Professor of Anthropology at Columbia University.

JAMES MERRYMAN is Professor of Sociology and Anthropology at Wilkes University.

SHAHMAHMOOD MIAKHEL is an Independent Photojournalist based in Washington, D.C.

LAURA NADER is Professor of Anthropology at the University of California, Berkeley.

BARBARA NIMRI AZIZ is Producer and News Reporter with Pacifica Radio Network and WBAI–New York.

DAVID PRICE is Assistant Professor of Anthropology at St. Martin's College.

ALI QLEIBO is head of the Faculty of Fine Arts at Al-Quds University (Jerusalem).

MARSHALL SAHLINS is Professor Emeritus of Anthropology at the University of Chicago.

NAZIF SHAHRANI is Professor of Anthropology and Central Asian and Middle Eastern Studies at Indiana University.

ZIEBA SHORISH-SHAMLEY is Executive Director of the Women's Alliance for Peace and Human Rights in Afghanistan.

ANNA SIMONS is Associate Professor of Defense Analysis at the Naval Postgraduate School.

NEIL SMITH is Distinguished Professor of Anthropology and Geography at the City University of New York Graduate Center.

IDA SUSSER is Professor at the City University of New York Graduate Center, Ph.D. Program in Anthropology.

WINIFRED TATE is a Ph.D. candidate in the Department of Anthropology at New York University, and a research fellow at the Washington Office on Latin America.

PERMISSIONS

The author is grateful for permission to reproduce the following copyrighted material:

ARTICLES

"Scientists as Spies" by Franz Boas. Reprinted with permission from the October 16, 1919 issue of *The Nation*.

"War Is Only an Invention—Not a Biological Necessity" by Margaret Mead. Reprinted with permission by Mary Catherine Bateson.

"Once You've Broken Him Down . . ." by Marshall Sahlins. Reprinted with permission from the October 25, 1965 issue of *The Nation*.

"Contemporary Anthropology and Moral Accountability" by Gerald D. Berreman. From *To See Ourselves: Anthropology and Modern Social Issues* edited by Thomas Weaver. Reprinted by permission of Pearson Education (Prentice-Hall Publishers). Used by permission of the publisher.

"Two Plus Two Equals Zero—War and Peace Reconsidered" by Laura Nader. Originally published in *The Radcliffe Quarterly*, March 1983. Reprinted by permission of the author.

"Dollars That Forge Guatemalan Chains" by Beatriz Manz. Originally published in *The New York Times*, March 18, 1985. Copyright © 1985 by The New York Times Company. Reprinted by permission.

"Anthropologists as Spies" by David Price. Reprinted with permission from the November 20, 2000 issue of *The Nation*.

"Abuse of Power by the Advocates of Reason" by Pierre Bourdieu. Copyright © 1998 *Acts of Resistance: Against the Tyranny of the Market* by Pierre Bourdieu. Reprinted by permission of The New Press. (800) 233-4830.

"West Must Correct Its Mistakes in Yugoslavia" by Robert M. Hayden. Originally published in *The Baltimore Sun*, August 16, 1992. Reprinted by permission of the author.

"No Exit from Somalia" by Anna Simons. Originally published in *The Washington Post*, May 15, 1991. Reprinted by permission of the author.

"Our Abysmal Ignorance about Somalia" by Anna Simons. Originally published

"Our Legacy of War" by Catherine Lutz. C 'ginally published in *The Chronicle of Higher Education,* September 28, 2001. Reprinted by permission of the author.

"Local Horror/Global Response" by David Harvey, Talal Asad, Cindi Katz, Neil Smith, and Ida Susser. Originally published in *The Chronicle of Education Online Colloquy,* 2001. Reprinted by permission of the author.

"A War Our Great-Grandchildren Will Be Fighting—Understanding Bin Laden" by William O. Beeman. Originally published by Pacific News Service, September 14, 2001. Reprinted by permission of the author. All rights reserved.

"What Have the 9/11 Investigators Overlooked?" by Janet McIntosh. Originally published in *The Christian Science Monitor,* July 11, 2002. Reprinted by permission of the author.

"For a Global Declaration of Interdependence" by Wade Davis. Originally published in *The International Herald Tribune,* July 6, 2002. Reprinted by permission of the author.

"Nation Is Home to Afghans, Mujahedeen, Taliban, Afghan-Arabs, to Name a Few" by Robert Canfield. Originally published in *The St. Louis Post-Dispatch,* September 23, 2001. Reprinted by permission of the author.

"The Folly of Quick Action in Afghanistan" by Ashraf Ghani. Originally published in *Financial Times,* September 27, 2001. Reprinted by permission of the author.

"Afghanistan Can Learn from Its Past" by Nazif Shahrani. Originally published in *The New York Times,* October 14, 2001. Copyright © 2001 by The New York Times Company. Reprinted by permission.

"Women in the New Afghanistan" by Amy Goodman with Zieba Shorish-Shamley. Copyright © 2001 by Pacifica Radio and Democracy Now! Reprinted by permission of the broadcast network.

"Enlisting Afghan Aid" by David Edwards and Shahmahmood Miakhel. Originally published by People's Geography, 2001. Reprinted by permission of the author.

"Pakistan's Dilemma" by Kamran Asdar Ali. Originally published by Middle East Research Information Project (MERIP Press Information Note 69), September 19, 2001. Reprinted by permission of the publisher and the author. Online information at www.merip.org.

"War Destroyed Chechnya's Clan Structure" by Francesca Mereu (with Sergei Arutyunov and Ian Chesnov). Originally published by *Radio Free Europe/Radio Liberty,* January 4, 2002. Reprinted by permission of the publisher.

"U.S. Anti-Terrorist Message Won't Fly in Islamic World" by William O. Beeman. Originally published by Pacific News Service, October 11, 2001. Reprinted by permission of the author. All rights reserved.

"Terror and Indigenous Peoples: War without End" by David Price. Originally published in *CounterPunch,* November 3, 2001. Reprinted by permission of the author.

"Afghan War Could Be Recruiting Tool for Terrorists" by John Burdick. Originally published in *The Post-Standard,* November 8, 2001. The Herald Company © 2001 The Post-Standard. All rights reserved. Reprinted with permission.

ILLUSTRATIONS

INDEX